Palgrave Studies in Professional and Organizational Discourse

Titles include:

Rick Iedema (*editor*)
THE DISCOURSE OF HOSPITAL COMMUNICATION
Tracing Complexities in Contemporary Health Care Organizations

Louise Mullany
GENDERED DISCOURSE IN THE PROFESSIONAL WORKPLACE

Keith Richards
LANGUAGE AND PROFESSIONAL IDENTITY

H. E. Sales
PROFESSIONAL COMMUNICATION IN ENGINEERING

Forthcoming titles include:

Edward Johnson & Mark Garner
OPERATIONAL COMMUNICATION

Cecilia E. Ford
WOMEN'S TALK IN THE PROFESSIONAL WORKPLACE

Palgrave Studies in Professional and Organizational Discourse
Series Standing Order ISBN 0–230–50648–8
(*outside North America only*)

You can receive future titles in this series as they are published by placing a standing order. Please contact your bookseller or, in case of difficulty, write to us at the address below with your name and address, the title of the series and the ISBN quoted above.

Customer Services Department, Macmillan Distribution Ltd, Houndmills, Basingstoke, Hampshire RG21 6XS, England

Also by Louise Mullany

THE ROUTLEDGE COMPANION TO SOCIOLINGUISTICS
(*ed. with C. Llamas and P. Stockwell*)

Gendered Discourse in the Professional Workplace

160401

Louise Mullany
University of Nottingham, UK

First published in 2007 by
PALGRAVE MACMILLAN
Houndmills, Basingstoke, Hampshire RG21 6XS and
175 Fifth Avenue, New York, N.Y. 10010
Companies and representatives throughout the world.

PALGRAVE MACMILLAN is the global academic imprint of the Palgrave
Macmillan division of St. Martin's Press, LLC and of Palgrave Macmillan Ltd.
Macmillan® is a registered trademark in the United States, United Kingdom
and other countries. Palgrave is a registered trademark in the European
Union and other countries.

ISBN-13: 978–1–4039–8620–7 hardback
ISBN-10: 1–4039–8620–7 hardback

This book is printed on paper suitable for recycling and made from fully
managed and sustained forest sources. Logging, pulping and manufacturing
processes are expected to conform to the environmental regulations of
the country of origin.

A catalogue record for this book is available from the British Library.

A catalog record for this book is available from the Library of Congress.

10 9 8 7 6 5 4 3 2 1
16 15 14 13 12 11 10 09 08 07

Printed and bound in Great Britain by
Antony Rowe Ltd, Chippenham and Eastbourne

To Matthew

Contents

List of Tables and Diagrams

Tables

Diagrams

Acknowledgements

I am deeply indebted to Ron Carter for his encouragement, advice and constant enthusiasm at the various stages of the production of this book, as well as for his insightful comments on a draft version of the manuscript. He is a true inspiration to all who work with him, and I feel very lucky to be one of his colleagues. Particular thanks also to Jill Lake at Palgrave for all her help and support, as well as for helping to make this publication possible in the first place. I am also grateful to Francesca Bargiela and Sandra Harris for sharing their expertise with me, particularly at the crucial early stages of this project. Carmen Llamas and Peter Stockwell have been key sociolinguistics colleagues and friends of mine over the years. I have learnt a great deal from them, and I will always be grateful to Peter for sparking my initial interest in language and gender studies. Thanks also to all other members of the Modern English Language staff at the University of Nottingham for helping to provide such a fruitful and friendly research environment. Special thanks are also due to my work-place informants for allowing me to intrude into their daily working lives.

My thinking on the topic of language and gender in the workplace has benefited greatly from the input of a number of other colleagues, as well as from discussions at various conferences and presentations. In particular I wish to thank Derek Bousfield, Chris Christie, Jennifer Coates, Bethan Davies, Karen Grainger, Janet Holmes, Lia Litosseliti, Miriam Locher, Catriona McPherson, Susan McRae, Andrew Merrison, Sara Mills, Janet Maybin, Elizabeth Morrish, Dalvir Samra-Fredericks, Helen Sauntson, Joan Swann, Tony Watson and Dom Watt. I am also grateful to the organizing committee of *Discourse, Communication and the Enterprise III* for inviting me to give a plenary presentation at PUC Rio, Brazil on the material presented in this book.

I also wish to express my gratitude to all MA students who have taken my language and gender module at the University of Nottingham, including the current cohort of distance-learning MA students in Buenos Aires, who made extracts of the data that appear in this book such a joy to teach on my visit to Lenguas Vivas College.

Two other crucial people to mention are my parents Chris and Ted for their continual encouragement and interest in my work. Finally, a special mention for my husband, Matthew. I would not have been able to complete this project without his love and support, and I feel truly privileged to share my life and work with him.

Transcription Conventions

(.) indicates a pause of two seconds or less

(-) indicates a pause of over two seconds

(xxx) indicates material that was impossible to make out

{xxx} indicates material that has been edited out for the purposes of confidentiality

[#] closed brackets indicate simultaneous speech

% % percentage signs indicate material was uttered quietly

RIDICULOUS Capital letters indicate material was uttered loudly

((laughs)) Material in double brackets indicates additional information

= Equals signs indicate no discernible gap between speakers' utterances

1
The Professional Workplace as a Research Site

Why choose the professional workplace?

Within the flourishing field of language and gender studies, the number of researchers who have examined the complex interplay between gender and discourse within the institutional, public sphere of the workplace has greatly increased in recent years. Such investigations have highlighted the fruitful nature of conducting research in this particular arena, but there is still much work to be done. This book presents a sociolinguistic study of gendered discourses in the professional workplace which adds new empirical evidence to this expanding field.

In a recent work which outlines the key, defining principles of twenty-first century sociolinguistic language and gender research, McElhinny (2003: 32) argues that it is essential for sociolinguists to examine the language of social institutions, of which the professional workplace is a prime example, in order to explore the role that linguistic strategies play in terms of social inequality based upon gender grounds. The growth of interest in professional workplace studies can be seen in part to be a consequence of the changing workforce demographic, which has resulted in more women entering the professions than ever before (Burke and Vinnicombe 2005). Most crucially, this transition has brought with it a range of social and political problems, resulting in gender inequalities, which warrant investigation from a sociolinguistic perspective. Analysing language and gender in the professional workplace can lead to an assessment of the role that language plays in the creation and maintenance of gender inequalities in the workplace, including the difficulties women face in attaining promotion to the highest echelons of power, frequently referred to as the *glass ceiling* (Morrison et al. 1987). Furthermore, as a great deal of us spend a large proportion of our lives engaged in workplace communication, it is essential for such sociolinguistic investigations to be carried out within the workplace context (cf. Vine 2004).

This volume adds to the prospering field of professional workplace research by investigating language and gender within the institutional setting of corporate businesses. In particular, the focus is upon managerial professionals, ranging from junior managers right through to company directors, in UK organizations.

The vast majority of early work in this field focused on professionals interacting with lay persons (see Kendall and Tannen 1997), and whilst a handful of studies did examine professional–professional interaction, this tended to be only on discourse within universities (Eakins and Eakins 1979; Edelsky 1981). In the late 1980s and 1990s, studies focusing upon professional–professional interaction in the business world started to emerge (see Mullany and Litosseliti 2006 for an overview). At the present time, linguistic studies focusing on professional–professional business communication are beginning to thrive. The largest and perhaps most well-known contemporaneous project is the New Zealand *Language in the Workplace* study, run by Janet Holmes and colleagues. Their project has a core sociolinguistic focus, and a good deal of research concentrates on gender and professional–professional communication, including a range of business interactions involving managers (Holmes and Stubbe 2003a; Holmes and Marra 2004; Holmes and Schnurr 2005; Holmes 2006a). Other recent works on gender and business communication include Baxter (2003) and McRae (2004) in the United Kingdom, Tannen (1999) and Kendall (2003, 2004, 2006) in the United States, Martin-Rojo and Gómez Estaban (2002, 2005) in Spain and Thimm et al. (2003) in Germany.

Research is now also starting to emerge from locations other than the Western world (Yieke 2005). As Thimm et al. (2003: 531) point out: 'talk at work has received attention from feminists worldwide, reflecting the growing importance of professional communication for women in different countries'. Furthermore, language and gender studies on professional communication outside of businesses have also blossomed. Investigations have been produced within the political sphere (Walsh 2001; Wodak 2003; Shaw 2006), law (McElhinny 1998; Ehrlich 2003) and the broadcast media (Mullany 2002; Walsh 2006; Litosseliti 2006).

Some commentators have gone as far as to argue that researchers need to focus solely on investigating talk that takes place in institutional, public spheres, in order to move sociolinguistic investigations away from a focus on informal settings amongst intimates/friends. Gal (1991) criticizes studies in informal, non-institutional settings for giving the impression that gendered talk is something that belongs only to individuals, neglecting the fact that gender is a crucial, organizing principle *within* institutions. Indeed, there has been a noticeable move within language and gender studies from conducting investigations within the private sphere, which dominated much early research (classic examples are works such as Fishman's 1978 study of heterosexual couples and Coates's 1988 investigation of women's friendship groups) to researching the public, institutional sphere, particularly as women's participation within public contexts continues to grow. Research in the professional workplace thus far has only just scratched the surface, and there is a large amount of crucial evidence that needs to be uncovered and brought to the fore in order to enable gender inequalities to be fully addressed. It is vital to investigate gender within institutions as it plays such a critical role in the process of social organization.

However, in adopting this position, it is not my intention to critique researchers who continue to produce studies within informal, non-institutional spheres, or that I am setting up conflict between the current study and language and gender studies that take place in private spheres. On the contrary, power and ideologies which lie at the root of gender inequalities can be just as easily observed within non-institutional, informal interaction. A prime example of this is Coates's (1996, 1997, 1999, 2003) more recent work on friendship groups which has shown how societal power structures and gender ideologies can be easily witnessed through talk in the private sphere.

Use of the binary terms 'public' and 'private' raises a range of issues within language and gender studies which are important to consider when carrying out workplace research. McElhinny (1997: 107) points out that the dichotomy between public versus private language and its associated linguistic counterparts of 'institutional' versus 'ordinary' language should be viewed as ideological labels instead of as concrete, definable spheres. As a result of the perpetual separation between public and private, she argues that 'relationships between occupations (including mothering) and gendered styles have been ignored' (1997: 108). She goes on to stress how the distinction 'obscures interpenetrations and relationships between home and work, home and state' (1997: 128). It is important for the public–private dichotomy to be viewed as an ideological label, deeply entrenched within Western societies' power structures in terms of the division of labour. Whilst I continue to use the term 'public' in this book, I do so in a reflexive manner, with a firm recognition that there is interpenetration between 'public' and 'private' spheres (cf. Baxter 2006a).

Indeed, the ideologically imposed separation between private and public spheres comes to the fore when considering the work–home balance of workplace professionals in corporate businesses (see Chapters 7 and 8). Furthermore, in reference to the dichotomy between ordinary versus institutional language, the analyses presented in Chapters 5 and 6 demonstrate how this distinction is wholly inaccurate, as the workplaces investigated in this study show ample evidence of allegedly 'ordinary' language (affective, non-referential talk) taking place within the institutional setting of the professional workplace.

It could be argued that use of the terms 'public' and 'private' should be abandoned altogether, as any usage may lead to reinscribing the dichotomies that language and gender researchers are striving to question. However, as Freed (2003) points out, our language system does not simply enable us to come up with alternatives, and whilst it is becoming increasingly common to problematize and deconstruct a range of dichotomies (Talbot 1998), most prominently the dichotomies of sex and gender, researchers often continue to use these specific, named categories. Whilst dichotomies are responsible for reinscribing stereotypes, another fundamental reason for continuing to use them is because they are drawn upon in everyday life to justify gendered inequalities based upon a wholly inaccurate biological rationale, and it is vitally important for academic researchers not to lose sight of this. Holmes and Meyerhoff (2003) make the following crucial observation regarding sex and gender in twenty-first century society:

> No matter what we say about the inadequacy or invidiousness of essentialized, dichotomized conceptions of gender, and no matter how justifiable such comments may be, in everyday life it really is often the case that gender is "essential". We can argue about whether people ought to see male and female as a natural and essential distinction, and we can point to evidence showing that all social categories leak. However, that has not changed the fact that gender as a social category *matters*. There is extensive evidence to suggest that gender is a crucial component of people's social world; many people really do find it vital to be able to pigeonhole others into the normative, binary set of female– male, and they find linguistic or social behaviors which threaten the apparent stability of this "essential" distinction extremely disturbing. (Holmes and Meyerhoff 2003: 9, emphasis in original)

Similarly, Cameron (2006: 6) argues that the dichotomies of public–private and male–female are both crucial 'principles of social organization' in

Western societies. Cameron details how the public–private dichotomy was gendered by the seventeenth century, with a sexual division of labour firmly in place, associating women with the private sphere and men with the public sphere. Whilst Cameron highlights that this dichotomy does ignore some exceptions, such as women talking in market-places, women were on the whole excluded from speaking in public arenas. Whilst women have now gained entry to public spheres since the mid-nineteenth century, Cameron argues that women's participation has been far from easy. Her work is published as part of a recent collection (Baxter 2006a), focusing on the female voice in the public sphere. In the volume introduction, Baxter (2006b) points to the problems that persist when women interact within public spheres:

> Despite at least 30 years of equal opportunities and educational reforms, more noticeably in the western world, women still struggle for acceptance within institutional settings such as government, politics, law, education, the church, the media, and the business world. (Baxter 2006b: xiv)

There is clearly much research that still needs to be conducted in a range of public spheres, including businesses, if real equal opportunities are to be achieved. We will now turn to a consideration of interdisciplinarity, which foregrounds the importance of investigating social and political problems within gender research.

Interdisciplinarity

Fifteen years ago, Eckert and McConnell-Ginet (1992a: 88) urged language and gender researchers to develop 'an interdisciplinary community of scholarly practice'. They argued that, if language and gender research is to have any kind of 'social or political responsibility', it is no longer acceptable to dismiss social theory simply on the grounds that we are 'just linguists' (1992a: 88). Their position is very similar to Cameron's (1996) belief that critical social theory should be integrated within sociolinguistics in order to move language and gender studies forward (see Chapter 2). The influence of such calls for interdisciplinary research has certainly had an impact, and by the end of the 1990s, interdisciplinary collections of language and gender research started to emerge (Bucholtz et al. 1999). In their highly influential *Handbook of Language and Gender*, Holmes and Meyerhoff (2003: 1) argue that its contents are 'truly interdisciplinary', citing anthropology, cultural studies, sociology, social psychology and organizational communication as examples of the range of areas covered.

In order to attempt to properly address social and political problems, I take an interdisciplinary approach in this volume. Whilst my primary basis is within sociolinguistics, influence from a range of other disciplines is also evident, including social theory, sociology, organizational studies, management studies and anthropology. However, one criticism that can be cited at studies which describe themselves as 'interdisciplinary' is that too often the term is used without being properly clarified. It is crucial for language and gender researchers to define the type of 'interdisciplinary' research that they are producing, in order to avoid confusion and opaqueness. The differing ways in which the term can potentially be used is elucidated by van Leeuwen (2005). He defines three different models of interdisciplinary research: *centralist*, *pluralist* and *integrationist*. Whilst these are not totally discrete categories, they are useful for providing clarification of the interdisciplinary approach taken here.

The centralist model is defined as one where a single discipline still remains at the centre of knowledge, but maps this knowledge in relation to other fields in order to gain knowledge from them. This is often due to crossover in subject matter. The pluralist model places particular issues and problems that require investigation at the centre, and brings together all disciplines equally. The integrationist model follows the view that no single discipline can address problems for investigation by itself, and thus disciplines become interdependent. This approach involves collaborative team work amongst researchers.

The main approach that I adopt in this book fits most clearly with the centralist model. A sociolinguistic approach is at the core of the study, but influence is taken from a range of other disciplines where there is crossover in terms of subject matter. Arguably there is some slippage here into the pluralist category, as one of the key reasons for subject matter crossover is that these disciplines are placing particular social and political problems relating to gender at the core of their studies. Fundamental problems in the professional workplace including the glass ceiling, unequal pay and the problem of workplace sexualization, are focused on in disciplines including sociology (Halford and Leonard 2001; Fitzsimons 2002), organizational studies (Gherardi 1996; Alvesson and Billing 1997; Jones 2000; Brewis 2001; Ashcraft and Mumby 2004; Burke and Vinnicombe 2005) and management studies (Davidson and Burke 2000; Mavin 2000; Olsson 2000; Appelbaum et al. 2002; Olsson and Walker 2003; Powell and Butterfield 2003; Powell and Graves 2003; Vinnicombe and Singh 2003; Drew and Murtagh 2005).

Influence from these disciplines is drawn upon throughout this investigation (see Chapter 2). However, all disciplines are not given equal weight, and ultimately it is the subject matter of gender inequalities in the workplace that can be seen as shared, thus leading to the centralist classification. The methodology of this study is heavily influenced by anthropology (see Chapter 3), though again this should be classified as a centralist approach, with sociolinguistics remaining as the core focus.

A degree of cross-fertilization already exists within these disciplines in terms of drawing upon the same theoretical frameworks, which can be seen as gesturing towards an integrationist model. As van Leeuwen (2005: 9) points out, within the humanities and social sciences, there is 'an increasing tendency for the same theoretical canon to be drawn upon in a range of different disciplines'. In particular, this is where critical social theory comes in, with the theoretical influence of Michel Foucault and Judith Butler being witnessed across all of the aforementioned disciplines that investigate gender in the workplace. This provides the current study with a consistent theoretical base which lies behind investigations outside of linguistics, thus hopefully easing the way for the progression of interdisciplinary research.

The linkage between various disciplines and linguistics has also greatly increased in recent years owing to the 'linguistic turn' that has taken place in a range of social sciences including organizational studies and management studies in particular (Grant et al. 1998). This 'turn' encourages interdisciplinary research in the specific setting of the professional, managerial workplace, and again moves some way towards van Leeuwen's integrationalist interdisciplinary model, where areas of expertise become blended with one another. In addition to the linguistic turn within social science disciplines, it is notable that within professions themselves there has also been a turn towards focusing on language and the importance of effective communication. Gunnarsson et al. argue the following:

> Probably due to the ongoing differentiation and specialization of professions, more and more people are becoming aware of the importance of effective communication among organizations and individuals in business ... efficient communication ... is absolutely vital for society to function properly. (Gunnarsson et al. 1997: 1)

They go on to stress that the growing interest in communication from professional practitioners is reflected in an increase in multidisciplinary academic studies (citing the disciplines of linguistics, sociology, psychology, communication studies and anthropology) in different professional contexts. Their use of the term 'multidisciplinary' directly accords with van Leeuwen's (2005) centralist category within his interdisciplinary model. The move towards producing interdisciplinary research is therefore not just coming from within language and gender studies, and indications are that such an approach – be it centralist, pluralist, integrationist or a combination of these – is emerging in various investigative areas in the social sciences and humanities.

Furthermore, when producing analyses of empirical workplace data in the current study, whilst being firmly positioned within the interactional sociolinguistic tradition of analysing patterns of interaction in discourse (Wodak and Benke 1997), influence from other linguistic sub-disciplines has also been taken, including analytical categories from (critical) discourse analysis and pragmatics in particular (see Chapter 4). By crossing over sub-disciplinary boundaries within linguistics, this study aims to produce a multilayered linguistic analysis through an integration of different approaches (Sarangi and Roberts 1999; Silverman 1999).

The transition towards interdisciplinary research within language and gender studies accords with calls within sociolinguistics more generally to produce interdisciplinary research. Coupland et al. (2001: xv) argue that 'a shift towards a more outward-looking sociolinguistics and to a more genuine interdisciplinarity must be the discipline's future'. Their collection focuses in particular on the role that social theory should play within sociolinguistics. Heller (2001) advocates that social theory, combined with traditional empirical sociolinguistic research, can be perceived as the way forward for the discipline as a whole. Roberts (2001) argues that, whilst critical social theory will not help sociolinguists decide on specific methodologies, it is still 'good to think with'. Her comments echo Eckert and McConnell-Ginet's (1992a) commitment to social and political responsibility:

> [I]t can provide warrants for a personal orientation to social justice. It sharpens our political senses and provides illuminating metaphors as thinking tools ... 'orders of discourse' and so on are the tropes which shed light on wider social and cultural processes. (Roberts 2001: 327)

This volume embraces the critical social theories of Butler (1990, 1993, 1999) and Foucault (1972, 1978, 1981), and applies them to an empirical, sociolinguistic examination of managerial business discourse (see Chapter 2).

Workplace research ethics

Within sociolinguistic study, Milroy and Gordon (2003: 84) point to a distinction between 'ethical research', based on dealing with problems of intrusion and confidentiality issues, and 'advocacy research', following Cameron et al. (1992). The advocacy position is defined as the principle that academic research should be 'with' and 'for' the community under study instead of simply producing work 'on' particular subjects (Cameron et al. 1992: 15). Holmes and Meyerhoff (2003) praise Cameron for her long association with this position. They stress the importance of academics being 'directed by the needs and interests of the communities of speakers studied', as opposed to producing research simply for the sake of 'academic appetite' (Holmes and Meyerhoff 2003: 10). Therefore, instead of conducting a study simply because you are interested in producing knowledge on a specific topic (a 'pure' approach, according to Sarangi 2006), language and gender scholars are advised to consider very carefully the research questions they pursue, and engage in a process of negotiation with those being researched in order to find out what kind of investigations could be of practical relevance to them. Holmes and Meyerhoff question the overall purpose of conducting academic work that does not abide by such principles:

> There seems little point to our academic interests if they do not at some stage articulate with real-world concerns and enable us or our readers to identify, for example, certain employment practices as unfair and ill-informed, based more on stereotypes and prejudice than they are on people's actual behavior in the real world. At some point, our research has to be able to travel out of the academy in order to draw attention to and challenge unquestioned practices that reify certain behaviors as being morally, or aesthetically, better than others. (Holmes and Meyerhoff 2003: 14)

I firmly endorse this perspective, and it is one of the key principles followed in this book.

It is an oft-cited criticism of traditional sociolinguistic (variationist) studies that they are merely descriptive (Fairclough 2001; Boxer 2002), and thus not interested in attempting to provide solutions to social problems. Whilst this criticism is applicable to some sociolinguistic research, it is important not to overlook the fact that key figures in the field of variationism, including William Labov and Peter Trudgill, have often followed such an 'advocacy' principle. A classic example is Labov's work on the Ann Arbor case, where his sociolinguistic evidence helped win a court battle on behalf of African American parents whose children were being unfairly disadvantaged in the educational system as a consequence of their speech patterns. The case brought about a change in educational practice. Milroy and Gordon (2003: 84) highlight Labov's commitment to the following principles of sociolinguistic research which are used to motivate investigators into taking social action:

The principle of error correction

A scientist who becomes aware of a widespread idea or social practice with important consequences that is invalidated by his [sic] own data is obligated to bring this to the attention of the widest possible audience.

The principle of debt incurred

An investigator who has obtained linguistic data from members of a speech community has an obligation to use the knowledge based on that data for the benefit of the community, when it has need of it. (Labov 1982: 173)

These principles are followed in the current study. The principle of 'error correction' will apply to attempting to change any ideas/social practices, including linguistic practices, which are not backed up by my data analysis. The principle of 'debt incurred' refers to the importance of making research of practical relevance. However, it is important to point out here that, as well as the crucial importance of research being of practical relevance to the immediate community under study, it should also have a wider applicability to the academic discipline as a whole, as well as a broader social and political relevance. Often this can be a difficult balance to strike, and careful negotiations between the researcher and the researched need to take place in order to ensure that the investigation fulfils these aims (see Chapter 3).

A commitment to practically relevant outcomes has always been evident in feminist language and gender research in a general sense, through a shared desire to bring about gender equality. However, Philips (2003: 266) points to the problem of 'a loss of a broader practical political perspective' within more recent investigations. It is essential that this problem is redressed, with academic research needing to reassert itself as a form of 'social activism' (Holmes and Meyerhoff 2003: 14). Holmes and Meyerhoff also argue that academic work is increasingly being held accountable in terms of what it gives back to the community that funds it in the first place. This should be viewed positively, with greater transparency hopefully resulting in jointly negotiated projects which strike a balance between academic credibility on the one hand and practical relevance on the other. Indeed, research of practical relevance has started to emerge from professional workplace studies. Janet Holmes and colleagues have produced publications aimed at a range of different audiences from their *Language in the Workplace* data, including materials for workplace practitioners and professionals themselves (Holmes 2003a, Holmes 2003b; Holmes and Stubbe 2003b). Baxter's (2003) work with telecommunications business managers in the United Kingdom also had a practical relevance component built into it and she developed practical resources designed to improve the efficiency of a mixed-sex managerial group.

An interconnected issue to the practical relevance question is a problem raised by Freed (2003). She highlights the large discrepancy that exists between the findings of current language and gender research and public perceptions of language and gender which still profess the outdated findings of the 'difference' approaches, collectively used here to refer to the deficit, power/dominance and culture/difference frameworks (see Cameron 1996 and Bergvall et al. 1996 for a thorough critique of these approaches). All of these frameworks take the search for gender differences as a starting point, and then catalogue these differences. Freed (2003) argues that academics are partly to blame for the existence and perpetuation of this problem, due to precisely the issue raised above, a lack of communication between researchers and the wider population outside of academic circles. She convincingly argues that researchers have not focused enough on popular perceptions of language, sex and gender. One way to change this is to follow the principles for sociolinguistic research just outlined, setting up a dialogue with those being researched in order to make the research process more of a joint endeavour. By involving those outside of academia in research questions and design, academics can investigate issues that are of concern to the population under study, as well as hopefully beginning to disseminate the newer findings of language and gender research in the public eye (see also Mullany 2008).

Cameron (2006: 18) summarizes the importance of practical relevance and a commitment to bringing about social change, stating that feminists need to perceive the theorizing of problems affecting women as a 'political as well as an intellectual enterprise'. She goes on to outline two key questions: 'it is proper to ask not only what explains the existence and nature of this problem?' but also, 'what is to be done?' (2006: 18). Indeed, I would argue that Cameron's second question should be adopted as a fundamental guiding principle for feminist sociolinguistics as a whole. Investigations should contain answers to these crucial questions, and such answers should ideally be aided by a process of negotiation between the researcher and the researched.

Producing research of practical relevance is not just a focus within sociolinguistics, but has also become a focus from within 'applied' linguistics more broadly. Sarangi and Roberts (1999: 40) urge linguists working within professional settings, including investigations of management, to follow Cameron et al.'s (1992) aforementioned principles. Sarangi and van Leeuwen (2003: 3) point out that recent transitions within applied linguistics have resulted in projects where people are no longer 'objects' who are 'left in the dark as to the effect that the research might have on their life and/or work'. Instead, the researched have become active participants who play influential roles in shaping the research process, with applied linguistic study now focusing on 'real world problems' (Sarangi and van Leeuwen 2003: 2). The work of Christopher Candlin, Celia Roberts and Srikant Sarangi in medical settings provides seminal examples of how applied linguistics is developing in particular relation to the professions (see Roberts and Sarangi 2003, 2005; Sarangi and Candlin 2003). Indeed, Sarangi (2006: 207) argues for a broadening of applied linguistics research to include a specific sub-field entitled 'Applied Linguistics of Professions'. The current study can be identified as part of 'applied sociolinguistic' research (Trudgill 1984), taking place within the broader field of 'Applied Linguistics of Professions', with real world problems being investigated and the results then applied to the community of participants who have been researched. Commitment to this 'applied' position opens up a range of methodological issues surrounding the negotiation of the relationship between the researcher and researched, as well as a number of key questions regarding research outcomes and deliverables. These issues are thoroughly explored in Chapter 3. At this point it is important to give further detail to the particular political and social problems that this study will investigate.

Workplace inequalities in management

There have been dramatic increases in the number of women entering workplaces at a professional, managerial level since the 1970s in the United Kingdom, and this pattern is replicated in numerous other countries across the globe (Powell and Graves 2003). As Adler (2003: x) points out, 'women worldwide now comprise a greater proportion of both workers and managers than in any previous era'. The British

Equal Opportunities Commission (EOC) publishes annual statistics revealing who occupies positions of power in private and public sectors in the United Kingdom, entitled the *Sex and Power Index*. Its 2006 publication coincided with the 30th anniversary of the *Sex Discrimination Act*. The report reflects upon the transitions that have taken place in the work-place demographic since the Act was passed. Statistics reveal that in 1974 only two per cent of women occupied managerial positions, and one per cent of women were company directors. In 2006, a third (33.1 per cent) of managerial positions are occupied by women in the United Kingdom, and on average, one in seven women are directors (14.4 per cent). Despite these inroads, the statistics highlight that if pro-gression continues at the current rate, it will take another 40 years for an equal number of female directors to be in place in FTSE 100 (*Financial Times Stock Exchange*) companies. This index is most frequently used when compiling UK workplace statistics – it contains the 100 largest companies on the London Stock Exchange.

Furthermore, there is still a very worrying difference in the amount of pay that females and males receive for doing exactly the same job. In 2006, women in full-time work were being paid 17 per cent less than men. This level of inequality increases to 38 per cent in part-time work. Whilst this situation was worse for women in full-time employment in the 1970s, when they were paid 29 per cent less in 1975, the percentage for part-time work has only decreased very slightly, from 42 per cent in 1975 to 38 per cent today. Furthermore, the *Equal Opportunities Commission* also reports the rather shocking figure that, every year, up to 30,000 women lose their position of employment for being pregnant.

In February 2006, the British Government published a report compiled by its *Women and Work Commission*, comprising 15 representatives including members of equality groups and representatives from education and industry. The Commission was set up in 2004 to examine the experi-ences of women in the workplace, and in particular to investigate the problem of the glass ceiling. The primary issue reported by the media from this report was the 17 per cent gap in pay (*BBC News*, 27 February 2006; *The Guardian* 27 and 28 February 2006). Many trade unions had called for compulsory pay reviews in order to attempt to redress this problem, but the Commission unfortunately stopped short of recommending the implementation of such a policy. The Commission also found that sex-segregation of job roles was still taking place, and suggested that girls should receive far more encouragement at school to enter non-traditional occupations. At the present time of writing, the British Government is in the process of devising an 'action plan' to attempt to redress the problems that the Commission has uncovered.

Powell and Graves (2003) point out that shifts in the global economy from a manufacturing to service-based industry, social policies such as equal opportunities and the fact that more females are both entering and succeeding in higher education than ever before, firmly indicate that the increase in women's managerial participation will continue. However, despite these factors, the glass ceiling is still firmly in place. A key driving force behind this book is to investigate the persistence of the glass ceiling. Despite the well-documented and continuing increases in women entering managerial jobs, and despite the fact that they have all of the necessary qualifications, women are still experiencing difficulties attaining promotion to the most senior positions in organizations (Burke and Vinnicombe 2005). The most recent statistics in the United Kingdom, published in October 2006, highlight that out of the FTSE 100 companies, only 10 have women directors (*The Guardian* 2 October 2006). Powell and Graves (2003) point out that the problem of the glass ceiling is not one that will simply rectify itself over time, or one that can be attributed to women's preference not to join the higher ranks of management.

One serious consequence of the persistence of the glass ceiling, according to Burke and Vinnicombe (2005), is that women are becoming increasingly disillusioned with managerial careers:

> The slow progress made by talented, educated, ambitious women is now having some negative effects on management and the professions as a career. Fewer women are entering MBA programs, thus reducing the pipeline for career advancement, despite efforts of MBA schools to attract more women students. In addition, more women in mid-career are leaving their corporate jobs, opting for a career in small businesses or full-time investment in family. (Burke and Vinnicombe 2005: 166)

A number of reasons why the glass ceiling is still in place is highlighted by Powell and Graves (2003). They begin by pointing out that there is often no systematic or transparent route in organizations for promoting candidates. Biased decisions can thus be made without fear of accountability. Another key reason is the 'cognitive processes' of those in decision-making positions, which includes 'stereotypes, prototypes and preference for similar others' (2003: 194). Therefore, if those already at the top of the ladder are male, other males will be preferred for promotion as they are similar to those currently occupying the gatekeeping positions. Another reason can be attributed to a self-fulfilling prophecy: if women think they will be disadvantaged, they may not put themselves forward for promotion. A further problem is the work–home balance, where a lack of family-friendly policies tends to disadvantage women managers far more than men. This can also be as a consequence of the deeply ingrained societal expectation that women should be responsible for more childcare than their male partners.

Overall aims and objectives

A crucial part of successfully fulfilling a managerial role is one's ability to enact power and authority. As Wajcman (1998: 1) points out, occupying a managerial post 'is a repository of power and authority, the site of decision-making and rule-making within organizations'. In order to be perceived as successful, managers need to be able to enact power and authority effectively, and crucial to this is a manager's ability to make decisions and rules. A primary focus of this publication falls on the manner in which managers perform their gendered and professional identities in order to enact power and authority. The higher up the organizational hierarchy managers climb, the greater their institutional power becomes in terms of the enactment of authority and gatekeeping. Focusing on professionals at a number of managerial levels will enable a range of different managerial positions to be explored, and this includes a focus on those few who have broken through the glass ceiling into the higher echelons of senior management.

There has recently been a surge of interest in examining leadership in language and gender workplace research (see Holmes 2006a, Marra et al. 2006, Baxter forthcoming), and examining women who have broken through the glass ceiling will add to this. This study will investigate both women and men managers in the businesses under scrutiny. Whilst early language and gender research was dominated by a focus on the language of women, more recently researchers have also examined men and masculinities (Johnson and Meinhof 1997; Baxter 2003; Coates 2003). As Johnson (1997) points out, whilst the predominance of studies on women in early language and gender research is understandable from a historical perspective, empirical evidence is required in order to examine how language and power are really constructed. It is thus essential for this study to investigate men managers as well as women, particularly for the glass ceiling to be properly investigated. McElhinny (2003: 26) stresses the importance of conducting sociolinguistic research in areas where women and men have entered non-traditional fields in order to examine 'how the boundaries between those spheres are actively maintained, how gender is policed, how people resist those boundaries, and perhaps what transformation requires'. The higher positions of leadership within organizations (senior management/directorships) are still very much non-traditional fields for women managers. Therefore, by focusing on those few who have broken through the glass ceiling, it is the intention that the boundaries to which McElhinny refers can be thoroughly investigated.

Powell and Graves (2003) further highlight that, in addition to enacting authority, managers also spend time working within managerial teams with status equals. This is the case with some of the data in this study. Therefore, whilst a key concentration of this book is upon how women and men managers enact authority, on occasions, managers also engage in identity performance when interacting with those at the same status level as themselves. However, there will be some observable slippage here, as managerial colleagues often need to utilize linguistic strategies in order to get their status equals to fulfil tasks for them. Furthermore, even when working in a team of status equals, authority in terms of local positions of power within specific contexts, such as chairing business meetings, or being responsible for a particular agenda item, will be apparent. These are careful considerations that are taken into account when analysing the data.

In order to produce a thorough analysis of the interplay between language and gender at a managerial level in corporate businesses, this study adopts a model of 'gendered discourses'. This framework enables both managerial interactions and broader issues of gendered power and ideologies to be thoroughly examined, with the overall aim of assessing current social and political problems in order to make suggestions to bring about social change. Whilst this approach is contained within an overarching sociolinguistic framework, the influence of other disciplines, including social theory, sociology, management studies and organizational studies is evident, as well as the influence of analytical tools from within (critical) discourse analysis and pragmatics. This overall approach will now be thoroughly detailed in the next chapter.

2
Gendered Discourses: A Critical Sociolinguistic Approach

Introduction

Wodak and Benke (1997) argue that sociolinguistic studies focusing on gender can be classified into two different types: variationist work that examines phonological (and grammatical) patterning, and the broad category that this study falls into, the examination of patterns of interaction within discourse, often termed interactional sociolinguistics. As part of this overall sociolinguistic approach, researchers often utilize techniques of discourse analysis to analyse the relationship between language and gender (Speer 2005). By adopting a sociolinguistic approach as the foundation of this study, one aim is to go some way towards raising the prominence of interactional sociolinguistic studies further, in order to challenge the mistaken assumption that exists, particularly in North America, that variationism is 'the whole of sociolinguistics' (Singh 1996: 7–8).

However, whilst this study does fall under the category of interactional sociolinguistics, another key aim is to try to push the boundaries of investigation further by not just adopting a pre-existing approach. As pointed out in Chapter 1, whilst a sociolinguistic approach is at the core, a centralist interdisciplinary approach is taken, with the overall aim of encouraging 'an interplay between multiple-voices' (Baxter 2003: 3). Instead of researchers pigeon-holing themselves within a particular sub-discipline, combining approaches and methodologies is far more fruitful (Holmes and Meyerhoff 2003). It also avoids the problem of research being placed into 'armed camps' (Silverman 2000), where analysts get embroiled in battles between whose approach is best, instead of concentrating on the social and political issues that should be the focus of the research. Battling about whether one particular paradigm is more acceptable than another runs the risk of 'damaging the spirit of enquiry' (Holmes and Meyerhoff 2003: 15). Combining approaches can thus be a very rewarding endeavour which can lead to pushing the discipline forward. Furthermore, as Baxter (2003: 3) points out, there are dangers in simply following an already well-established framework, which can result in 'an unquestioning and overrespectful adherence' to particular models just because they are associated with 'certain revered experts'.

When considering interdisciplinarity in Chapter 1, I highlighted that a combination of social theory with the collection and analysis of empirical sociolinguistic data can be perceived as the way forward for the discipline of sociolinguistics as a whole. From within this centralist interdisciplinary perspective, the approach taken here can be broadly perceived as a 'critical' sociolinguistic approach (Heller 2001: 119), integrating sociolinguistics with social theory (Foucault's discourse theory), along with concepts from recent feminist social theory (Butler's theory of performativity) and social theories of learning (Lave and Wenger's communities of practice theory). Influence is then also taken from disciplines where researchers have embraced one (or more) of these critical social theories, including organizational studies, management studies and sociology. The approach combines a fine-grained, interactional sociolinguistic analysis with a model which examines wider discourses and power structures in society. In doing so, the intention is that the abstractness of Foucault's social theory will have some grounding in empirical linguistic data, whilst at the same time, the linguistic evidence will be viewed from a perspective that questions essentialist social categories and gives a wider societal grounding through which the linguistic performance of social identities can be observed. Social practice provides the link between social theory and sociolinguistics, with the communities of practice (CofP) approach providing a 'bridging' model. This perspective accords with Bucholtz's (2001: 166) argument that any investigation of discourse needs to pay attention to 'large-scale cultural forces, to local contexts of practice and to the fine details of discursive form and content', as well as to Heller's (2001: 117) view that 'local linguistic practices' should be linked to 'processes of social structuration' in sociolinguistic analyses.

Despite the prime association within linguistics of 'critical' being associated with 'critical discourse analysis' (CDA), it can be convincingly argued that any research from a feminist perspective, regardless of the specific discipline to which it belongs, can be described as 'critical' in orientation (Cameron 1997a: 21). Wodak (1997a: 7) makes a similar point, arguing that 'feminist scholarship in every discipline is characterized by its *criticism* of science and its *criticism* of an androcentric view within traditional science' (my emphasis). Furthermore, Sunderland and Litosseliti (2002: 33) state that their edited collection suggests both the 'importance' and 'appropriacy' of producing *critical* analyses of gender and language, whether or not these happen to be located in a CDA framework. These perspectives reflect Billig's (2000) definition of 'critical' research as an analysis of the social, and in particular, an analysis of social inequality. Heller (2001: 117) also highlights that the aim of a critical approach is to identify and explain 'the construction of relations of social difference and inequality'. My commitment to exploring social and political inequalities in the professional workplace, outlined in Chapter 1, thus adds weight to the classification of this study as 'critical sociolinguistics'.

The principle of reflexivity, the need to acknowledge the vital role that your subjectivities as a researcher play in the research process, has become crucial in studies that take such a 'critical' approach. From a sociolinguistic perspective, the importance of reflexivity can be traced back to Hymes (1974). Rampton et al. (2004: 3) argue that it is crucial for 'researchers' own cultural and interpretative capacities' to be acknowledged in the sense-making processes involved in conducting research. Hammersley and Atkinson (1995: 16) point out that commitment to producing reflexive investigations means that researchers acknowledge how their orientations are 'shaped by their socio-historical locations, including the values and interests that these locations confer upon them'. Whilst the reflexive approach is a principle that runs throughout the book, this chapter in particular will outline my alignment with a third-wave feminist approach to conducting academic research (Mills 2003; Baxter 2006b), which is a crucial part of the socio-historical location within which I have conducted this work; Chapter 3 specifically details the importance of being reflexive when considering the relationship between the researcher and the researched.

Over the last fifteen years, with the development of post-structuralist, third-wave feminist theories, the term 'critical' has also acquired a more local meaning within feminist linguistic studies. Talbot (1998: 150) argues that, as well as CDA, the social constructionist view of gender can also be perceived as a critical approach. Indeed, the perception of gender as a performative social construct, along with the CofP approach, developed as critiques of the earlier deficit, power/dominance and culture/difference approaches to language and gender studies. The term 'critical' therefore has a two-fold meaning here. It refers to gender and social inequality being examined from a feminist perspective, and in a more local sense it refers to the perspective that is adopted which critiques earlier approaches to language and gender.

In this chapter, I will begin by contextualizing the broad foundational sociolinguistic approach that is taken, and then illustrate how influence from other disciplines is drawn upon and applied. This incorporates a full explanation of how the crucial terms gender, discourse and gendered discourses are being defined and applied in this study.

From variationism to social construction and social practice

Variationist studies have long dominated sociolinguistic research, and it is possible to see how current theoretical and methodological approaches in interactional sociolinguistic language and gender studies have been influenced, in part, by frustrations with some key concepts within the variationist paradigm. McElhinny (1997, 2003) argues that feminist sociolinguistic researchers have now for some time been critiquing the ideological underpinnings of sociolinguistics by questioning and redefining key analytical concepts. She observes how traditional sociolinguistic terms (associated with variationist research), had to undergo a process of re-evaluation if gender was ever to be taken seriously. The 1990s was a time of great transition within feminist sociolinguistics, a consequence of high-profile figures such as Cameron (1996: 49) urging sociolinguists to 'challenge our co-optation' by those who would set narrow agendas for 'sociolinguistics proper'. The impact of these key developments will now be discussed.

Romaine (2003: 100) points out that within variationist research the concept of social class is fundamental, with gender differentiation being 'derivative' of social class. This is highly problematic, particularly because of the masculine bias contained within early social stratification research, whereby women were classified according to their husband's occupation or, if unmarried, their father's (Labov 1972; Trudgill 1974). At present, the problem of social class categorization persists, as women and men still have unequal relations with one another within the class structure. Despite the professional, managerial focus of this book, and despite the fact that there are now more women in the workforce than ever before, it should not be overlooked that there is still a higher concentration of women in lower-paid occupations than men (Romaine 2003). The solution that Romaine (2003: 115) puts forward is for sociolinguistic research to undergo 're-examination from a new, non-class-based standpoint'. I agree with Romaine that social class should not be the fundamental starting point of a sociolinguistic study, which represents a clear departure from traditional variationist research. This view also signifies a key difference from CDA (Fairclough 1989, 1992), whereby social class is seen as the primary concern, thus again over-shadowing the importance of gender as an investigative focus (Mills 1997; Walsh 2001). As Walsh (2001: 28) points out, viewing gender inequalities as stemming simply from 'capitalist oppression' buries 'cross-class fraternal alliances which have supported the exclusion of women from a number of public and civil spheres and activities' including the workplace. Similar to Romaine's perspective, Walsh (2001: 27) further argues that Fairclough's work fails to acknowledge how the concept of class has become a 'highly contested site', and thus a very difficult category to define.

Another criticism that can applied to traditional variationist research is the view of linguistic differences as 'neutral', with inequality simply resulting from difference being suppressed or stigmatized. Cameron argues that such a relativist argument surely overlooks the following crucial concern:

> [T]he issue is not so much whether this way of speaking is as good as that, as whether the division of labour has significant political consequences, systematically empowering some groups at the expense of others ... this argument implies that inequality can give rise to difference, rather than the other way around. The fact that different discourse strategies often appear in single-sex peer groups in no way detracts from the important point that *the difference arises in a context of unequal gender relations*. (Cameron 1996: 44, emphasis in original)

The problem of gender inequality therefore runs far deeper than an intolerance of gender differences, which have themselves been subject to question in language and gender studies, as highlighted in Chapter 1.

However, it is important to realize that not all variationist sociolinguistic research follows this model of relativism. The Milroys (Milroy 1987; Milroy and Milroy 1997) offer a different perspective. Their work is associated with a *conflict* model of power in society, whereas Labovian-influenced research presumes what has come to be known as a *consensus* model: the view that lower-class speakers simply share the values of the upper-middle classes. The alternative, conflict model directly accords with Cameron's (1996) criticisms of linguistic relativism. Milroy and

Milroy (1997) argue that there are distinct divisions between unequal social groups in society, maintained by language ideologies, which result in conflict. Such conflict is hidden by the promotion of a consensus view of shared linguistic norms.

One fundamentally important criticism that can be cited at all of the aforementioned variationist studies, including Milroy's (1987) work, is the manner in which gender is conceived. The problem here is the conceptualization that 'language reflects already existing social identities rather than constructs them' (Romaine 2003: 109). Speakers are classified as either male or female, and then linguistic behaviour is categorized as a consequence of this. It is therefore more accurately sex, not gender that is used as a categorization device within this variationist work (Wodak and Benke 1997). A number of works call for a major re-evaluation of the manner in which gender is conceived within sociolinguistic studies. Cameron (1996) attacks sociolinguistics for failing to provide language and gender studies with the theoretical apparatus necessary to interrogate the relationship between gender and language. She argues that feminist sociolinguistics requires a theory of gender which challenges 'academic renditions of received wisdom' (1996: 49). She points out that for too long sociolinguistics 'has taken gender for granted by treating it as a demographic category that is given in advance ... *gender is a problem not a solution*' (1996: 44, emphasis in original). Cameron urges sociolinguists to look towards critical social theory and integrate this with detailed linguistic analyses, echoing the arguments outlined in Chapter 1 when defining the centralist interdisciplinary position.

In particular, Cameron points to Butler's (1990) view that gender should be perceived as a performative social construct, instead of being seen as a fixed social category. Indeed, the social constructionist, performativity approach has had a significant impact on language and gender studies. Kendall and Tannen (2002) remark that this perspective now prevails in gender and discourse research, and this is still the case five years on. Another popular framework is the notion of CofP, which represents a move away from quantitative, correlational methods to qualitative, ethnographic research. Indeed, gender is conceptualized from a social-constructionist perspective in this volume, and the CofP framework is also utilized. Romaine (2003: 116) argues that these recent transitions within sociolinguistic language and gender studies illustrate how approaches have moved forward, and her summary reflects the perspective taken here, that research has moved beyond 'simplistic correlations between language use and sex to focus on the symbolic and ideological dimension of language ... both gender and language comprise rather complex social practices and performances'.

Gender as a social construct

According to Butler (1990: 25), gender can be perceived as a *performative* social construct because it is 'always a doing' and there is 'no gender identity behind the expressions of gender ... identity is performatively constituted by the very "expressions" that are said to be its results'. Butler therefore believes that masculinity and femininity are effects we perform by the activities in which we partake, not predetermined traits we possess. She draws heavily on Foucault's work, particularly on his perceptions of identity and power. As Jones (2000: 194) points out, Butler (1990, 1993) has appropriated the work of Foucault as 'it offers ways out of what seems like the intractable problem of collapsing back into unchangeable stereotypes whenever we talk about gender differences'.

One of the key advantages of Butler's model is that it completely reconceptualizes how identity is perceived within sociolinguistics. It can be viewed as turning traditional sociolinguistic acts of identity on their head (Cameron 1996). Cameron (1996: 47) argues that instead of the essentialist, sociolinguistic, variationist perception that your linguistic behaviour represents 'who you (already) are', Butler alternatively argues that 'who you are, and are taken to be depends on your repeated performance over time of the acts that constitute a particular identity'. Butler's notion of performativity has been very influential in feminist linguistics (for example, see Bergvall, Bing and Freed 1996; Cameron 1997a, 1997b; Livia and Hall 1997; Talbot 1998; Mills 2002, 2003).

The argument of viewing gender as a social construct was also made by Wodak and Benke (1997) in their detailed discussion of gender as a sociolinguistic variable. They posit that individuals should be seen as 'doing gender', following West and Zimmerman (1987), as opposed to viewing gender as a fixed and stable social category from which linguistic behaviour can be statistically ascribed, as with the variationist approach. The conceptualization of 'doing' gender enables the full complexity of enacting identities to be seen. As Litosseliti (2006: 41) points out, the view of 'doing' gender shows how identities are 'multiple, multilayered, contextualised, shifting and often contradictory or dilemmatic'. Baxter (2006b : xvi) also makes this point, as well as stressing that the performativity approach has enabled gender identities to be perceived as co-constructed 'through social interactions and practices'.

A major advantage of the performative model is that it allows for speakers' agency and creativity, in contrast with the older 'difference' approaches which view women and men simply acting like 'automata', drawing on rigid and pre-determined speech patterns (Cameron 1997a: 30). However, Butler (1990: 33) openly states that repeated acts take place within a 'rigid regulatory frame', thus acknowledging that there are norms and constraints which govern how speakers decide to perform traits of femininities or masculinities. As Cameron (1997b: 49) argues, Butler 'insists that gender is regulated and policed by rigid social norms', but women and men are not viewed as totally trapped by these norms. Cameron (1997b: 50) makes the crucial point that Butler's perspective enables speakers to 'engage in acts of transgression, subversion and resistance', though this may occur at 'some social cost' to the speaker who breaks the gendered norms typically associated with their sex. The persistent problem of negative attitudes/evaluation can be seen as part of what is referred to as 'social cost' here, and will be more fully discussed later.

Both Ehrlich (2003) and McElhinny (2003) point out that Butler's 'rigid regulatory frame' has been critiqued for being too abstract. Ehrlich (2003: 647) argues that there needs to be a focus on how 'dominant gender ideologies often mold and/or inhibit the kind of gendered identities that women (and men) produce' in order to avoid such abstractness. Kotthoff and Wodak (1997), Baron and Kotthoff (2001) and Walsh (2001) also argue that there is a danger with Butler's approach in that some researchers may interpret her work as implying that speakers can do and say whatever they like, thus neglecting larger societal forces which constrain speakers' linguistic behaviour. In response to these debates, I wish to follow Mills's (2002: 71) position of adopting performativity in a 'modified' form, whereby 'the force of stereotyping and perceptions of sex-appropriate roles' is acknowledged but also combined with the view that these stereotypes are not impenetrable, as they can also be challenged and resisted (cf. Cameron 1997b).

The enthusiasm and rapidity with which the social constructionist approach has been embraced by feminist sociolinguists indicate the levels of dissatisfaction that were felt with the variationist approach in general, but also with previous theoretical paradigms within feminist sociolinguistic research, the deficit, power/dominance and culture/difference approaches. These paradigms share the variationist approach's conceptualization of sex/gender identity as something static and pre-existing. McElhinny (2003: 24) summarizes current positions on gender and difference in feminist sociolinguistics, highlighting that the move towards social constructionist perspectives has resulted in a change of research questions: analysts are no longer asking 'what are the gender differences?', but instead, the questions being posed, and ones that are posed in this book are 'what difference does gender make?' and 'how did gender come to make a difference?'

As well as perceiving gender as a social construct, Butler (1990: 17) also believes that sex is a social construct produced in discourse. Bing and Bergvall (1996) draw on Butler's perspective to argue that such an approach gets beyond binary thinking and avoids reinforcing gender polarization. However, Wodak (1997a: 12) questions the rather 'dogmatic' perspective put forward by Butler (1990), asserting that the role of feminist researchers is not to get bogged down in a discussion of whether the biological category of sex is real or not. Researchers instead should be aiming to expose the 'arbitrary construction of this binary opposition', as sex is used as a 'powerful categorization device' in society (Wodak 1997b: 12). She illustrates this with the example of the pay gap between women and men in the workplace, a prime example of gender inequality, already highlighted in Chapter 1. Sex in such contexts is perceived as a natural biological category, and not as a social construct.

This is a crucial point, and I fully endorse Wodak's position, which echoes the key quote of Holmes and Meyerhoff (2003) cited in Chapter 1, that essentialism is rife in wider society, and thus needs to be given full consideration in language and gender research. Wodak and Benke (1997) provide an excellent discussion on the topic of sex and gender and I follow their perspective on the interconnectedness between the two concepts. During the socialization process, children's gender identity develops around the biological sex label that has been assigned to them at birth. Therefore, 'biological differences become a signal for, rather than a cause of, differentiation in social roles' (Wodak and Benke 1997: 129). These differences are maintained by societal norms. This leads them to suggest that it is better to talk of plural *genders* instead of a singular gender, as what it means to be women or men changes according to social variables such as age, ethnicity, class, religious affiliations, and so on. More recently Coates (2007: 67) highlights the importance of viewing gender as a pluralized concept, arguing that 'at any point in time, there will be a range of femininities and masculinities extant in a culture, which differ in terms of class, sexual orientation, ethnicity, and age, as well as intersecting in complex ways'. However, there are crucial issues of power that should not be overlooked here, and the plurality of gender will be discussed at a later stage.

Following Meyerhoff (1996), Holmes (2000a) argues that gender identities, along with other forms of social identity, are constantly being performed and enacted by participants when engaging in spoken discourse.

Like Holmes (2005: 46), I believe that gender is omni-relevant in every interaction. As Eckert and McConnell-Ginet (2003: 50) point out, 'the force of gender categories in society makes it impossible for us to move through our lives in a nongendered way, and impossible not to behave in a way that brings out gendered behavior in others'. Stubbe et al. (2000: 237) make a similar point, drawing on Bem (1993) to highlight that the manner in which we perceive one another is 'automatically filtered through a gendered lens'.

Finally, coming back to variationist sociolinguistic research, Cheshire (2002) examines the labels of 'sex' and 'gender', pointing out that variationist studies still tend to examine sex, based on an essentialist approach, instead of gender. Cheshire's (2002: 424) perspective accords with Wodak (1997a) when she argues that, as the binary opposition between female and male appears to be 'a fundamental organizing principle' in society, it is reasonable to expect this 'to guide our evaluations of our own and others' speech'. However, she goes on to make the point that adopting a male–female distinction will not result in providing any explanations for *gender* and language variation. In order to examine gender, she advises researchers to follow a local, community-based approach, and also to examine the wider social forces that may be constraining linguistic behaviour.

Communities of practice

The CofP framework has already been successfully applied to analysing language and gender in the workplace (Holmes and Marra 2004; Holmes and Schnurr 2005; Holmes 2006a), and a number of researchers have made a connection between gender as a social construct and the CofP approach. Holmes and Meyerhoff (1999: 180) point out that the CofP approach is clearly more 'compatible' with the social constructionist view of gender than other, 'less dynamic or activity focused concepts'. Cameron (1996) also provides an illuminating illustration of the compatibility of the two frameworks:

Throughout our lives we go on entering new communities of practice: we must constantly produce our gendered identities by *performing* what are taken to be the appropriate acts in the communities we belong to – or else challenge prevailing gender norms by refusing to *perform* those acts. (Cameron 1996: 45, my emphasis)

The CofP approach focuses on localized social practices, examined by conducting qualitative, ethnographic research. This represents a clear theoretical and methodological shift away from early variationist studies (see Mullany 2007a for further discussion). Indeed, Eckert and McConnell-Ginet (1992a) accuse quantitative, variationist studies of over-generalizing differences between male and female speech patterns, resulting in the perpetuation of stereotypes.

This study follows Eckert and McConnell-Ginet's (1992a, 1992b) now classic definition of a community of practice:

> An aggregate of people who come together around mutual engagement in an endeavor. Ways of doing things, ways of talking, beliefs, values, power relations – in short – practices – emerge in the course of this mutual endeavor. (Eckert and McConnell-Ginet 1992b: 464)

In a later work, Eckert (2000) argues that a CofP is defined simultaneously by its membership and by the shared practices in which its members partake. The immense value of the CofP as a theoretical construct rests on 'the focus it affords on the mutually constitutive nature of the individual, group, activity and meaning' (2000: 35). Communities of practice (CofPs) can survive changes in membership, be a variety of sizes and can come into existence and go out of existence. Individual members can be either *core* or *peripheral* depending on how integrated they are in a CofP. Eckert and McConnell-Ginet (1992a: 95) believe that individuals and CofPs change constantly, and that our gendered sociolinguistic identities are transformed as we change and expand 'forms of femininity, masculinity, and gender relations'. Gender is produced and reproduced in different memberships of CofPs, and an individual's exposure or access to a CofP is related to other categories of social identity as well as gender, including age, class, ethnicity, and so on. Gender is also produced and reproduced in differential forms of participation in a CofP, and this is crucially linked to the place of such groups in wider society.

According to Wenger (1998: 73), the three dimensions of 'practice' that need to be fulfilled in order to make up a 'community of practice' are *mutual engagement*, a *joint negotiated enterprise* and a *shared repertoire*. In his later work, he emphasizes the visibility and importance of CofPs in the specific context of the workplace:

> Workers organize their lives with their immediate colleagues and customers to get their jobs done. In doing so, they develop or preserve a sense of themselves they can live with, have some fun, and fulfil the requirements of their employers and clients. No matter what their

official job description may be, they create a practice to do what
needs to be done. (Wenger 1998: 6)

Similarly, Holmes and Meyerhoff (1999: 177) emphasize the value of
using the CofP approach for examining workplace interaction, arguing
that it can be used to assess different practices within and across different
workplaces, being of use to both employees and those 'outsiders' who
wish to interact with company members. This integrates well with this
study's aims of practical relevance, outlined in Chapter 1. Furthermore,
Holmes and Stubbe (2003b) point out that the approach can be utilized
to explore workplace culture in conjunction with gender, as well as to
provide a basis from which individuals' gendered identities can be seen
as being balanced with the enactment of acceptable professional roles
within workplace CofPs.

Eckert and McConnell-Ginet (1999) point out that the notion of a
CofP can also extend to more global communities, such as academic
fields, religions or professions. However, they stress that, due to both the
'size' and 'dispersion' of these global communities, 'face-to-face interactions never link all members', and 'their "focal" practices are somewhat
diffuse' (1999: 189). There is thus a need to concentrate on how meaning is made at a more local level, using ethnography (see Chapter 3).

Bucholtz (1999a: 221) summarizes the overall usefulness of the CofP
approach, pointing out that it is through CofPs that individuals' 'local
identities and the linguistic practices that produce these identities
become visible to sociolinguistic analysis as the purposeful choices of
agentive individuals, operating within (and alongside and outside) the
constraints of the social structure'. McElhinny (2003) also highlights
how the CofP approach can be seen to bridge the gap between local
practices and the overall macro power structures in society:

> Communities of practice articulate between macro-sociological struc-
> tures such as class and everyday interactional practices by considering
> the groups in which individuals participate and how these shape their
> interactions. The groups in which they participate are in turn deter-
> mined and constituted by their place within larger social structures.
> The notion of community of practice thus serves as a mediating
> region between local and global analysis. (McElhinny 2003: 30)

In an effort to link the local and the global, Wenger (1998) coins the
notion of *constellations* of practice, whereby individual CofPs come
together to make up an overall collective grouping, such as a company,

with different CofPs striving towards the same profit-making goals (in theory at least). Wenger (1998: 131) argues that, in the context of 'constellations' of practices, the local and global are 'related levels of participation that always co-exist and shape each other'.

However, whilst a crucial mediating role is played by the CofP framework, within workplace studies, it is essential that the gender of institutions is given full attention, and the CofP approach does not quite go far enough. Examining gender within activities will provide a focus on the gender performance of individuals, but these activities also need to be viewed as being situated within larger social structures and systems, where gender also needs to be analysed at an overarching, institutional level (McElhinny 2003). Bergvall (1999: 288) posits that researchers need to go beyond the CofP approach in order to produce a more comprehensive theory of language and gender, arguing for 'theories that extend beyond local communities of practice: there are forces larger than communities of practice, where influences go beyond mutual engagement in the shaping of public opinions'. In later work, Eckert and McConnell-Ginet (2003: 32) also demonstrate the importance of analysing the overall social structure in society, coining the term 'the gender order', maintained by ideologies and social conventions, within which gendered behaviour takes place and is maintained. It is within this 'gender order' that gender continues to be dichotomized. Indeed, they point out that gender as a binary category remains at the centre of the social order, due to our own hegemonic compliance in keeping it there (Gramsci 1971, see later).

Therefore, the CofP approach can take us some way, but we need an additional analytical component in order to assess how gender operates at an overarching, institutional level. In this study, to ensure that gender is also examined at the level of social structuration, an analysis of 'gendered discourses' is adopted. It is the intention that this will enable the primary aim of twenty-first century sociolinguistic language and gender research to be achieved, with this study challenging 'dominant ideologies where they help perpetuate inequities' (McElhinny 2003: 36). The manner in which the crucial concept of gendered discourses is defined in this study will now be carefully explicated.

Defining discourse, defining gendered discourses

In conjunction with the social constructionist approach to gender and the CofP framework outlined above, a dual definition of discourse is adopted in this study. First, discourse is conceptualized in its traditional linguistic sense, as 'language beyond the sentence' (Tannen 1989: 6). Second, in order to examine language and gender fully at a global level of social structuration, discourse is conceptualized in a much broader sense, following Foucault's discourse theory (1972; 1981), which has been heavily influential in feminist linguistic study in recent years (Coates and Jordan 1997; Mills 1997; Coates 1999; Baxter 2003; Sunderland 2004). 'Discourse' in this sense will be analysed according to the oft-cited Foucauldian definition of pluralized discourses as 'practices that systematically form the objects of which they speak' (Foucault 1972: 49). Mills (1997) presents a clear guide as to how broader, Foucauldian discourses can be identified:

> A discursive structure can be detected because of the systematicity of the ideas, opinions, concepts, ways of thinking and behaving which are formed within a particular context, and because of the effects of those ways of thinking and behaving. (Mills 1997: 17)

Sunderland (2004) draws attention to a number of publications which are titled 'Gender and Discourse' including Wodak (1997b), Walsh (2001), and Litosseliti and Sunderland (2002). She argues that these have all demonstrated how 'discourse *is* gendered' (2004: 20, emphasis in original). She underlines this even more clearly by fusing 'gender' and 'discourse' together, turning gender into an adjective to come up with the phrase 'gendered discourse'. She argues that the term 'gendered' is much stronger than the descriptive term 'gender-related', as it signifies that 'gender is already a part of the "thing" which gendered describes' (2004: 20–21). Sunderland's description of 'gendered' is extremely useful, and when the term 'gendered' is used in this book, gender should already be seen as belonging to the 'thing' which is being described. Sunderland (2004: 6) defines the 'discourse' part of her term very broadly as '*ways of seeing the world*', following Fairclough (2003) and Foucault (1981).

In this study, a dual definition of gendered discourse is adopted, though the two levels are inextricably interlinked. The first definition of gendered discourse is at the level of interactional style (i.e. discourse above the level of the sentence), whereby speech styles are conceptualized as being stereotypically gendered. This perspective builds upon Ochs's (1992) ground-breaking work on indexing, which has been an influential perspective in recent suggestions for the future of sociolinguistic language and gender studies (McElhinny 2003). The second, and overarching manner in which gendered discourses are conceptualized draws upon the Foucauldian-influenced definition of discourse. Following Mills (1997) and Sunderland (2004), gendered discourses are defined in this sense as the boundaries of social practice through which appropriate gendered behaviour is regulated. Gendered discourses work as parameters through which women and men 'are represented or expected to behave *in particular gendered ways*' (Sunderland 2004: 21, emphasis in original). Gendered discourses are maintained by gender ideologies. Gendered interactional styles should be perceived as belonging within the second, overarching definition, as the speech strategies that women and men draw upon are important ways in which they are judged to be acting (in)appropriately for the particular identity and social role that they are enacting. These two strands of analysis and the manner in which they are crucially interlinked will now be fully elucidated.

Gendered discourses: Interactional styles and social practices

The turn towards social constructionist approaches to gender has resulted in a transition away from cataloguing gender differences between women's and men's speech styles. One way beyond the differences search which researchers including Freed (1996) and McElhinny (1998, 2003) have taken is to view speech as something that is indexed with gender, following Ochs (1992). The indexing approach has been advocated as the way forward for sociolinguistic language and gender studies, as it turns around recent concerns of debating 'when' gender may be relevant in analysis, to instead considering '*how* gender is relevant' when analysing interactional styles (McElhinny 2003: 35). It enables the powerful role that stereotypes play, in terms of ideologically prescribing behaviour, to be observed, providing reasons as to why some linguistic strategies are deemed to be appropriate for some speakers but not others, thus linking a 'local' linguistic analysis with global, overarching considerations of the role of gender at the level of social structuration.

Ochs's (1992: 341) theory is based on the view that very few linguistic forms directly index gender. Examples are a handful of items such as pronouns 'she/he' and titles including 'Mrs'. As a consequence, linguistic strategies should be seen as being *indirectly* indexed with gender (this can also apply to other aspects of our social identities). As a consequence, speech styles should not simply be catalogued according to sex. Instead, Ochs (1992: 341) points out that 'linguistic features may index social meanings (e.g. stances, social acts, social activities), which in turn help to constitute gender meanings'. Language can be indexed at a whole range of different linguistic levels, including interactional styles

(Sunderland 2004). A crucial component of Ochs's (1992: 342) position is her argument that knowledge of how language relates to gender should consist of a 'tacit understanding' of 'norms, preferences and expectations regarding distribution of this work vis-à-vis particular social identities of speakers, referents and addressees'. Ochs's (1992) theory therefore enables us to view the interface between language and gender as follows: whilst indices are non-exclusive, i.e. the same style can be used by women or men (which integrates nicely with the performativity approach), there are linguistic norms for women and men, maintained by 'linguistic and cultural ideological expectations about femininity' (and masculinity) which influence our language preferences when interacting (McElhinny 2003: 35).

These indexicalized norms also crucially influence expectations of speech, and thus affect the manner in which interactants are assessed and evaluated. Ochs (1992: 343) highlights a distinction between 'unmarked' and 'marked' linguistic forms, the former being those that accord with expectations of behaviour, whilst the latter refers to instances where speakers do not perform the interactional style that is expected of them. Consequently, speakers may be viewed as deviant and negatively evaluated. These views interconnect with Butler's (1990: 33) aforementioned 'rigid regulatory frame' that constrains appropriate acts of identity, and Holmes's (2005: 57) view of gender as always being relevant as a 'background framing construct', which works by 'unobtrusively influencing people's unconscious interpretation of what is considered appropriate in workplace interaction'.

It also raises the issue of the double bind (Lakoff 1990, 2003), namely that women are placed in a doubly difficult situation in the workplace and other public spheres: if they interact in a stereotypically feminine manner they will be negatively evaluated for being an incompetent professional, whereas if they interact in a stereotypically masculine manner, using 'marked' linguistic forms, they will be negatively evaluated for being overly aggressive (see Mullany and Litosseliti 2006). As Lakoff (1990: 206) argues, a professional woman faces a no-win situation: 'she can be a good woman but a bad executive or professional; or vice versa. To do both is impossible'. I will come back to consider these crucial issues of evaluation more fully later.

To summarize, the indexicality model reconceptualizes the manner in which linguistic forms relate to social identity. As McElhinny (2003: 35) observes, indexicality changes the way identity is perceived in that a female speaker does not use a tag question simply because she is a female speaker. Instead, she may use a tag question because she is abiding by 'cultural and ideological expectations about femininity'. Conversely, if a woman does not abide by these expectations, then she can be seen as resisting such cultural and ideological expectations, for which she may experience negative evaluation for operating outside of the 'rigid regulatory frame' of societal expectation. As previously mentioned the indexing perspective interlinks well with the notion of performativity. As Sunderland (2004: 20) argues, the 'performance or construction of a particular identity involves indexing. Language users, however, do not and cannot index an identity directly themselves, but do so rather through indexes.' Holmes's (2005: 47) notion of *covert* gendered discourse has much in common with Ochs's view of indirect indexicality. Holmes defines this discourse as when gender has a powerful effect on interactional strategies without being the direct topic of conversation or without being explicitly referred to (i.e., without being directly indexed, or *overt*, to use Holmes's term). Holmes argues that analysing covert gendered discourse can reveal much about how 'gender plays a part in taken-for-granted assumptions about the way power relations are constructed in workplace interaction', a key role played by the indexicality approach taken in this study.

In their investigations of gender and managerial workplace interaction, Holmes (2000a) and Holmes and Stubbe (2003a) have listed as a starting point typical 'feminine' and 'masculine' interactional styles, based on the findings of older sociolinguistic language and gender studies which followed the deficit, power/dominance and culture/difference approaches. Holmes (2000a) and Holmes and Stubbe (2003b) argue that such lists are of much analytical use for workplace gender research as they present the features of women's and men's speech that govern people's *stereotypical expectations* of what speech *should* be produced by women and men managers. These discourse patterns, (produced in Table 2.1), can thus be viewed as those that have been indirectly indexed with gendered meaning, and can therefore be utilized as a guide to stereotypically gender*ed* speech styles.

As Holmes and Stubbe (2003a) point out, the list does oversimplify, and does not take into account a range of contextual factors, issues of social power and other features of social identity apart from gender that can affect the performance of speech styles. However, producing such lists is still very useful as it does provide evidence of social and cultural expectations regarding what are considered appropriate interactional norms for women and men to use. When viewed from this perspective, perhaps it is unsurprising that so many earlier language and gender studies found distinct gender differences in speech, as interactants can

Table 2.1:   Widely cited features of 'feminine' and 'masculine' interactional style

Feminine	Masculine
■ indirect	■ direct
■ conciliatory	■ confrontational
■ facilitative	■ competitive
■ collaborative	■ autonomous
■ minor contribution (in public)	■ dominates (public) talking time
■ supportive feedback	■ aggressive interruptions
■ person/process-oriented	■ task/outcome-oriented
■ affectively oriented	■ referentially oriented

Source: Holmes and Stubbe 2003a: 574.

be perceived as producing discourse patterns that are deemed appropriate for them in order to avoid negative evaluation or stigmatization. Indeed, as Holmes and Stubbe (2003a: 575) point out, whilst there have been criticisms of early studies for oversimplification, much of this research was 'well-conceived and carefully executed', and, they follow Cameron (1997a: 49) in emphasizing that such findings have proved to be 'remarkably robust'.

This approach of utilizing stereotypes of feminine and masculine speech as analytical resources has also been put forward by Cameron (1992), Bucholtz and Hall (1995) and Talbot (2003). Cameron (1992) postulates that whilst researchers should never lose sight of the fact that folklinguistic beliefs are inaccurate, they do nevertheless give vital information on powerful ideologies and stereotypes about women and men's language use within society. Bucholtz and Hall (1995: 5) argue that, instead of simply dismissing folklinguistic beliefs, such as those expressed in Lakoff's (1975) work, analysts should utilize these as a resource as they aptly highlight 'the dominant cultural expectations of gender appropriate behaviour'. Talbot (2003: 475–476), cites a very similar dichotomous list of speech patterns to the one presented in Table 2.1. She highlights how these stereotypical speech styles support gender ideologies, and can thus be viewed as ideological prescriptions for how individuals *should* act when engaging in interaction, as individuals need to 'respond to the stereotypical roles expected of them' (2003: 472). Therefore, by utilizing lists of stereotypical gendered speech styles as lenses to analyse what takes place in actual interactions, researchers will be able to investigate language ideologies in conjunction with the realities of linguistic practices.

In this study, these stereotypical, gendered speech styles will be investigated by comparing them with actual usage in workplace interactions to assess how women and men managers perform their identities at work. Conducted from a CofP perspective, this analysis will assess the enactment of these indexicalized gendered speech styles, and ensure that the full range of social identity features and contextual factors which influence choice of interactional strategies for identity performance are fully evaluated. In order to assess the full impact of power and ideology, these findings will then be viewed from within the second, overarching layer of analysis of gendered discourses, following the Foucauldian-influenced definition. This includes a detailed analysis of how women and men managers are assessed and evaluated by themselves and by one another on the basis of their identity performance.

To illustrate how the framework of gendered discourses comes together, we will consider the importance of viewing stereotypical gendered speech styles from within the dominant 'discourse of gender difference' (Sunderland 2004). As its name suggests, this discourse heavily emphasizes the differences between women and men in society, including differences in language use. As Sunderland (2004: 52) points out, the discourse of gender difference 'is a significant "lens" for the way people view reality, difference being for most people what gender is all about'. Therefore, whilst the argument about viewing gender in a pluralized sense has been made, as mentioned earlier, within academic studies (Wodak and Benke 1997; Coates 2007), it is essential to point out that the dominant discourse of gender difference seeks to emphasize *homogeneity* within *singular* categories of femininity and masculinity, stressing instead the differences *between* women and men, as opposed to the differences *within* groups of women and groups of men.

Furthermore, Cameron (2003: 450) argues that one of the most persistent ideological perspectives on gender and language is that 'there are clear-cut stable differences in the way language is used by women and by men. In many versions of this ideology the differences are seen as natural, and in most cases, they are seen as desirable.' This explains the persistence of the view in wider society that women and men speak differently, as well as explaining the multitude of empirical findings of gender differences in speech styles. It also accounts for the popular success of books which draw on gendered stereotypes of appropriate language use, such as John Gray's Mars and Venus book series, which now includes *Mars and Venus in the Workplace* (2002). Arguably such publications become best sellers because readers claim to recognize their behaviour in such books.

By conducting this research, directly interrogating the dominant societal norms surrounding feminine and masculine language use in the workplace, it is my intention that this study may go some way towards

Freed's (2003) call to bridge the discrepancy between popular perceptions of language and gender and academic language and gender studies, as part of the overall aim of producing findings of practical relevance. Evidence of the dominant discourse of gender differences in language use, along with a range of other dominant gendered discourses that may work to place women managers at a disadvantage in the professional workplace will be carefully analysed in this study.

The decision to consider gendered discourses from within this overarching, Foucauldian-influenced analytical perspective has not just come from within linguistic study. As pointed out in Chapter 1, Foucault's influence is also prevalent within a range of disciplines including organizational studies, management studies and sociology. For example, management researchers Olsson and Walker (2003) draw on the work of Bem (1993) to observe through interview data that women and men executives 'perceive the executive world through a gendered lens and constitute themselves and men through a more general discourse on gender difference'. Fitzsimons (2002) has also drawn on the concept of gendered discourses in her sociological research to demonstrate why gender inequalities still persist in the workplace.

Baxter (2003) uses a similar two-pronged definition of discourse in her 'Feminist Post-Structuralist Discourse Analysis' (FPDA), and the following observation helps to summarize how analysis of the two different levels of discourse are crucially interlinked:

> [D]iscourses are forms of knowledge, or powerful sets of assumptions, expectations and explanations, governing mainstream social and cultural practices. They are systematic ways of making sense of the world by inscribing and shaping power relations within all texts, *including spoken interactions*. (Baxter 2003: 7, my emphasis)

Analysis of any texts, including spoken interactions, that is, analyses of language beyond the sentence, should be viewed within the second, broader definition of discourses in order to help elucidate dominant social practices which govern social and cultural ideological norms and expectations of what is deemed as appropriate behaviour for women and men within institutions. Following Foucault, Baxter (2003: 7) goes on to point out that discourses are 'always inextricably linked with concepts of power. Not as a negative, repressive force but as something that constitutes and energises all discursive and social relations'. Conceptualizing power from a Foucauldian perspective is a complex but beneficial endeavour from a feminist point of view, and will now be further explored.

Discourse and power

Foucault (1978: 101) argues that 'discourse transmits and produces power; it reinforces it, but also undermines it and exposes it, renders it fragile and makes it possible to thwart it'. He points out that discourse should not be seen as divided between a dominant group and a dominated group, as power is not simply an oppressive tool. Furthermore, as Deetz (1992: 252) points out, Foucault believes that power is 'omnipresent as it is manifest and produced in each moment'. Following Foucault, Mills (2002, 2003) makes the crucial point that power is both enacted and contested in every interaction and as such it should be viewed as a 'web'/'net' instead of a possession. Baxter (2003: 8) also draws on the 'net' metaphor, arguing that power is not something that a person has, but rather it is a ' "net-like organization" which weaves itself discursively through social organizations, meanings, relations and the construction of speakers' subjectivities or identities'.

In this volume, power is conceptualized as enacted and contested in every interaction. A key positive of Foucault's theorization of power for feminist linguistics is that it enables resistance to the norms of gender stereotyping to be brought to the fore of analysis, as opposed to viewing women simply as oppressed and passive victims (Coates 1997, 1999; Coates and Jordan 1997; Mills 1997, 2003; Walsh 2001). Pluralizing masculinities and femininities in conjunction with a Foucauldian perspective on power has enabled women and men to be more accurately perceived as complex, diverse groups.

However, whilst there is empirical evidence of women resisting and subverting gender stereotypes through resistant discourses, alongside this there are also examples of oppressive, dominant discourses, including, as we have already seen, the persistent and overarching 'discourse of gender difference'. Additionally, two other mainstream and also conflicting discourses are a 'patriarchal, or androcentric discourse' and a more 'radical, feminist discourse' (Coates and Jordan 1997: 216). Whilst I agree that these are also two important discoursal categories, instead of the term 'patriarchal', I favour the term 'masculinist hegemonic discourse', following Walsh's (2001: 17) argument that patriarchy is problematic as it implies 'a monolithic and totalising system of oppression in which all men dominate all women'. Walsh instead draws on Foucault's concept of orders of discourse, the sets of norms and conventions through which discourse is produced, to argue that discourses should instead be perceived as 'masculinist'. This perspective is also fully endorsed by researchers including Mills (2002) and Baxter (2006b). 'Masculinist hegemony' is defined by Walsh (2001: 17) as a concept which enables a dominant discourse to be viewed as 'diffuse', 'embedded in impersonal discursive practices and institutional structures commonly associated with men'. Gramsci's (1971) theory of hegemony, based on how power is enacted in society through means of gaining consent, refers to how power is found in 'everyday routine structures, emphasizing that the most effective form of domination is the assimilation of the wider population in ones' worldview' (Eckert and McConnell-Ginet 2003: 43). Baxter (2006b: xvi) recently observes that rejecting patriarchy has the advantage of placing key emphasis upon female agency and 'resistance to localised, masculinist discourses', as opposed to seeing all women oppressed by all men within a patriarchal system.

The overarching discourse of gender difference can be identified as a masculinist hegemonic discourse. If we come back to the stereotypical feminine and masculine interactional styles in Table 2.1, these can be seen as part of a hegemonic discourse of masculinity and a hegemonic discourse of femininity, contained within the overarching hegemonic discourse of gender difference, which de-emphasises differences within the gendered categories of women and men and instead maximises differences between a singularly defined masculinity and femininity to the extent that they appear naturalized. It thus hides differences and therefore the pluralities that exist *within* the heterogeneous categories of femininities and masculinities.

Coming back to Foucault, Mills (1997: 78) also points out that his view of power has been heavily influential with feminist theorists since it seems to make possible the developments of a complex model of power relations which deal with other social variables, such as race and social class, without having to prioritize one of these over the others. However, whilst there are clear advantages to adopting Foucault's view of discourse and power, this is not without problems for work of a feminist nature. Whilst his notion of orders of discourse is very useful, as is his fluid model of power, as Mills (1997: 78) points out, there is a difficulty in 'formulating a clear political agenda' from Foucault. This is clearly problematic for research with a feminist aim in general, and, in particular, for the kind of sociolinguistic work outlined in Chapter 1, where a clear political aim is central.

Foucault's work raises a number of difficulties in terms of structure and agency. As Bucholtz (2001: 173) argues, a major problem with his notion of discourse is that 'agency resides both everywhere and nowhere', which is highly problematic if you are examining social inequality with the intention of bringing about social change. If Foucault's theory is taken to its logical conclusion, then power appears to be agentless. At the extreme end of Foucault's theory is a view of discourse as completely disembodied (Mills 1997: 85).

A major reason for apparent agentless power can be attributed to the fact that Foucault (1979: 36) openly resists the concept of ideology in his theory of discourse. Mills (1997) examines the categories of Foucauldian discourse and ideology, arguing that the former has been used as an alternative to distance oneself from the heavily Marxist-laden category of ideology. However, she also points out that many researchers do not draw such a clear delineation between the two terms, and continue to use ideology successfully within discourse theory. Numerous examples of such work can be found (for example, Graddol and Swann 1989; Deetz 1992; Fairclough 1992, 1995, 2001; Hennessy 1993; Coates 1997, 1999; Coates and Jordan 1997).

In this study, I also wish to follow a framework that conceptualizes ideology as an 'integrated' approach to conceiving notions of power and discourse (Christie 2000: 52). Following Sunderland (2004: 6) and Mills (1997), discourses should be perceived as *'carrying* ideology' (emphasis in original). However, unlike the Marxist undertones that accompany a CDA approach, it is perfectly feasible to use the term ideology in a non-Marxist manner (Graddol and Swann 1989). I take Heller's (2001: 120) view that discourses in a Foucauldian sense 'are obviously linked to the notion of ideology, insofar as ideologies are understood as means of structuring and orienting domains of activity, and therefore inform discursive production and content'. This position accords with Bucholtz's (1999b: 20) emphasis on the importance of retaining the concept of ideology in feminist linguistics so that speakers' socially constructed identities 'are inflected by ideologies of gender and other social constructs'.

To clarify the relationship between ideology and stereotypes, I draw upon Talbot's (2003: 470) definition that stereotypes 'are ideological prescriptions for behaviour', with the process of stereotyping involving 'simplification, reduction and naturalization'. Stereotypes work to maintain the 'social and symbolic order ... they play an important part in the hegemonic struggle' (2003: 471). Stereotypes present us with simplistic presentations in light of which judgements are then made.

In particular reference to structure, agency and gender, following other feminist work influenced by Foucault, there is what Walsh (2001: 29) terms a 'creative dialectic that exists between structure and agency'. Walsh draws on Mills's (1995) conceptualization of gender ideologies to summarize this perspective:

> Ideologies of gender are not solely oppressive, they are not simply imposed on women by men. Women and men construct their own sense of self within the limits of these discursive frame-works, and build their pleasures and emotional development, often in conscious

resistance to, as well as in compliance with, these constraints. (Mills 1995: 2)

Another important point that I will take into account is Eckert's (2003: 396) observation that 'age-related ideology is inseparable from gender ideology, as well as from ideologies of class, race, and ethnicity'. Instead of analysing chronological age, Eckert (1997) argues that the social construction of life-stages is the way forward in sociolinguistic research. Such 'life-stages' are inflected by age ideologies that operate in society, which co-occur with gender and professional workplace identities. Ideologies of age do co-occur with gender ideologies when professional managers discuss their attitudes and evaluations of themselves and others (see Chapter 7). It is thus important that gender ideologies are also viewed alongside other ideologies that relate to further aspects of our social identities. Furthermore, Halford and Leonard (2001) and Powell and Graves (2003) point out that there is still a stereotypical expectation of managers as white middle-class males, due to the traditional domination of such individuals in the professional workplace context. In her consideration of linguistic politeness, Mills (2003) turns not just gender but also class and race into adjectival forms, imbuing them with the same meaning as Sunderland's definition of 'gendered', that politeness is classed and raced and thus already a part of the thing that is being described (see Chapter 4). Management can thus traditionally be seen as stereotypically gendered (masculine), classed (middle-class) and raced (white).

Sunderland (2004: 48–50) provides a very useful framework through which gendered discourses can be categorized. The gendered discourses which I have highlighted so far can be incorporated into her system. Her categorization starts with discourses of *substance*, and this includes the categories of a dominant hegemonic 'discourse of femininity' and a 'discourse of masculinity' which can be seen within the overarching 'discourse of gender difference'. The second category refers to *relational* discourses, where the term describes the relationship between different discourses, such as 'competing discourses'. The next category is *functional* discourses, whereby the explicit observable function of the discourse is part of the term, such as a 'liberating discourse' or 'subverting discourse'. Coates and Jordan's (1997) definition of 'resistant discourses' can be placed in this category. There are also a range of other, context-dependent discourses, which Sunderland terms *specific* discourses, that have been coined by various researchers depending upon what type of context and topic they have investigated, such as a 'mother as main parent' discourse, or, of particular relevance to this study, an 'equal opportunities discourse' (Sunderland 2004: 50).

There are thus a whole range of gendered discourses which fulfil different functions, and these categories outlined above will be used as an overall systematic guide to analysing gendered discourses at this all-encompassing level. The first layer of analysis of gendered speech styles will be assessed within the overarching level of gendered discourses, including the discourse of gender difference, enabling ideological expectations of language and gender to be assessed. Furthermore, Sunderland (2004: 7) points out that gendered discourses can also be fruitfully analysed within the language that women and men managers use to represent their 'ideas, opinions and concepts'. In this study, gendered discourses will also be examined within interview data with managers in order to gain access to their 'ideas, opinions and concepts' about gender and language, as well as on issues of gender more generally within their workplaces. This accords with Holmes's (2005) categorization of *overtly* gendered discourse, where gender becomes the actual topic of the interaction. Discussing the topic of gender in direct relation to language will enable stereotypical, folklinguistic beliefs to be directly accessed, through which dominant gendered discourses can be viewed (Talbot 2003). Within organizational studies, Brewis (2001: 293) neatly demonstrates how a Foucauldian-influenced discourse analysis can be successfully conducted by analysing interview data, as 'listening to females talking about organizations allows an exploration of their discursive positioning', which can highlight if they are being disadvantaged and/or treated differently due to dominant gendered discourses.

Sunderland (2004: 21) observes a shift in the manner in which she analyses 'gendered discourses', from examining the 'gendered how' to the 'gendered what' in language and gender investigations. She elaborates on this, claiming that from an analytical perspective 'the *substance* of what is said is more important than the *style*' (2004: 18). Gendered beliefs have therefore replaced language in use as the topic of analysis in her publication. In contrast, this book investigates both the 'gendered how' and the 'gendered what', with language in use, that is, analysis of gendered interactional styles (the first level of gendered discourse), taking place in conjunction with gendered substance/beliefs (the second, overarching level of discourse). To utilize Halliday's terminology (cf. Walsh 2001; Sunderland 2004), both the *interpersonal* and *ideational* levels of analysis are investigated. It is a long-standing tradition within discourse-orientated sociolinguistic research to examine language in use, and more specifically, it is the job of sociolinguists to focus on how workplace identities are constructed through communicative interaction (Marra et al. 2006). Analysing authentic language in use also gives the researcher real-life data from which practically relevant suggestions can be made. By adopting the indexicality approach and analysing managers' interactional styles as part of an overarching analysis of broader gendered discourses, it is the intention that the fruitful nature of this integrated approach will bring to the surface reasons as to why gender inequalities in the professional workplace still exist, and identify the role that language and gender ideologies play in perpetuating such inequalities.

In summary, the particular critical sociolinguistic approach taken here integrates a range of different approaches, bringing together Butler's (1990) notion of performativity, the CofP framework, Foucault's (1972; 1981) conceptions of 'power' and 'discourse', as well as Ochs's (1992) indexicality model. By combining these approaches, this study can therefore be seen as firmly belonging within the third-wave feminist category.

Gendered work

Combining Ochs's (1992) indexing theory with the overarching notion of gendered discourses also enables specific social contexts to be viewed as gendered, along with social roles and social activities. In specific reference to indexicality, Freed (1996) draws on Ochs to produce the following argument:

> [S]etting and associated communicative tasks become an index of a 'gendered style' ... not only can a particular linguistic feature be an index of a social meaning (which in turn is attached to gender), but certain social activities themselves may be indexed for certain types of talk. These activities and practices may then themselves become symbolically gendered if they are regularly and consistently associated with either women or men. (Freed 1996: 67)

This 'symbolic' gendering can be perceived within the dominant overarching perspective of gendered discourses, with social and cultural norms and expectations dictating whether women or men are thought to be best suited to particular social roles, activities and overall practices. Similarly, McElhinny (1998: 309) argues that workplaces are gendered due to one sex being more dominant than the other, along with 'the cultural interpretations of given types of work which, in conjunction with cultural norms and interpretations of gender, dictate who is understood as best suited for different sorts of employment'. Mills (2003: 5) refers to the work of Freed (1996) and McElhinny (1998) collectively as a model of 'gendered domains', whereby gender is enacted within settings 'which are themselves gendered by association'.

Coates (1995) and Kendall and Tannen (1997) have argued that the dominant speech norms in the workplace are masculine, as historically men have made up the vast majority of the workforce. Kendall and Tannen (1997: 86) add that the predominance of men, both in general but particularly at more senior levels of professions, along with stereotypical 'cultural interpretations', dictate who is thought to be best suited to carry out a particular professional role. These factors operate to ensure the maintenance of professional workplace norms as masculine norms.

Similar observations regarding 'gendered' workplaces and particular employment roles as gendered have also been made within organizational studies and management studies. Wajcman (1998) argues that both managerial posts and organizations are gendered. She points out that 'managerial competence' is intrinsically linked to qualities associated with men, a point also made by Hearn and Parkin (1988). Accordingly, managerial ideologies are masculinized. In organizational studies, Brewis (2001: 288) draws heavily on Foucault (1972) to suggest that women's experiences within organizations have been marginalized by a dominant masculinized perspective, which has become accepted as the 'truth' for all organizations, 'that they are neutral, non-discriminatory environments in which relations are governed by objectivity and rationality ... to ensure that there is no reward for anything other than individual merit'. She argues that the 'discourse of gender difference' is of particular relevance to this version of the organizational 'truth', in conjunction with what she terms 'the discourse of scientific modernism', a discourse of *substance* according to Sunderland's (2004) classifications. This discourse depicts the workplace as an arena where objectivity and rationality must prevail in order for success to be achieved. Brewis (2001: 293) argues that the discourse of gender difference and the discourse of scientific modernism work together to promote 'understandings and representations of women as being less suited to organizational life', since the discourse of gender difference positions women as 'irrational, emotional and inevitably subjective in decision making'.

Within sociology, Fitzsimons (2002) has drawn upon Foucauldian notions of discourse and Gramsci's hegemony to identify a typology for a 'hegemonic discourse of femininity' and a 'hegemonic discourse of masculinity'. These typologies identify men with professional occupations, always in the public sphere, and include management, whereas women are instead identified with caring, either in a domestic setting, or, if in the public sphere, within professions such as nursing. In reference to character traits, Fitzsimons (2002: 152) lists the hegemonic traits of femininity as emotional, maternal, close to nature, devious, sly, untrustworthy and bitchy. This sits in direct opposition with the typology of the hegemonic discourse of masculinity which contains character traits of independence, rationality, competitiveness, and power and control over emotions as well as over other men, women and children (2002: 103).

Sex-role stereotyping has also been identified as a problem for women managers. When women gain positions of power within the workplace, arguably there are a limited number of identity roles they can adopt which enables them to enact their professional roles legitimately. Sociologists Halford and Leonard (2001: 108–109) draw on the original work of Kanter (1977) to map out these social roles. The first is the 'mother role', whereby women give emotional support and care for their colleagues and subordinates. Adopting this role runs the risk of being assessed as too emotional as opposed to being professional. The mother role can also be negatively evaluated by those who may feel they are being patronized (Tannen 1994). Another role is the 'seductress', which can be enacted consciously or unconsciously. As Halford and Leonard (2001) argue, this role is often accompanied with much suspicion, and negative evaluation as a whore usually results. Adopting such a role often causes resentment from other men who are status equals in the business, particularly if senior men are involved. From the 'seductress' perspective women's competence and professional abilities are extinguished by her sexuality. The 'pet' is another category, whereby women can be 'adopted' by men and treated like one of the boys. Such women often engage in humour and fun but they are never really taken seriously. The final category is the 'iron maiden', the tough, aggressive feminist, characterized by Tannen (1994: 164) as 'the dragon lady'. Enactment of this role most often leads to the double bind and negative evaluation for being overly aggressive, unemotional and thus unnatural. These categories for women are seen in direct opposition to the male as norm, maintained by the dominant discourse of masculinity.

Despite these identity categories and dominant gendered discourses, it is important to acknowledge that changes within the workplace demographic have now been afoot for some time, and despite the persistence of the glass ceiling, women do nevertheless make up a third of all managerial positions in the United Kingdom. Recent work has suggested that this is starting to impact upon managerial speech styles, as well as on the manner in which managerial roles and particular organizations are viewed. Holmes (2000a) argues that women managers display a 'wide-verbal-repertoire' (Case 1988; 1995), drawing on both stereotypically masculine and feminine speech styles. Holmes and Stubbe (2003a) assess the concept of the gendered workplace. Their work indicates that the observations made in older studies such as Coates (1995) and Kendall and Tannen (1997), of workplace speech norms being masculine norms, are now out-dated. Holmes and Stubbe (2003a) investigate some organizations in their corpus from the perspective of being stereotypically 'feminine', with the 'feminine' interactional styles outlined in Table 2.1 being dominant, as well as more traditional, stereotypically 'masculine' workplaces, with masculine speech norms being dominant. However, they do argue for a context-sensitive, CofP analysis in order to reveal the complex range of factors that affect the discourse styles that managers use in the workplace.

Marra et al. (2006: 241) also draw attention to women using a wide-verbal repertoire, arguing that, despite the predominance of the stereotypical view of leadership as masculine, a 'complete leadership "package"', which includes both transactional and relational goals, and thus a combination of stereotypically masculine and stereotypically feminine strategies, is found. They argue that their data show how effective leaders 'do leadership' by invoking strategies 'which have been associated with both normatively masculine and normatively feminine ways of talking' (2006: 242). A useful framework is their continuum of masculine and feminine CofPs. The continuum stresses 'the ways in which gendered patterns of communication are sustained in the shared practices of each community' (2006: 244). To illustrate, they identify a workplace CofP which shows a collaborative style, egalitarian philosophy, frequent use of indirectness and supportive discourse strategies as being towards the feminine end of the CofP continuum, whereas a team frequently enacting competitiveness, challenges to one another and individualism is identified towards the masculine end of the continuum.

In particular reference to sex-role stereotyping highlighted earlier, Wodak (1997a) observes a transition as far as the 'mother role' is concerned, arguing that it has now become legitimized. She examines the discourse strategies of three women head teachers chairing school meetings, discovering that they utilize powerful and authoritarian discourse strategies through 'patterns of maternity' (1997c: 367). Whilst it may be the case that the mother role is more acceptable in teaching professions where there is already a caring, nurturing expectation built into role responsibility, Stubbe et al. (2000) and Holmes and Stubbe (2003a) also comment on how the 'mother role' can provide women managers with a legitimate social role through which authority can be enacted in professional workplaces without experiencing negative evaluation.

Coming back to interactional discourse styles, Mills (2003) observes a recent shift in the manner in which women's communicative strategies have been re-evaluated, reflected in the workplace through certain companies' communication training. She reports that this now tends to draw upon key aspects of stereotypically feminine speech styles. Within organizational studies, Appelbaum et al. (2002) also observe a transition to stereotypically 'feminine' communication skills as the superior style for managers to now adopt. Similarly, Cameron (2000, 2006) demonstrates that there has been a recent transition towards adopting stereotypical feminine speech styles as effective models of communication in late modern societies. She accords this with Fairclough's (1992) theory of the *conversationalization* of public discourse, whereby speech strategies associated with the private sphere, that is, those stereotypically associated with feminine speech styles, are permeating their way into the public sphere. Fairclough bases this on the *democratization* of discourse, whereby markers that overtly signal asymmetry are being eliminated in organizational cultures and replaced with flatter structures. Instead of being exercised through coercion, Fairclough argues that power is instead exercised through consent, in a *repressive* as opposed to *oppressive* manner (Pateman 1980). He accords consent power with Gramsci's (1971) hegemony, highlighting that ideology works as a primary means of 'manufacturing consent' (Fairclough 1989: 4). Sarangi and Roberts (1999) refer to these transitions in workplace practices as the *new work order*, following the work of Gee et al. (1996).

However, it is important not to get carried away here. As Cameron (2003: 462) argues, such transitions towards the promotion of feminine communicative styles as effective in workplaces are seen as part of powerful 'communication ideologies', and although they bring 'new representations of gendered language', they do not necessarily work in favour of women. Regardless of how much this new ideology stresses the important qualities of 'feminine' communication skills, it has not been motivated by a desire to bring about equality, but instead through a desire to fulfil the needs of contemporary consumerist capitalism. Just because stereotypically feminine strategies are favoured does not mean that women are being placed at an advantage. In fact, these new ideologies can be very damaging for women. As Cameron (2003) observes, such moves in contemporary society are often based upon ideas of widely discredited notions of biological essentialism, which work to reinforce gender dichotomies and inequalities. Furthermore, and most importantly, 'the individuals who most closely approximate the new ideal in the real world are often men: men who combine the traditional "masculine" qualities of authority, enterprise and leadership with a command of the more "feminine" language of emotional expressiveness and rapport' (Cameron 2003: 463). Cameron observes that, when men enact 'feminine' communicative styles such as 'emotional expressiveness', they are 'applauded' for it. In contrast, women are subject to the double bind, being seen as too emotional for the workplace. Similarly, Appelbaum et al. (2002) observe the following:

> When there seems to have been some merit in what would normally have been considered a 'female' approach, men adopt it as their own. What was weak is now thought of as flexible; what was emotional now combines with rational to bring balance. (Appelbaum et al. 2002: 49)

Holmes (2005: 56) also makes this observation about interpretations of male behaviour, based on her large workplace corpus, arguing that men in several workplaces they observed 'operated in traditionally "feminine" ways without any evidence that their behaviour was perceived as out-of-line'.

This difference in assessment is a prime example of the discourse of gender difference in action: when men are seen in a positive light for adopting feminine strategies, women will not receive the same evaluation. Indeed, women may in fact be seen as too emotional for the public sphere. Both Brewis (2001) and Lakoff (2003) have pointed out that women expressing emotions in the workplace are negatively evaluated, seen as acting irrationally, and are thus subject to the double bind.

Whilst empirical evidence of feminine speech strategies or a combination of feminine and masculine strategies being used by managers in workplaces has started to be found, evidence indicates that women and men are still evaluated very differently. Such deeply ingrained beliefs work against women and result in the perpetuation of gender inequalities. Indeed, recent studies have found that women and men are evaluated differently even when acting in exactly the same manner. Appelbaum et al. (2002: 45) observe how 'the same leadership behaviour is often evaluated more positively when attributed to a male than a female', an argument that is also made by Marra et al. (2006). Wajcman (1998: 61) too highlights how the same actions can be evaluated very differently depending upon whether they are enacted by a man or woman manager: 'A particular action or experience might be defined as "firm", "decisive" and "rational" when constructed in relation to a man, and as "bossy", "hysterical" and "irrational" when a woman is involved.' Furthermore, as Olsson and Walker (2003: 395) point out, whilst women are negatively evaluated due to gender stereotyping, the stereotypes about men and masculinity do not 'damage their power', including the levels of effectiveness and competence with which they are perceived to be doing their job. Furthermore, a frequently cited finding from within management studies research is the continual persistence of the problem that has come to be commonly identified as 'think manager, think male' (Olsson 2000; Olsson and Walker 2003; Powell and Graves 2003). In matched-guise tests and tests that assess managerial effectiveness, both women and men managers continually evaluate men and stereotypically masculine traits as more effective and successful.

Overall, this chapter has emphasized that there are a range of complex aspects to take into account when conducting a study of language and gender in managerial workplaces. Social and political changes in terms of transitions in workplace practices and demographics have now been afoot for some time, and recent research has shown that older studies of male dominance are now out-dated. However, the visibility of women in management has not resulted in gender equality. In order to investigate the complex manner in which language and gender interrelate in managerial workplaces, this study will examine the gendered speech styles that are being used in managerial interactions, which includes a thorough assessment of whether recent transitions that have been witnessed in other aforementioned studies can be witnessed in the organizations under study. In conjunction with this, the CofP approach will be followed in order to ensure that the complexities of how managerial identities are performed in specific workplace contexts are examined. The manner in which managers are evaluated and assessed as a consequence of the identities they enact needs to be carefully scrutinized as part of this approach. Adopting the dual model of gendered discourses outlined in this chapter enables both interactional styles and broader gender ideologies that operate in society to be assessed. In order to fulfil these aims and objectives, a multi-method approach to data collection is required. This is detailed in the next chapter, along with consideration of the broader issues at stake when collecting workplace data in general.

3
Collecting Workplace Data

Restricted research sites

Sarangi and Roberts (1999: 40–41) stress the importance of the need for researchers to 'fight against the temptation to collect what is easily collectable' and persevere in attempting to gain access to restricted research sites. The workplace is a prime example of a restricted research site, and a range of challenging obstacles need to be overcome if access is to be gained. Furthermore, commitment to producing research which is of overall political relevance to wider society, including being of value and practical use to those who are being researched, poses a range of complex problems that need to be carefully negotiated when deciding upon research methodologies. The methodological approaches taken in my study are outlined in this chapter. This enables consideration of the variety of negotiations and compromises that take place when conducting a research project within any institutional research setting. As well as detailing the choices I made and justifications as to why I did this, other avenues that could be pursued by researchers wishing to conduct investigations in the workplace are also highlighted.

It is thus my intention that this chapter can be of practical use to investigators conducting empirical research projects in any institutional setting where researcher access is restricted. This will commence with consideration of a traditional starting point for methodological decision-making, an overall consideration of quantitative and qualitative methodologies in particular relation to language and gender workplace research.

Qualitative and quantitative methodologies

Holmes and Meyerhoff (2003) observe a noticeable transition to qualitative, ethnographic methodological approaches in language and gender studies in recent years, seen to be a consequence of their compatibility with the theoretical approaches outlined in the previous chapter. Drawing on the work of Gal (1995), Cameron (1997b: 28–29) argues that any study of linguistic acts needs to be accompanied with broadly ethnographic descriptions of 'the local contexts and belief systems within which language use is embedded'. A more general shift from quantitative to qualitative methodologies has also been observed as a trend in numerous disciplines in the social sciences, including organizational studies and management studies (Alvesson and Deetz 2000).

However, despite the current popularity of qualitative approaches, Holmes and Meyerhoff (2003) also argue that there is still a place for quantitative as well as qualitative research in language and gender studies. They believe that integrated approaches which combine methodologies are highly productive. Such integration enables overall patterns to be highlighted by a quantitative analysis, emphasizing the 'gendered norms' (2003: 15) that speakers are drawing upon, which can then be used as background for producing fine-grained linguistic analyses of data. They believe quantitative research has been unfairly penalized as it is not currently fashionable. These are valid points, and Holmes and Meyerhoff are not alone in their endorsement of utilizing combined methodological approaches. Wodak and Benke (1997), Bergvall (1999), Swann (2002) and Swann and Maybin (2008) all argue that, where possible, language and gender research would benefit from combining both qualitative and quantitative methods (see Eckert 2000).

It is important to emphasize that, by following a qualitative, ethnographic approach I am not setting this study up in opposition with quantitative approaches. As Silverman (2000: 11) argues, the dichotomy which exists between qualitative and quantitative approaches is 'highly dangerous', resulting in researchers being unwilling to learn from each other. In the same vein as his argument regarding researchers avoiding placing one's work into 'armed camps', emphasized in Chapter 2, Silverman (2000; 2001) advocates that academics should build bridges between different social science traditions in an effort to move disciplines forward by sharing ideas. Similarly, Sarangi and Roberts (1999: 40) highlight a general tendency in academic debate to 'marshal arguments around two opposing camps', which often has the unfortunate consequence of masking opportunities for more integrated methodological approaches to research.

This study takes a 'multi-method' approach to data collection, in that a range of different methods is used within an overall ethnographic approach. These multi-methods are: analysis of audio-recorded business meeting data, analysis of audio-recorded interview data, analysis of field notes of informal talk and other recorded background information gained whilst shadowing, along with analysis of written documents. Within the linguistic data analysis of meetings, what Silverman (2001: 241) terms 'basic calculating techniques' are utilized to survey the overall patterning of the data. As he points out, just because a qualitative approach is adopted does not mean that such techniques cannot be used. Indeed, he argues that such an approach enables the 'whole corpus of data' which is 'ordinarily lost in intensive, qualitative research' to be surveyed. This overall survey is then followed up with a more detailed, fine-grained qualitative analysis of the data enhanced by ethnographic observation. Whilst this does not by any means amount to a combined quantitative and qualitative approach to which aforementioned language and gender researchers refer, it can be seen as integrating qualitative and quantitative *tools of analysis* to some degree within the confines of an ethnographic framework. Employing such techniques to the analysis of business meeting data goes some way towards minimizing the problem of anecdotalism (Silverman 2001), a charge that is often cited at qualitative research. Silverman goes on to point out that it is extremely difficult for qualitative methods to be combined with quantitative surveys, which require a large research team, substantial funding and a great deal of time to be successful. Holmes and Meyerhoff (2003) make a similar point, observing that there are significant costs that go along with blending together quantitative and qualitative research methods, including the investment of many years of work.

Overall, it is essential to realize that methodological decisions should be based on more complex decisions than theoretical preferences and trends. Practical issues including size of research team, the amount of financial support and the length of the project are all factors, as well as the influence that the 'researched' will have on the project, as research questions and access undergo the process of joint negotiation within applied sociolinguistic studies. Access problems also play a critical role when deciding upon what kind of methods can be deployed, and my decision to take a qualitative approach in this study is also influenced by the difficulties of initial access to workplaces. From the outset it was thought that only a handful of businesses would be willing to take part in the project, and thus qualitative methods seemed far more appropriate, as well as more practicable for a sole researcher. Therefore, instead of simply assigning oneself to a methodological paradigm out of pre-established traditions within a discipline, researchers should be driven by practical factors when deciding upon methodologically appropriate approaches. Theoretical influences should not be overlooked, however, and part of the decision to conduct qualitative research was still due to the trends that have taken place in language and gender studies in recent years, resulting in my desire to conduct an in-depth, qualitative study of the role that language can play in producing and reproducing gender inequalities, in conjunction with the other practical constraints mentioned above. Methodological decisions are thus made up of a complex balance of a range of factors.

Sociolinguistics and ethnography

Within sociolinguistics, ethnography has been traditionally associated with the ethnography of communication (Hymes 1974) and interactional sociolinguistics (Gumperz 1974; 1982). The methodological principle of needing to gain a deeper understanding of context through an ethnographic approach runs through a range of work on language and gender, including Gal (1979), Brown (1980), and more recently, work in the collections of Bucholtz et al. (1999) and Baron and Kotthoff (2001). It is also important not to overlook the fact that variationist sociolinguistic research has also utilized ethnographic methods, including Milroy (1987), Cheshire (1982) and Eckert (2000).

Another factor which influenced my decision to produce ethnographic studies was Sarangi and Roberts's (1999) view, from within applied linguistics, that a *thick description* (Geertz 1973) should be used to provide a comprehensive examination of workplace interaction. One of the approaches they suggest for achieving a thick description is ethnography. They summarize the advantages of taking such an approach:

> [It] reaches down to the level of fine-grained linguistic analysis and up and out to broader ethnographic description and wider political and ideological accounts. Such a holistic description attends to the smallness of things and aims to understand them in all of their interpretative complexity. It acknowledges the overarching social order in which they interact and which binds and regulates as it reinvents itself. (Sarangi and Roberts 1999: 1)

They therefore propose that researchers include both 'an interaction based notion of talk' and 'an ideologically based notion of institutional order' when conducting analysis (Sarangi and Roberts 1999: 1). The approach taken in this book can be described as a thick description in this sense: a linguistic analysis of gendered speech styles is enhanced by ethnographic description, gained through a CofP approach, which is then examined as part of and in conjunction with wider gender ideologies, gained by an analysis of overarching gendered discourses which operate at an institutional level.

Defining ethnography

Hammersley and Atkinson (1995) point out that 'ethnography' refers primarily to a specific set of methods, identified as follows:

> The ethnographer [participates] overtly or covertly, in people's daily lives for an extended period of time, watching what happens, listening to what is said, asking questions – in fact, collecting whatever data are available to throw light on the issues that are the focus of the research. (Hammersley and Atkinson 1995: 1)

Whilst the notion of an 'extended period of time' is quite vague, within anthropology, this has often meant absorbing oneself in a community for many years, and often such communities have tended to be rather 'exotic' and remotely located (Duranti 1997). However, from a sociolinguistic perspective, Swann and Maybin (2008) point out that it is very uncommon for researchers to embrace ethnography in this traditional, anthropological sense, perhaps with the exception of Eckert (1989; 2000). Following Green and Bloome (1995), they argue that it is far more common for sociolinguists to follow an *ethnographic perspective* which is still strongly influenced by crucial ethnographic principles, including insider observations based on ethnographic methods. The ethnographic approach taken in this study follows the sociolinguistic tradition more than the anthropological tradition. A range of ethnographic methods are used, including the crucial concept of insider observations. The length of time in the field was arrived through complex negotiations between myself as researcher and those being researched. Full details of this are documented later from a reflexive perspective.

Coming back to Hammersley and Atkinson's quotation, the process of the ethnographer taking part in 'people's daily lives', or the process of 'insider participation' is commonly known throughout the social sciences as *participant observation*. Stewart (1998) argues that, whilst there can be a variety of approaches to the process of ethnographic data collection, participant observation is the key research tool of any ethnographic study. Alvesson and Deetz (2000) point out that participant observation, accompanied with loosely structured interviews, make up the most fundamental elements of ethnography, with further methods including engagement in informal talk and examination of materials, including written texts. In particular relation to management studies, they document that the focus of ethnographic research will typically fall upon a particular organization or specific department within an organization. The importance of conducting informal interviews and engaging in spontaneous talk with managers is seen as an essential part of the fieldwork process. Without the information gained via these modes it is very difficult to comment on 'the meanings of and ideas guiding particular behaviours and practices' (Alvesson and Deetz 2000: 76). Sarangi and Roberts (1999: 27) argue that the adoption of an ethnographic approach 'involves a triangulation of data sources including traditional participant observation, audio and video recording and the collecting of documentary evidence'. Both Alvesson and Deetz's (2000) and Sarangi and Roberts's work has been influential when deciding which specific ethnographic methods I wished to follow, as well as being influenced by the requests, needs and restrictions of those being researched. The multi-methods adopted can be seen as a form of triangulation, implemented in order to attempt to gain as much detail as possible from differing sources in order to produce a convincing interpretation of the data under scrutiny.

The ability to make audio or video recordings of workplace practices that are being observed is a crucial element of conducting an ethnographic study from a *linguistic* standpoint. It was essential that the companies I approached would agree to me recording encounters to undergo transcribed linguistic analysis, so that I was not just a participant observer in the traditional sense, with only a notebook as a tool for recording speech events (see Duranti 1997 for a critique of ethnographies that do not analyse recorded language data). Although some workplace researchers have used video as a form of recording, including some of the meeting data obtained by Holmes and Stubbe (2003b) and their team in New Zealand, audio recording was chosen as I perceived this to be a less intrusive method than videoing, and thus one that may not affect participants' behaviour as much as the presence of a video recorder. Furthermore, I believed that companies would be more willing to grant me permission to record workplace interactions if I used audio equipment instead of video equipment. Duranti (1997: 117) observes that video seems far more likely to trigger the effect of the observer's paradox than audio recording. Whilst the inescapable fact remains that the presence of tape recording equipment may still affect participants' actions, it is hoped that this influence was kept at a minimum. The observer's paradox will be thoroughly discussed later.

Approaching and negotiating with organizations

In order to be considered as a data source, the only prerequisite prospective businesses had to have was to employ women at a managerial level, and grant me permission to audio-record interactions. I did not restrict the companies I approached in any other way; for example, I did not specify a particular sector or company size, due to the difficulties I expected to face in terms of gaining access. Alvesson and Deetz (2000: 75) point out that, in order to gain initial access to managers when conducting ethnography, it is common for the researchers to establish close contact with a 'key informant' who then guides the research. It was thought that personnel departments within companies would be the best points of initial contact, as those working within this section often play a gate-keeping role in terms of access (Bargiela-Chiappini and Harris 1997).

Furthermore, it is the personnel departments within businesses who have overall responsibility for equal opportunities, and thus it was integral to have them involved in the project from its inception. However, despite these crucial advantages of using members of personnel departments as my initial points of contact and as key informants, one potential danger of this is that other managers may perceive me to be working on behalf of personnel. It was thus important to assure all participants that this was not the case, and stress instead how the findings that I would produce and any practical recommendations that resulted from this study would be open and available to all, not just written for the benefit of personnel. Personnel departments of a wide variety of businesses from different sectors were thus approached, with the hope of finding a key informant to guide the research process. I decided that approaching a female at a middle/senior level of management within a company would be the best point of initial contact, based on the view that females may be more sympathetic to the aims of a project on gender.

A number of crucial issues surrounding the initial point of contact between a workplace and the researcher are highlighted by Sarangi and Roberts (1999), and these points can be a useful practical guide. They argue that, if researchers 'present themselves through discourses that are seen as threatening, obfuscating or irrelevant', barriers may come down almost immediately (1999: 42). It is vital for the managers in companies to understand and appreciate the overall purpose of the research, not perceive the researcher as a threat or challenge, be able to see that they can have input into the direction and aims of the research, as well as perceiving how the research can be of potential practical relevance overall.

Initial contact with companies was made by posting them a written outline of the project, which aimed to be as clear and concise as possible for a non-academic audience. The practical relevance that the project could have, particularly in relation to issues of gender inequality, was clearly highlighted. The outline emphasized how the project aimed to provide evidence of changes in role and identity that women and men managers may have experienced in recent years, focusing in particular upon 'workplace communication'. Investigating the impact that language may have on the glass ceiling was highlighted as a key practical aim. As the glass ceiling is a well-known and oft-cited problem of workplace gender inequality in popular culture and the mass media, as well as in the academic world, I thought that this issue in particular would highlight how the research could be of key practical relevance to organizations. Assurances of complete confidentiality were also given. Posting the outline was followed up with a telephone call a few days later to see if the recipient was interested in taking part. If the personnel manager agreed, a face-to-face meeting was set up.

The starting point for approaching companies was based on geographical location, with the aim of gaining access to businesses located within a reasonable travelling distance (within fifty miles). A potentially fruitful starting point for contacts was with companies who had had some contact with the university in the past, and thus, in theory at least, may be more open to participating in academic research. A list of personnel managers/directors who had enrolled students on undergraduate work experience programmes provided the first list of contacts. Female managers/directors who appeared on this list were approached, and one company was gained from this technique.

After this access had been secured, it became evident that the projected difficulties in terms of gaining access were well founded. Numerous workplaces were approached, but repeatedly the women managers reported that, whilst the project sounded interesting, they were too busy, or they were not happy about the audio-recorded aspect of the project or confidentiality issues in general. In some cases, no reply was received. Another identifiable barrier that emerged related to my identity as an academic researcher. Being a linguist located in an English department was a noticeable obstacle. Personnel managers expressed confusion as to why anyone in an English department would want to examine business communication. This issue draws attention to the preconceptions that non-academics have about university researchers and 'appropriate' arenas within which they can legitimately produce research. It is hoped that future interdisciplinary projects will provide more flexibility with researcher identities and affiliations and thus provide solutions to such difficulties (Mullany 2008 expands upon this issue). As a consequence of the barriers I was encountering, I decided to widen the catchment area for companies, and I also decided that male managers would be approached, as the appeal to female solidarity did not appear to be having much of an impact. Eventually, a second company was found. Interestingly, the personnel manager of this company was male.

Whilst the case for commitment to producing research of practical relevance has been firmly made in Chapter 1, there is a potential conflict here in terms of research having broader political applicability and relevance to wider society, and being committed to following the desires of those being researched. It is quite possible that the desires of those being researched may well be at odds with the overall political relevance for wider society, perhaps particularly in a corporate environment, where the need to makes profits is so essential. An interrelated point here is that the aims of the researched may well have been at odds with the researcher's own principles. It is also more than possible in institutional settings that different employees may have different ideas and needs in terms of the kind of topics that they would like to be researched.

In the companies that agreed to take part in the research, I was fortunate in that none of their requests conflicted with my own principles. As gender inequality is a problem that stretched across all different departments in the companies, it was hoped that this overarching topic would enable all different departments in the companies to feel both included and that the research may be of benefit to them. In order to maintain the wider political importance of the study outside of the companies, so that my aims were met, it was important for me to ensure that the research focus did not stray away from the focus on workplace communication and gender inequality. The potential for conflict in terms of differing research needs only arose once, when a male manager told me that the primary focus of my study should be on the crisis of masculinity and the 'decline' of the male manager as opposed to focusing on women managers' problems in breaking through the glass ceiling (see Chapter 7 for further discussion).

The real negotiation of research aims in terms of producing findings that can be of practical relevance to the community under study took place within the face-to-face meetings with personnel representatives, resulting in agreement of access and methods. My desire to conduct research using ethnographic methods, based upon recent transitions in the discipline, as well as upon the limited number of companies that had agreed to take part, would only be possible in practice if careful negotiation took place. As I had approached the businesses and initiated the potential research link, what Sarangi (2006: 199) aptly refers to as 'self-imposed' research as opposed to 'invited' research, there was an expectation that I would inform them of the benefits to getting involved in the project, as well as present them with suggestions for the type of access that I would require in order to fulfil the negotiated research aims. During such meetings I presented details of how the glass ceiling and other potential gender inequalities could be investigated from a linguistic perspective, as well as detailing the qualitative, ethnographic methods that I thought would be best suited to investigating these issues, in non-technical language.

In terms of the negotiation of research aims and questions, both companies were very interested in the glass ceiling and issues of women's career progression in general, and these were cited as key reasons why both companies had decided to get involved following the details provided on the project résumé. Whilst both businesses had equal opportunities policies in place, the glass ceiling was clearly evident in these organizations, and they were thus interested in learning more about the role that language and communication could potentially play in causing and maintaining such gender inequalities. The importance of managers possessing 'good communication skills' was key in both companies. This ties in with the point made by Gunnarsson et al. (1997), emphasized in Chapter 1, that businesses themselves have recently become very much aware of the importance of communication, and it has become a key part of corporate business training in order to improve the overall effectiveness and productivity of organizations. Both companies were also interested in the impact that gender can have on managerial effectiveness, and the manner in which managers are assessed and evaluated. Therefore, it was agreed that I would develop a study focusing on the role that gender can play in affecting workplace communication, how managers perceive the role that gender and language play in their own careers, as well as how gender more generally affects their assessments and evaluations of other colleagues. It was the negotiated intention that the results of the project could then be integrated into training programmes on gender and managerial communication.

It was of key importance within these initial meetings to gain agreement to audio-recording. I suggested my preference for recording business meetings and interviews, though any speech event could potentially be recorded in order to provide me with linguistic data. Firm assurances of confidentiality were vital at this stage. The personnel representative was assured that a copy of the tape could be requested by all participants at any time. Audio-recorded material which participants were unhappy with would be deleted immediately on request, including the option of deleting entire meetings or interviews. Initial agreement with both companies was for me to shadow/observe managers, attend and audio-record business meetings, as well as conduct and audio-record interviews. Audio-recording of any other speech events, such as interaction that took place during shadowing, was not permitted. Both companies thought that this would be an invasion of privacy, and may also result in feelings of antagonism/suspicion towards me. It was agreed that field notes could be used in place of audio-recording encounters, provided that informants were told and that I was not noting things down whilst managers were talking in case this adversely affected them in terms of going about their everyday tasks.

Both companies agreed that I could spend a full week with them initially and then regularly re-enter the organization for day visits to continue with shadowing, recording meetings and interviews. Both organizations agreed that it would be beneficial for me to go through the induction process that a new employee would experience on the first day that I entered both companies to begin the fieldwork proper. This was a very beneficial starting point for my participant observation as I was immediately immersed in the metadiscourse of the different workplace cultures. Whilst my relationship with the two companies developed differently, I did end up with the same aforementioned multi-method approach in both companies. In terms of coming to an agreement about what form my feedback would take, it was negotiated that I would provide the companies with a written report documenting my findings, aimed at everyone who had taken part (not just the personnel department), and also offer presentations on the findings and one-to-one feedback to all who took part.

The first organization was a manufacturing company. After the initial meeting of research negotiation had taken place, my research proposal was officially approved by the company's board of directors. The female personnel director then passed me over to one of her subordinates, a female personnel officer, who became my key informant and helped drive the research process forward. The second organization was a retail company. After my initial meeting, again approval also had to be secured from their senior managerial board. The male personnel manager then handed the project over to one of his female subordinates, interestingly based on the principle that she would find it more 'applicable' than him. She then became my key informant. This organization was stricter about my movements within the company than the manufacturing company. My key retail informant maintained close control over the people I shadowed, the meetings I attended and the interviews I was allowed to conduct. She developed official written schedules for me every time I entered the business. In contrast, I was given far more freedom in the manufacturing company. My key informant gave me an email list of all managers within the business, and I was allowed to contact any of these individuals and make my own arrangements with them. It thus appeared that the retail company wished to have more control over my observations and recordings than the manufacturing company. It is important to bear this in mind when considering the findings, and these points will be discussed later in light of the continual negotiation of the relationship between the researcher and the researched, and when considering the practical impact of my findings on these companies (see Chapter 8 and Mullany 2008).

Participant observation

Milroy and Gordon (2003: 68) summarize the advantages of producing ethnographic work within sociolinguistics via the method of participant observation, arguing that its key benefits are 'the amount and quality of data collected' and 'familiarity with community practices gained by the investigator'. They characterize the key aim of participant observation within ethnography to be 'the pursuit of local cultural knowledge' (2003: 68). Duranti (1997: 99) draws a distinction between the different 'modes' that participant observation can take, ranging from 'passive participation' to 'complete participation'. He argues that whilst 'complete participation' can be very beneficial to the research process by providing fieldworkers with the opportunity to 'directly experience the very processes they are trying to document' (1997: 100), it may not always be possible or ethically appropriate to conduct this kind of research. Furthermore, he highlights that there is an inherent difficulty associated with becoming a complete participant, in that it is possible to become distracted by one's own role within the interaction, and thus lose sight of one's task as a researcher.

Duranti thus suggests that observers should resist the temptation to become complete participants. Instead, he argues that it may be more beneficial for the researcher to adopt the position of an 'accepted by-stander' or a 'professional overhearer' (1997: 101). By taking up these positions, the potential problem of the project's results being skewed by the researcher 'going native' and thus being unable to say anything that will be of 'wider theoretical interest' can be avoided (Alvesson and Deetz 2000: 83).

My own participant observer position can best be described as being towards the passive participation end of Duranti's scale. During the meetings that I observed, I aimed to be a 'professional overhearer', sitting in an unobtrusive position, with the intention that participants should carry on as they normally would if I were not present. In practice, it soon became clear that I could not do this throughout the duration of the meeting. At the commencement of meetings, I often had to introduce myself, assure participants of complete confidentiality and also give them the opportunity to ask any questions they might have about the project. My presence at the meeting was also formally recorded in the minutes. Furthermore, on occasions I would be directly referred to within meetings, and this would often involve participation on my behalf. On the majority of occasions this took the form of laughter to signal that I had appreciated the humour being used by the meetings' participants. I firmly believe that participation at these points was essential in order to build/maintain a rapport with meeting participants whom I wished to shadow, interview and talk to informally during the rest of my time within the company. My role thus moved along the continuum of participation depending upon what was demanded of me in the particular circumstances.

In addition to Duranti's different modes, it is also useful to conceptualize my role from within the perspective of the CofP approach. My own membership of these organizations can be categorized as being between a peripheral member and an 'outsider', beyond the bounds of the CofP (Wenger et al. 2002: 57). My initial contact began by being immersed in the induction process for new employees, and can be best categorized as peripheral, as it would for any new recruit who undergoes induction and thus enters a CofP for the first time. This included full health and safety training with both companies. In the manufacturing company, a task that all new managerial employees have to fulfil is to make one of the products that the company manufactures, so that managers know what it is like to work on the factory floor. I completed this task as part of my own induction. These induction activities can also be identified as further towards the 'complete participation' end of Duranti's scale. However, it is important to emphasize that all company members knew that I was not participating in the manner of a 'proper' apprentice, that I would not be with the company on a permanent basis, as well as the fact that I did not belong to the company in any formal way. In this sense, I could always be classified as an 'outsider'.

Whilst shadowing employees and conducting interviews, my role can be seen as moving further along Duranti's continuum in the direction of complete participation. During these periods, I was fully participating by engaging in sustained periods of talk with the participants I was observing. When engaging in talk whilst shadowing, topics were generally based around managerial role in the workplace, including asking managers to explain their role more thoroughly. This would also involve a good deal of small talk, as the conversations moved from work-related talk to social talk (Holmes 2000d). On occasions, I would also be participating in the activity at hand, for example, eating lunch, and would fully participate in social talk on non-work-related matters, such as sport and hobbies.

Meetings

Holmes and Stubbe (2003b: 57) characterize meetings as 'the very stuff of "work"' in white-collar organizations. In particular relation to management, meetings have been characterized as 'the essence of managerial praxis' (Bargiela-Chiappini and Harris 1997: 30). Furthermore, Boden (1994: 81) categorizes meetings and '*the* interaction order of management'. She suggests that meetings enable researchers to witness 'the very social action through which institutions produce and reproduce themselves', as they are an arena where both individual roles and institutional roles are located and legitimated. Mumby (1988: 68) makes a similar point, arguing that meetings are 'one of the most important and visible sites of organisational power'. The usefulness of utilizing meetings as contexts where displays of power can be observed is also highlighted by Holmes et al. (1999) and Marra et al. (2006). The meeting as a speech event thus appears to be an ideal context from within which to observe how managers enact their identities through the spoken discourse strategies they use. Sarangi and Roberts (1999: 10) argue that, due to the new work order, there are now considerably more meetings held in workplaces than ever before, and many of these take place at 'an interprofessional level with blurred hierarchies – which result in the renegotiation of old identities and the formation of new ones'. Another influential factor in the decision to analyse meetings was that, by focusing on observing and recording one particular speech event, different types of meetings can then be compared, both within the same company, and between companies, thus providing a direct framework for comparison.

There are various ways in which a meeting can be defined. Boden (1994) provides an excellent working definition of meetings which documents its key features. All of the speech events classified as meetings in this study meet her criteria:

> A planned gathering, whether internal or external to an organization, in which the participants have some perceived (if not guaranteed)

role, have some forewarning (either long-standing or quite impro-
visatorial) of the event, which has itself some purpose or ' reason', a
time, place and, in some general sense, an organizational function.
(Boden 1994: 84)

Meetings from this perspective would be classified as 'formal' according
to Holmes and Stubbe's (2003b) classifications. Schwartzman (1989)
makes a number of important points concerning the structure and
organization of meetings which can be explored to gain further crucial
ethnographic information. She highlights how status within particular
communities can be assessed by whether or not particular individuals
have been invited to attend. Boden (1994: 88) too makes this point,
arguing that meetings can be perceived as *membership categorization
devices*. Schwartzman (1989: 284) highlights that the time participants
arrive and depart from meetings can be illuminating in terms of 'communicating status, allegiance, support and opposition'. Any occasions
where participants arrive late or leave early will thus be carefully
analysed. She also makes reference to the fact that individuals may be
attending meetings to represent both themselves and others, which can
include their subordinates, superior(s), or status equals, depending upon
meeting type and participant's role. These are all important considerations to bear in mind, and will be carefully analysed within a CofP
framework.

Interviews

Utilizing the method of interviews in order to gain research data is
common practice in a multitude of disciplines throughout the social
sciences (Hester and Francis 1994). The motivation behind conducting
interviews as a source of spoken language data was to gain further
ethnographic background information, and in particular, to gain evidence
of the wider gendered discourses operating both within and on the
workplace, as pointed out in Chapter 2. An overall distinction has been
drawn between two basic types of interview encounters: the *standardized*
interview, where researchers ask the same question in the same manner
to every interviewee to avoid 'contaminating' the answers informants
produce, and the *active* interview, where interviewers take a more flexible
approach to questioning and ask more open-ended and less structured
questions (Holstein and Gubrium 1995). The former is typically associated with quantitative, survey-based interviews, whereas the latter is
associated with qualitative research methods, including ethnographic
interviews. Like all dichotomies, the 'standardized' versus 'active' interview
tends to oversimplify, and would be better conceptualized as a continuum.

That aside, within sociolinguistics (variationist sociolinguistics in particular), the main problem with interview studies is that they are often used as the *only* method through which to gain data, and these data are then often treated as if it they were naturally occurring talk.

Whilst techniques have been developed to make sociolinguistic interviews more like spontaneous talk, such as the famous Labovian 'danger of death' question, just using interviews as speech events through which all sociolinguistic data is gathered is highly problematic. As Duranti (1997: 103) argues, analysing data derived from the interviews alone is a poor substitute for observing and recording actual interactions. The multi-method approach taken here gets around this problem by combining interview data analysis with audio-taped analysis of business meetings, along with other ethnographic, observational methods of actual events.

Duranti (1997: 102) points out that, in the loosest sense of the term, interviews are constantly being conducted in an ethnography, with fieldworkers frequently posing questions to their informants. If this general definition of an 'interview' is followed, then data of this nature can be seen in my field notes recording informal talk whilst shadowing. However, on specific occasions, informants can be presented with a series of 'more or less structured, partly pre-planned questions' (Duranti 1997: 103). It is these encounters that are referred to as interviews in this study, where time is specifically put aside to elicit data in a context officially termed an 'interview' by both the researcher and informant(s). Hammersley and Atkinson (1995) point out that a key difference between ethnographic and standardized interviews is that in the former there are no sets of questions prepared beforehand. Instead, they usually consist of a list of topics that need to be covered, but there will be variety in the manner in which each question is asked.

For the purposes of my study, I decided to conduct semi-structured interviews, in that I designed a set of questions/topics which provided guidance for the discussion in each encounter. However, I took a very flexible approach to asking these questions, and my overall intention was to bring up particular topics and then engage participants in conversation on this topic to elicit as much detail from them as possible. This involved a range of interactive strategies from me which were not nor could they be pre-planned in any way, and they differed significantly in every interview. Alvesson and Deetz (2000: 73) argue that getting engaged in 'real' conversation with 'empathetic understanding', can make the research interview a 'more honest, morally sound and reliable' encounter. Respondents should be treated as if they are on a level footing with the interviewer, which should reduce the need interviewees may feel to give a good impression. A conversational style interview, if conducted in a co-operative manner, may also result in the interview being more informal, hopefully inclining interviewees to produce a more 'realistic' picture of events. Indeed, overall I aimed to take what Sarangi and Candlin (2003: 279) have termed the 'researcher as befriender' approach, where the interviewer aims to be as unselfconscious as possible in order to put interviewees at ease and make the encounter relaxed and friendly. A previously proven technique that I followed was to gain interviewees' opinions and perceptions from specific instances of their own experience in the form of life histories and/or narratives (Musson 1998, see Mullany 2006b). Overall, the interviews can be seen as being towards the active, ethnographic end of the interviewing continuum.

The interview questions/topics focused on three areas. The first was on general managerial role, the second more specifically on gender and the third on the particular topic of gender and language in business meetings. I thought that initially asking managers general questions about their role in the company would make them more at ease by asking them to discuss something familiar. It was also the intention that this section be a key source of additional ethnographic information on particular CofPs and overall workplace culture. The gender section questions focus on career choice and career progression, designed to assess perceptions of the glass ceiling, along with the topics of perceptions and evaluations of gender identity in the workplace in terms of subordinates, status equals and superiors, in order to gain as much information as possible on participants' representations of gender, through which relevant gendered discourses can be analysed. The final section was a continuation of this, though it did focus on eliciting opinions on gender and language in particular, concentrating specifically on the context of meetings to assess managers' linguistic perceptions of one another within this context. In Chapter 7, where the analysis of interview data takes place, all discourse is included, not just the interviewee's responses. Indeed, the importance of viewing interviews as speech events where discourse is jointly produced has become more common in recent years, partially as a consequence of the recent 'linguistic turn' which has taken place in the social sciences, highlighted in Chapter 1. This has led to a range of methodological debates concerning interviewing techniques. Indeed, Hammersley and Atkinson (1995: 156) argue that researchers need to be wary of simply accepting what interviewees say as being a reflection of truth, and instead realize that what they have produced during an interview, through the joint process of discourse with the interviewer, should be used as 'a source for information about events' or as 'revealing the perspectives and discursive practices of those who produced them' (Hammersley and Atkinson 1995: 156). Indeed, the aim of the interviews in this study is to assess the discursive practices of interviewees, with particular regard to the production of gendered discourses.

Duranti's (1997) argument that linguistic anthropologists can use interviews to ask participants for clarification about what they thought was happening in particular speech exchanges should be treated very cautiously. Whilst this method has been used within feminist linguistics (Mills 2003), as Silverman (2000) points out, just because this technique of respondent validation has been used does not mean that researchers can then claim that they now have the 'truth' of a particular utterance, or that participants' intentions have now been clearly documented. Instead, such responses should be treated as simply another source of data, a point which Mills (2003) clearly acknowledges. In interviews with informants who partook in the meetings recorded, any comments they make regarding their behaviour in business meetings will be treated with caution. It is not the intention to ask participants directly what they thought their intentions were behind particular utterances in meetings due to the above reasons, and also additionally due to the time it takes to produce detailed linguistic transcripts of multi-party talk. By the time transcripts were produced, it was thought that informants would not be able to remember what their intentions were anyway. Furthermore, it would have been practically impossible to convince busy managers to give up their valuable work time in order to attempt to help me come to a conclusion about their intentions behind something they said in an old meeting. Time is very much of essence in business, and often this does not accord with the slower process of linguistic recording, transcribing and analysis (see Chapter 8 for further discussion).

Field notes

The intention behind making field notes was to have a written record of all events and talk that took place during shadowing as an additional data source of 'documentary evidence' (Sarangi and Roberts 1999: 27), so that as much ethnographic description as possible could be drawn upon. However, field notes are inevitably not as reliable as audio-recorded data. In an attempt to make my notes as accurate a record as possible, I made them as soon as I could after the event had taken place, either within my allocated office space within the companies, or as soon as possible after I had left the building for that day. The data provided by field notes are treated cautiously, and no formal linguistic analysis is carried out on any talk recorded via field notes only. However, these notes have proved very useful when compiling a picture of workplace participants, their attitudes and evaluations of one another, background information on the company, and the workplace culture as a whole. Also, field notes were used as an additional source of recording information during all audio-recorded business meetings to aid the transcription and data interpretation process. The field notes for this study have been compiled in the form of a chronological record of my time in both organizations.

Documents

I decided to request any documents detailing background information on gender in the workplaces I entered once I had begun to establish relationships with participants. Furthermore, any written documents that I could be given to aid my interpretation of the meetings I attended were also requested. I aimed to receive a copy of meeting agendas and a written record of the minutes from previous meetings to gain as much background detail as possible on the speech events that I would be observing.

These written resources were extremely valuable sources of background information on encounters. On occasions, the meeting's turn-taking system was roughly pre-allocated on a detailed agenda, and this proved to be a very useful reference tool when transcribing the data. I was also given access to companies' equal opportunities literature, as well as to their mission statements and promotional literature. Access to such documents thus enriched my analysis, providing additional ethnographic information which I used to enhance my interpretations. Whilst it is difficult to make direct reference to this material due to issues of confidentiality, I do this where possible to illustrate how written documents have been utilized to enhance the data analysis.

The observer's paradox

The crucial issue of the observer's paradox has already been mentioned in relation to the presence of the tape recorder and the influence that this may have on participants' actions. As Milroy (1987: 59) points out, 'the very act of recording is likely to distort the object of observation'. Duranti (1997: 117) argues that the problems raised by the observer's paradox, if carried to their logical conclusions, suggest that 'it would be better *not to be there* at all' (emphasis in original). He points out that there are two ways in which such a proposition can be realized. The first option is to abandon the study of people altogether, whilst the second option is to record covertly, not informing participants that their behaviour is being recorded. However, he points out the pitfalls with both of these options:

> The first option is self destructive [as] ... it implies that we should not improve our understanding of what it means to be human and have a culture (including a language) simply because we cannot find the ideal situation for naturalistic-objective observation. The second proposal is first of all unethical and, second, impractical under most circumstances outside of laboratories with two-way mirrors. (Duranti 1997: 117)

Duranti's reaction demonstrates that, whilst the observer's paradox is a deeply problematic concern, this does not mean that researchers should abandon analysing naturally occurring data. The unethical nature of covert recording is also highlighted by Milroy (1987) and Milroy and Gordon (2003), who argue that it is now essential for sociolinguistic studies to be carried out overtly, with covert recording and then asking for permission afterwards no longer being a viable option. Indeed, within institutional settings, such an option would not be available anyway due to lack of access, unless academic researchers were investigating their own institutions, which raises a whole host of other complex ethical issues. Surreptitious recording can result in damaged relationships, future access being denied by a group, and the quality of recording being poor if the tape recorder is concealed.

A possible way to minimize the effect of the observer's paradox for recorded meeting data would be to set up the equipment and leave the room. However, there are a number of practical advantages to my own observation in meeting settings. It greatly enhanced my interpretation of participants' interactional strategies, enabling a record of paralinguistic features to be kept, as well as a record of the ordering of speakers' utterances in multi-party talk. Valuable ethnographic data would thus have been lost had I not been present. Leaving the room also raises practical problems such as who would be responsible for turning the tape. A meeting participant could be assigned the role (see Holmes and Stubbe 2003b), but this runs the risk of losing valuable chunks of data if the person forgets. After each meeting, either in periods of informal talk or during recorded interviews with those present at the meetings I recorded, I asked participants whether they thought my presence had affected behaviour during the meeting. The overwhelming consensus was that it may have affected interaction right at the very beginning of the encounter, but after a short period of time, they became absorbed in the topic under discussion and they did tend to forget about me and the recording equipment.

Like Duranti (1997: 118), I believe that 'people are too busy running their own lives to change them in substantial ways because of the presence of a new gadget or person'. I believe this to be the case especially in institutional contexts such as the workplace, as when engaged in workplace interaction participants are often working to tight deadlines. During meetings managers are often engaged in discourse which either directly or indirectly has a financial impact on the company and affects how competent they are perceived to be at their profession. I believe these considerations are far more prevalent to participants than my presence. Furthermore, Duranti argues that neutral observation is an illusion anyway. He is not advocating that the observer's paradox be ignored, but rather he suggests that researchers should approach it 'with the awareness of its unavoidability' (1997: 118).

In order to aid meeting transcription, at the commencement of each encounter all participants were assigned a number, based purely on their sex and the physical position they occupied around the table (F1, F2, F3, M1, M2, M3, etc). I then used this codification system to attempt to keep track of all individuals' turns within the meeting. When speakers engaged in simultaneous talk, these instances were particularly challenging to transcribe, especially with larger meeting groups. Field notes were also taken during the meetings as an additional aid to identify speakers and also to characterize their communicative acts. These notes documented participants' paralinguistic features and any other features that would aid both the transcription process and my interpretation of the data. These notes were of great help in distinguishing different speakers when transcribing, aiding the accuracy of the transcripts, as well as providing essential additional ethnographic background information to aid interpretation of the results.

Introducing the companies

In the interests of confidentiality, the two companies will be referred to simply as the 'retail company' and the 'manufacturing company' throughout. Both companies are international organizations and their products have worldwide circulation. The number of employees for both companies is similar. The retail company employs approximately 175 people and the manufacturing company approximately 200 people. Both companies have requested that certain background details are not included in this study in order to maintain their anonymity. As stated above, the personnel managers who acted as my initial points of contact in both businesses perceived the glass ceiling to be in existence, and in the initial meeting wished for this to be investigated from a linguistic point of view. In the retail company, the managerial structure is split into a senior level (the store manager), followed by an upper-middle level, a middle-management level and a lower level. The lower level includes assistant/trainee managers. The most senior managerial position in the retail company is occupied by a male. In the upper-middle management team, out of 10 positions, 8 are occupied by males and 2 are occupied by females. At the middle level, the balance is exactly equal, with 15 female and 15 male middle managers. At a lower level, there are 2 male and 3 female assistant/trainee managers. A very similar pattern can also be observed in the manufacturing company. In the company's executive committee, at its most senior managerial level, only 2 directors out of 10 are female. The manufacturing company is similar to the retail company in that it has clearly observable upper-middle, middle and lower levels of management. At an upper-middle level, there are 8 male managers compared to no female managers. At the middle level, there are 32 males compared to 21 females. At the lower level, the gender balance equals out with 2 female and 2 male managers.

It has already been pointed out that this study did not aim to be a long-term one in the sense of many anthropological ethnographies. Access was carefully negotiated but very much restricted by the institutional setting and concerns with managerial time. Due to the negotiation of access to these companies and also the time-scale of my study I spent the equivalent of approximately one month's working hours within each company, entering both on at least 15 different days after my first full week to continue shadowing, observing and recording. The data collection took place over a period of six months in total. Whilst present, the companies allocated me a base in their main open plan offices, which also allowed me to observe from this position.

During this period I had observed the workplace interactions of 51 different CofP members belonging to six different CofPs, three CofPs from each company. Six of these individuals, however, were members of more than one CofP. My analysis therefore focuses in total on 46 different individual managers, 22 females and 24 males. The cross-over of these six individual managers represents an excellent opportunity to witness the same speakers interacting in different CofPs. Meetings were very difficult to get permission to record, and the sample on which the meeting discourse is analysed is based upon eight hours worth of recording, which consists of six different meeting encounters, one from each CofP. In the retail company there are two female-chaired meetings and a male-chaired meeting, and in the manufacturing company there are two male-chaired meetings and one female-chaired meeting. The female Chair in the meetings from the retail company is the same person, as she was the only female in the company senior enough to hold formal, pre-planned meetings, which arguably can be regarded as part of the findings of this study. These two meetings present the opportunity to analyse her chairing style in two different CofPs. Some encounters are female-dominated meetings whilst other encounters are male-dominated. A summary of the meeting data is provided in Chapters 5 and 6. All speakers were white, again, arguably part of the findings, and as was pointed out in Chapter 2, their social role as managers can be perceived as 'classed', aligning speakers with a middle-class identity (which, like any other form of identity, can be subverted or resisted).

The managers in both companies tended to be of a similar age. Generally the most senior participants at meetings were the eldest, as would be typically expected. In the retail company's meetings the chronological age of participants ranges from 29 to 37, with those managers who are in their mid-to-late thirties being both the most senior participants and also the meeting Chairs. In the manufacturing company, the age of participants is a little wider, ranging from 30 to 41. Again, the most senior participants/the meeting Chairs are the eldest speakers present. The age of all participants who took part in the study is presented in the Appendix. However, as was pointed out in Chapter 2, it is socially constructed 'life stage' and ideologies of age which are important to analyse in conjunction with gender, and not chronological age per se. Evidence of age and gender ideologies can be witnessed through the gendered discourses observed, particularly within interview data (see Chapter 7).

In terms of interview data, I aimed to conduct encounters with those members of the CofPs whose meetings I recorded, as well as participants who belonged to all of the other company's departments outside of these CofPs in order to build a picture of the retail company as a whole. I conducted 23 interviews in total, totalling over 19 hours worth of data. Nineteen of these interviews are with female participants and 4 are with male participants. In the retail company, I conducted 10 interviews, 8 with female managers and 2 with male managers. In the manufacturing company, I conducted 13 interviews, 11 with females and 2 with males. In the retail company, despite my requests to get more males involved, my key informant arranged more female interviewees than male interviewees because she thought my project would be more 'relevant' to them, and also because she thought they were more likely to agree to be interviewed. In this company, interviews were carried out with at least one participant from each departmental CofP within the business, including at least one participant whose CofP meetings had been recorded. In the manufacturing company, whilst I tried to arrange interviews with males, attempts were unfruitful apart from the co-operation of two informants. A key reason given was that they did not think that a study on gender was that applicable to them, or that they were too busy. In this company, again at least one representative from each departmental CofP was interviewed, and a wide range of participants who belonged to the CofPs who had their meetings recorded made themselves available to me for interview, as I had more control over who was approached. A summary of the interview data, including participants' gender, age, managerial position and departmental affiliation is also presented in the Appendix.

In summary, the overall complexities involved when conducting research in the restricted site of the professional workplace have been outlined. This has been illustrated in conjunction with presenting the development of my innovative, negotiated methodological approach, both to provide the necessary background information for this study, and also as a practical source of information for those researchers who are carrying out similar investigations in future projects.

4
Analysing Workplace Interaction

An integrated linguistic framework

In this chapter, the analytical frameworks designed to analyse workplace interaction are outlined. Whilst these frameworks are utilized in particular to focus on workplace meeting interaction, in principle they can be applied to interactional data in a range of institutional settings. As part of the centralist, interdisciplinary approach outlined in Chapter 1, analytical frameworks from interactional sociolinguistics are integrated with tools from pragmatics and critical discourse analysis (CDA). This aligns with Sarangi and Roberts's (1999) point that, in order to produce a 'thick description', researchers need to draw upon a combined analytical approach. Furthermore, Holmes et al. (1999) argue that an integrated analytical approach is essential in order to account for the fundamental role that power plays in governing workplace talk:

> Workplace interactions are seldom neutral in terms of power. The construction of professional identity in this context is therefore also inevitably concerned with the ways in which power and solidarity are enacted through discourse. (Holmes et al. 1999: 354)

They argue that interactional sociolinguistics, politeness theory and CDA provide productive explanatory frameworks. The overwhelming importance and influence of power at a global, overarching level has been emphasized in Chapter 2. As part of this, it is essential to ensure that power relationships are also carefully analysed at a local level, particularly due to the institutional power hierarchies present in workplace interactions. It is worth reiterating here that, from a social-constructionist, Foucauldian-influenced view, power needs to be enacted in discourse.

It is not something that a manager will simply possess just by virtue of occupying a superior position on the institutional hierarchy. As Holmes and Stubbe (2003b: 3) point out, participants in every workplace interaction should be seen as 'enacting, reproducing and sometimes resisting institutional power relationships in their use of discourse by means of a range of coercive and collaborative strategies'. The enactment of power is particularly important when focusing on managers, as their ability to enact power and authority effectively is crucial for them to be identified as successful professionals (see Chapter 1). It is vital for any empirical study of gender and language in workplace interaction to fully account for the crucial role played by power. As Holmes (2005: 57) points out, both gender and power 'must be attended to in order to fully understand "what is going on" in workplace interaction'.

Within my overall interactional sociolinguistic framework, politeness theory and speech act categories are integrated from pragmatics. As Sarangi and Roberts (1999: 31) argue, pragmatic concepts including politeness and speech acts 'can account for how meanings and identities are (not) negotiated in situated encounters in the workplace'. From CDA, I utilize the notions of 'oppressive' and 'repressive' discourse, based on coercive and consent power, respectively (Fairclough 1992, 2001, see Chapter 2), as categories through which the enactment of power, gender and managerial authority can be viewed. Bucholtz (2001) argues that, whilst CDA has been a heavily criticized approach, certain concepts can still be useful if combined within a hybrid framework. Integrating politeness theory with CDA has been successfully achieved by Holmes et al. (1999: 355), Holmes (2000d) and Holmes and Stubbe (2003b) in their analyses of workplace interactions.

Analysis of meeting interaction will enable usage of stereotypical gendered speech styles by women and men managers to be scrutinized. This includes an assessment of whether recently observed features of stereotypically feminine styles and wide, verbal repertoires combining stereotypically feminine and masculine speech styles can be observed. This analysis takes place within a community of practice (CofP) framework to ensure that contextual factors, including power and other features of social identity that can account for how women and men perform their managerial identities, are fully considered. Analysing these findings as part of overarching gendered discourses operating as social practices enables dominant gender ideologies and gender stereotypes to be carefully scrutinized.

To analyze business meeting data from the perspective of gendered speech styles, linguistic practices previously identified as gendered were selected. Table 2.1 in Chapter 2 was used as a key resource. Pateman's (1980) notions of oppressive and repressive power, utilized by Fairclough (1992, 2001) can be mapped onto these stereotypical gendered styles. Traditionally, managerial styles have been seen to be oppressive, exercised coercively through the stereotypical masculine interactional styles of directness, aggressiveness, competitiveness, autonomy and dominance (Coates 1995; Kendall and Tannen 1997; Holmes 2000a). In contrast, due to recent transitions towards power being enacted repressively, through consent, it can be exercised through stereotypically feminine strategies of indirectness, collaboration, facilitation and person-orientated styles which seek to minimize status and power differences, giving the (superficial) impression of flatter workplace structures (Gee et al. 1996).

Holmes (1995) uses politeness as an 'umbrella' term to analyse a whole range of linguistic features (Crawford 1997: 428). Whilst the approach to linguistic politeness that Holmes (1995) takes is arguably outdated, particularly due to its over-reliance on Brown and Levinson's (1987) model (discussed later), viewing a range of linguistic variables through the framework of politeness in such an encompassing manner is very useful, and can greatly enhance interactional analyses. All of the linguistic practices that are analysed in this study will be viewed from within the politeness framework that is adopted here. The decision to analyse managers' performance of speech acts enables the vast majority of stereotypically masculine and feminine speech styles highlighted in Table 2.1, to be analysed. Speech acts that are identified as indirect, performed in a conciliatory, facilitative or collaborative manner can be seen as part of a stereotypically feminine style, whereas those identified as being direct, performed in a manner which emphasizes confrontational, competitive or autonomous action will be identified as stereotypically masculine strategies. The specific speech acts that will be examined are defined and detailed later. Feminine supportive feedback versus masculine aggressive interruptions, cited in Table 2.1, are analysed as part of the turn-taking system. The final two listings, person-orientated versus task-orientated, and affectively orientated versus referentially orientated styles are investigated by analysing humour and small talk. Both of these linguistic practices are more commonly associated with non-serious, affective talk in more informal spheres.

Holmes et al. (2001) summarize previous language and gender research on humour, arguing that women's humour is 'cooperative, inclusive, supportive, integrated, spontaneous and self-healing', whereas men's humour is 'exclusive, challenging, segmented, pre-formulated and self-aggrandising' (2001: 85). The usual stereotypical dichotomies can thus be witnessed here, and, as with all other older findings, these features can be viewed as stereotypically gendered speech styles. However, humour is a very complex linguistic feature to analyse, perhaps particularly due to its ambiguous nature. Therefore, viewing humour from the perspective of gendered speech styles in the workplace is not as straightforward as the above listings suggest, and a model which characterizes the range of functions that humour can fulfil is developed and then applied to the stereotypical categories of gendered speech styles.

In contrast with humour, small talk can be solely identified as stereotypically feminine gendered discourse (Holmes and Marra 2004). It is traditionally perceived as empty, trivial talk, including gossip (Coupland 2000), as well as being stereotypically associated with private, domestic spheres, the arena historically associated with women due to the sexual division of labour. Despite such negative evaluation, small talk can fulfil a range of important functions in the workplace.

These frameworks for analysis will now be outlined, commencing with an exposition of how linguistic politeness will be defined and applied as an encompassing model through which all other linguistic practices can be viewed.

Conceptualizing linguistic politeness

The significant role played by politeness in workplace interactions has led to the application of linguistic politeness frameworks in a range of different settings (Holmes and Stubbe 2003b; *Journal of Politeness Research* special issue 2006). This also includes studies focusing on gender and professional communication, including the older work of West (1990), Tannen (1994) and Holmes (1995), and more recent research including Holmes and Marra (2004) and Holmes and Schnurr (2005). The aforementioned older gender studies, influenced by the power/ dominance or culture/difference approaches, present evidence which demonstrates that women are more linguistically polite than men, even when they occupy positions of power. Indeed, women in positions of authority are observed utilizing politeness strategies in order to minimize such authority. These older findings can be used as a basis upon which gendered speech norms can be witnessed. Enacting linguistic politeness strategies can be seen as being indirectly indexed with a stereotypically feminine gendered style. In contrast, failing to abide by politeness norms and conventions, or being impolite, can be identified as indirectly indexed with a stereotypically masculine interactional style.

This accords with Mills's (2003) conceptualization of politeness as something which is already gendered feminine.

The older work on gender and politeness cited above follows Brown and Levinson's ([1978], 1987) hugely influential work, where politeness is based upon Goffman's (1967) notion of *face*, defined as interactants' public self-image. Politeness strategies are used to mitigate demands or intrusions that need to be made on another person's face, known as face-threatening acts (FTAs). In this study, politeness is alternatively conceptualized from a CofP perspective, broadly following the work of Mills (2002, 2003), who criticizes work influenced by Brown and Levinson, focusing in particular on Holmes's (1995) publication. Mills argues that Holmes does not relate the polite acts she defines to a 'community which judges these acts and the people as polite' due to an over-reliance on Brown and Levinson's universals framework, resulting in the production of both 'abstract' and 'disembodied' analyses (2002: 77). Following Mills (2002, 2003), Brown and Levinson's theory needs to be adapted if the context within which interaction takes place is ever to be properly analysed. Alternatively, from a CofP perspective, politeness should be seen as 'a set of practices or strategies which communities of practice develop, affirm and contest' (2003: 9). Mills's view is that any notion of linguistic politeness in a feminist linguistic study should be conceived through a CofP framework:

> Feminist linguistics should be concerned less with analysing individual linguistic acts between individual (gendered) speakers than with the analysis of a community-based perspective on gender and linguistic performance, which in the case of politeness must therefore involve a sense of politeness as having different functions and meanings for different groups of people. (Mills 2002: 71)

In addition to its advantages in relation to context, the CofP approach is also advantageous over a Brown and Levinson-influenced approach as it enables politeness to be seen as emerging at a discourse level across utterances, as opposed to the now widely discredited view that politeness is simply contained within a sentence (see Harris 2001; Mills 2002, 2003). Additionally, this helps move politeness away from being a speaker-oriented model, also dictated by Brown and Levinson's position, to instead viewing politeness as enacted and produced within interaction *between* speakers and hearers (see Culpeper 2005; Mullany 2007b). Examining interaction *across* stretches of discourse ensures that responses to initial speaker utterances are also analysed. It is crucial to analyse responses (if given) in order to perceive how the hearer inter-prets the speaker's utterance. Furthermore, researchers including Spiers (1998) and Harris (2001) have questioned the usefulness of Brown and Levinson's categories of positive and negative politeness. Brown and Levinson split both the concept of face and politeness strategies into positive and negative categories, with the former signifying one's desire to be liked/admired, whilst the latter refers to one's need to be unim-peded. Spiers (1998) claims this positive–negative distinction cannot account for the multifunctionality of linguistic strategies, due to its rigidity. Harris (2001) further discredits their perspective by presenting evidence of positive and negative politeness strategies co-occurring within the same stretch of talk.

Furthermore, one of the most fundamental problems with Brown and Levinson's model is its neglect of impoliteness. This is due to an over-reliance on Grice's (1975) co-operative principle, which leads to their concentration on strategies for *avoiding* FTAs. A number of researchers including Culpeper (1996, 2005), Eelen (2001), Mills (2003) and Watts (2003) stress that it is essential for a model of politeness to also include impoliteness if it is ever to be deemed comprehensive. The CofP approach to politeness is advantageous in this respect as it enables notions of both linguistic politeness and impoliteness to be conceived. Participants within CofPs decide what is either polite or impolite against the norms and conventions they have for the specific communities in which their discourse takes place. Mills (2002: 79) argues that from a CofP perspective impoliteness exists 'when it is classified as such by cer-tain, usually dominant community members, and/or when it leads to a breakdown in relations'. The CofP approach thus enables key criticisms that have been cited at Brown and Levinson's model to be overcome. A useful concept when analysing impoliteness is Austin's (1990) face attack act (FAA), defined as an act which injures the hearer's face, uttered in a situation that could have been avoided, where reactions from the hearer indicate that the act has been perceived as intentional.

One key difference between Mills's CofP approach and the CofP approach to (im)politeness I am taking here is in relation to who is responsible for defining an act as (im)polite. Mills completely minimizes the role of the analyst, arguing that only those who belong to the CofPs being studied are able to define whether a particular stretch of discourse can be analysed as (im)polite or not. However, like Holmes and Schnurr (2005), I agree that whilst it can often be difficult to interpret particular stretches of interaction, particularly due to the multifunctionality of linguistic devices, this does not mean that analysts should no longer do this. Holmes and Schnurr (2005) argue further that such a suggestion goes against the foundational aims of sociolinguistics and discourse analysis. Following an approach where only members of CofPs can decide whether politeness or impoliteness has taken place is limiting in terms of the type of data that can be analysed. In practice, it seems that this will either restrict researchers to analysing contexts where they are themselves interlocutors, or stick to contexts where they are guaranteed that they can interview interactants after interactions have take place to attempt to elicit their intentions. The methodological problems with such an approach, particularly in terms of gaining data in institutional settings, have already been highlighted in Chapter 3. Taking an ethnographic approach enables a wealth of background information about particular CofPs under study to be utilized as a valuable tool to aid interpretation. Therefore, provided that the researcher is reflexive and uses all tools available to attempt to come up with the best interpretation possible, and provided they acknowledge that this is not an ultimate reading, but one which has been arrived at through careful consideration of all research tools available, then researchers can and should be making interpretations of the linguistic data that they collect.

Despite all of the drawbacks of Brown and Levinson's (1987) approach, I do utilize Goffman's (1967) notion of face as an analytical category, along with Brown and Levinson's FTA category, but only in conjunction with Austin's (1990) notion of FAAs, to account for instances where there is no co-operative intent from the speaker. However, based on the arguments made above, I do not regard splitting face or politeness into positive and negative categories to be either beneficial or valid. The practical application of this approach to linguistic (im)politeness, in terms of its influence on analytical frameworks to assess the enactment of stereotypically gendered speech styles in business meetings, will now be detailed.

Floorholding

It is important to recognize that there are different types of conversational floor that can operate during meeting interaction, following the ground-breaking work of Edelsky (1981). Edelsky coined a distinction between a *single* and a *collaborative* floor, thus breaking away from the traditional one-at-a-time notion of turn-taking associated with the seminal conversation analysis of Sacks et al. (1974). Coates (1988; 1996) has utilized these perspectives in her research, categorizing an *all-together-now* floor (ATN) and a *one-at-a-time* floor (OAT). According to Coates (2004), women are far more inclined to use the former type of floor, and it can thus be stereotypically associated with a feminine interactional style. The single, one-at-a-time floor can alternatively be classified with a stereotypically masculine interactional style.

These different types of conversational floor provide background to the analysis of other linguistic features which take place within these conversational floors. It is most often the Chair's responsibility to control the 'type' of floor that is in operation in meetings, though this will depend upon meeting type and function. On occasions, responsibility will shift to other participants, including those who have 'expert' power upon particular topics (Spencer-Oatey 2000; Holmes and Stubbe 2003b). The interactional features that are part of the techniques of floorholding will now be detailed.

Interruptions and supportive simultaneous talk

Within interactional sociolinguistics, the key difference between simultaneous speech functioning as a disruptive interruption and simultaneous speech functioning supportively is well established. In this book I follow Holmes's (1995: 52) definition of an interruption as a 'disruptive turn', and adopt Coates's (1996: 121) definition of supportive simultaneous talk as 'jointly constructed' utterances, where the voices of different speakers combine in the joint production of discourse. Holmes (1995) classifies disruptive interruptions as impolite (despite the lack of theorization of impoliteness in Brown and Levinson's model). Interruptions can thus be identified as stereotypically masculine strategies. On the other hand, supportive simultaneous talk can be identified as a strategy of politeness. It pays attention to face needs, being a co-operative device signalling solidarity with the speaker(s). It can thus be interpreted as a stereotypically feminine strategy. In order to provide a context-specific, CofP analysis, interruptions and supportive simultaneous talk will be focused on when they occur during speech act analysis or during periods of humour and small talk, as opposed to being analysed as free-standing variables in their own right. The CofP approach to politeness will assess how these strategies are being used in different communities of practice.

Finally, it is important to distinguish instances of simultaneous talk from overlaps, defined as 'instances of slight over-anticipation of the next speaker' (Coates 2004: 113). These often occur at transition-relevant places (TRPs) – points where the conversational floor is open to transition to another speaker, but current speaker will finish her/his turn (Sacks et al. 1974). Overlaps are a useful category to help distinguish instances of over-anticipation from either disruptive or supportive instances of simultaneous talk.

Speech acts

Holmes et al. (1999) demonstrate the value of using speech acts to examine how power and authority are enacted in workplace interaction. The speech acts they define are as follows:

1. setting the agenda
2. summarizing progress
3. closing an interaction
4. issuing directives
5. expressing approval
6. issuing criticisms
7. issuing warnings
8. issuing challenges (Adapted from Holmes et al. 1999: 358–364)

Functions 1–3, setting the agenda, summarizing progress and closing an interaction, demonstrate how superiors control the structure and development of meetings, whereas functions 4–8 reveal how managers actually manage and instruct their subordinates through the speech strategies they use. I will analyse how managers open and close meeting encounters to assess their skills at controlling meeting structure, including their ability to set the agenda. Additionally, the non-structural speech acts will also be focused on (points 4–8).

From the perspective of linguistic politeness, Brown and Levinson-influenced studies including Tannen (1994), Holmes (1995) and Kendall (2003) have argued that women in positions of authority will be more likely to issue directives in a face-saving manner, thus using tactics such as indirectness, in attempts to avoid potentially confrontational reactions. From the perspective of gendered speech styles, mitigating directives, criticisms, warnings and challenges by those in positions of authority can be seen as associated with stereotypically feminine strategies. In contrast, issuing directives, criticisms, warnings or challenges baldly, without mitigation, may directly threaten or attack face, and can thus be viewed as stereotypically masculine speech styles. As expressions of approval are face-enhancing, these can also be categorized as stereotypically feminine strategies.

The focus of the speech act analysis typically falls on Chairs, enabling managers in leadership positions to be examined. However, it is important to reiterate again that power is fluid and can easily change hands in an interaction. On occasions, subordinates may enact power by issuing directives, giving criticism, expressing approval or even by issuing warnings or challenges, particularly if the topic under discussion is their own specialism, an example of aforementioned 'expert' power. Other lower-level managers, or even meeting participants with low social status, such as secretaries, can enact power for themselves by using one or more of the above speech acts (cf. Mills 1997). A fine-grained CofP analysis, informed by additional ethnographic detail, is thus crucial in identifying such instances.

The overall total number of occurrences of speech acts and who elicits these within each CofP meeting will be presented to give an overall picture of what takes place in each meeting before the qualitative analysis of stereotypical gendered speech styles takes place. The individual speech act categories of directives, expressing approval, criticisms, warnings and challenges will now be further defined.

Directives

Directives are popular speech acts to investigate with researchers examining language and gender in professional workplaces (West 1990, 1995; Coates 1995; Stubbe et al. 2000; Kendall 2003; Vine 2004). Following Coates (1995) and West (1990), I adopt Goodwin's (1980: 157) definition that directives are 'speech acts that try to get another to do something'. In her study of doctor–patient interaction, West (1990) draws a distinction between *aggravated* and *mitigated* directives based on Labov and Fanshel (1977), distinguishing the former as acts which include 'orders and demands' and which imply that 'the speaker can legitimately impose on another by stating their requirements baldly', whereas the latter are identified as occasions when speakers 'avoid offending another by putting forth their wishes in downgraded ways'. Coates (1995: 18) draws on the aggravated–mitigated distinction, arguing that directives can range from the 'bluntness' of an imperative to more mitigated forms, and 'typically powerful participants will demonstrate their power (i.e. their ability to ignore the face needs of their addressees) by using direct commands'. In a later work, West (1995) accords aggravated imperatives, the form favoured by male doctors in her data, as 'impolite'. However, if (im)politeness is perceived from a CofP perspective, as just discussed, then this classification would be contested. If a speaker is imposing 'legitimately' then this does not automatically mean that he/she is being impolite. The lack of theorization of impoliteness can be seen as part of the reason why the term is just applied if a speaker is not being 'as polite' as another. From a CofP perspective, impoliteness would only be defined as such when the norms and conventions of politeness have been *broken* within CofPs, and when there is clear evidence to indicate this from both speakers and hearers. In order to clarify these distinctions, whilst I will follow the category of 'mitigated' directives, I wish to change the evaluative category of 'aggravated' to 'unmitigated' to account for any bald, on-record directive that is used by a speaker who has legitimate power, and have 'aggravated' as separate category. As the term 'aggravated' has negative connotations which strongly imply impoliteness, it is applied in this study if participant(s) have judged actions within that particular CofP to be impolite. From the perspective of gendered speech styles, face-threatening speech acts which have been mitigated show attention to face needs, and can thus be identified as stereotypically feminine speech strategies. In contrast, unmitigated directives, along with aggravated, that is, impolite directives, can be viewed as stereotypically masculine strategies. Mitigated tactics can be viewed as 'repressive' power strategies that draw on 'superficial' politeness behaviour, whereas unmitigated tactics can be seen as oppressive power strategies.

Goodwin (1980), West (1990), Holmes (1995) and Holmes and Stubbe (2003b) all outline a number of lexical, grammatical and syntactic features which can be used to mitigate directives. These categories are very useful and can be applied to all speech act categories outlined in this section, not just directives. These mitigation features are therefore utilized as an analytical framework for all of the speech act categories analysed in my study. It is important to ensure that both the form and function of all strategies are analysed to ensure that these forms are functioning as mitigation strategies due to their multifunctionality (Holmes and Stubbe 2003b). A close textual analysis will ensure this takes place. When they are being used to fulfil the function of mitigation, all of these features can thus be identified as being associated with stereotypically feminine speech styles. At a syntactic level, Holmes and Stubbe (2003b: 39) outline that, whilst the bald imperative form is the 'canonical' structure for directives, that is, the unmitigated, direct, and thus stereotypically masculine form, syntactically directives can be mitigated by taking the form of interrogatives or declaratives. Directives can be mitigated by rationalizations and justifications, hesitations and pauses. Holmes (1995: 74–75) further outlines a number of useful hedging tactics which speakers can use to mitigate directives, including 'tag questions and modal verbs, lexical items such as *perhaps* and *conceivable*, and pragmatic particles such as *sort of* and *I think*'. Goodwin (1980: 162) observes that linguistic forms commonly used to mitigate directives include 'let's', which 'signals a proposal rather than either a command or a request ... [it] shows neither special deference toward the other party nor claims about special rights over the other'. Other mitigating forms Goodwin highlights include the collective pronoun 'we', often accompanied with modals 'can' and 'could', indicating possibility rather than necessity.

The importance of analysing responses to directives was emphasized above. Goodwin's (1980) response categories of compliance, non-compliance and counters to proposals are utilized. Counters to proposals work like side sequences, and often take the form of questions that need to be answered satisfactorily before compliance can be gained. Responses can be used as part of the overall analysis of politeness at a discourse level to assess if a directive has been interpreted as (im)polite. However, in the specific context of business meetings, it is predicted that compliance with directives may not always be given verbally by those who are being issued with directives, due to the power differences that exist and also due to the confines of the meeting context, where there is usually an expectation that subordinates will receive directives. However, each CofP will have its own norms and practices, and responses to directives will thus be an interesting feature to monitor in the meeting analysis to reveal a good deal about particular practices and interactional relationships within CofPs.

Expressing approval

Holmes et al. (1999: 361) describe an utterance that expresses approval in Brown and Levinson's terms as a 'positively polite speech act'. Expressing approval enhances the face of the intended recipient(s), paying direct attention to their face needs, if the act is positively evaluated as such by the recipient(s) within the CofP in which it is performed. Holmes et al. (1999) document that part of a superior's role in workplace interactions is to express approval overtly and explicitly, as it is part of her/his responsibility to evaluate subordinates' performances. It can also be argued that expressing approval simultaneously maintains collegiality and group harmony within CofPs, supportively encouraging subordinates in their work. As highlighted above, expressions of approval can be seen as stereotypically feminine speech strategies. Along with being a speech act typically issued from a superior to a subordinate, Holmes et al. (1999) also found some evidence of approval being expressed between status equals, and from subordinates to their superiors. However, when those of lower status expressed approval to superiors, they interpret such occasions as subordinates agreeing rather than giving a direct evaluation of a superior's performance.

The strategy of expressing approval can be illuminated further through an examination of the speech act category of complimenting following Holmes's (1995) earlier work, but viewed in light of Mills's (2003) recent critique. In the formal context of business meetings, approval can be expressed by complimenting the skills and abilities of the recipient, whether this takes place from a superior to a subordinate, a subordinate to a superior or between status equals. Holmes (1995: 131) defines a compliment as a positively polite utterance that refers to 'something which is positively evaluated by the addressee'. Again, compliments can also be classified as a stereotypically feminine style, a further example of acting in a face-enhancing manner. The category of expressing approval in this study refers to speech acts that indicate praise of interlocutors by complimenting their skills, performance or abilities. Mills (2003) also points out that Holmes's use of Brown and Levinson's term 'positive politeness' with compliments is misleading. It implies that speakers are always being sincere when expressing approval, which may not always be the case. Examining responses may therefore be important for attempting to assess if and how expressions of approval are being used and received within particular CofPs. However, as with directives, it is predicted that, due to the specific meeting context, responses to expressions of approval may be rare, and it may be established practice not to respond. It will be interesting to see if this is the case in the data analysis, as this can be used to reveal established practices within particular CofPs.

Criticism

As a starting point for defining criticism, I draw upon the broad definition provided by social psychologists Mulac et al. (2000: 390) in their study of gender, management and criticism, that it is 'negative evaluation of some aspect of an individual that is communicated by others'. However, this definition needs expansion, as it is not just individuals that can be criticized. Criticisms can be much broader, and can be of other CofPs, the company itself, other companies or even of wider institutions. Criticism of their subordinates is most frequently expected from managerial superiors, since it is part of a superior's role responsibility to criticize subordinates if necessary. However, criticism can also take place between equals; it can also be given by subordinates to superiors in a contestive, subversive manner. In terms of politeness theory, Holmes et al. (1999: 361) argue that criticism functions as a 'negatively affective, explicitly face threatening' strategy. By following a CofP approach to politeness, I wish to drop the Brown and Levinson-influenced term 'negatively affective', and also replace their concept of a criticism being an FTA in favour of Austin's (1990) FAA category. Again, responses to criticisms (if any are given) are important to include in the analysis.

Superiors are legitimately entitled to criticize their subordinates due to their institutional role responsibility, though there is a range of different ways within which criticisms can be enacted. As with directives, criticisms can be issued baldly, in an unmitigated fashion. The aggravated category can also be applied to criticisms if they are issued in a manner that flouts politeness conventions of the CofP, and can thus be evaluated as an impolite act. Criticisms enacted in either of these ways can be interpreted as being associated with stereotypically masculine interaction. If criticisms are softened through form(s) of mitigation, they can be aligned with a stereotypically feminine speech style.

Warnings and challenges

Whilst it is also part of a manager's role responsibility to issue warnings and challenges if the need should arise, these speech acts can be explicitly face attacking, particularly if they are addressed to an individual(s) in front of other colleagues within business meetings. For example, they may occur at times when the company's productivity has been affected by an error which needs to be rectified as soon as possible. Again, responses (if any) will be included as part of the analysis. Warnings and challenges often co-occur with directives. Whilst it is possible for warnings and challenges to be issued with mitigation, which shows some concession to interlocutors' face needs and thus some evidence of a stereotypically feminine strategy, bald, on-record speech acts which are devoid of politeness may be used, and participants may also deliberately intend to break the norms and conventions of politeness with the performance of such speech acts, enacting impoliteness in order to get their point across, thus invoking stereotypically masculine styles.

Humour

In contrast with speech acts, humour is not absolutely necessary in order to get tasks achieved in the workplace. As Holmes and Stubbe (2003b: 110) point out, humour has more of an 'indirect' relationship with completing workplace goals. Similarly, Crawford (1995) reports the traditional view of humour being seen in direct opposition with seriousness (Mulkay 1988). However, the role of humour in the workplace should not be under-estimated. It can occur frequently in workplace interaction, and be used for a variety of different functions, including serious workplace goals. Humour can often co-occur with any of the speech act categories just outlined. Whilst many disciplines have highlighted the importance of humour in workplaces, including management and organizational studies, little research has drawn upon empirical linguistic evidence, instead favouring the rather questionable methods of field notes, questionnaires or self-reports (cf. Holmes 2000b). The work of Holmes and her colleagues has shown how fruitful linguistic investigations of humour and gender in the workplace can be in what is still an under-researched area (Holmes et al. 2001; Holmes and Schnurr 2005; Holmes 2006a, 2006b; Marra et al. 2006).

Defining exactly what constitutes humour is a complex undertaking. Drawing on Gumperz's (1982) interactional sociolinguistic perspective, I follow Kotthoff's (2000: 64) view that laughter is 'the contextualisation cue of humor par excellence'. However, as Holmes (2000b) rightly points out, laughter can sometimes be ambiguous, and a range of other contextual and linguistic features must also be examined. Although Holmes's (2000b) and Holmes and Stubbe's (2003b) work is heavily influenced by Brown and Levinson (1987), it is still useful. Holmes (2000b) foregrounds the role of the researcher in distinguishing humour, highlighting how analysts draw upon a range of 'paralinguistic, prosodic and discoursal clues' to determine if humour has taken place. Holmes (2000b: 163) assesses humour by examining speaker intention, arguing that humour is characterized as instances that are 'intended by the speaker(s) to be amusing and perceived to be amusing by at least some participants'. However, Holmes does acknowledge that her definition of humour is not comprehensive. In this study, I adapt and expand upon Holmes's (2000b) definition in order to move beyond a sole focus on speaker intention, a key criticism that has been cited at traditional Brown and Levinson-influenced studies. Identifying whether an instance is humorous or not should instead be seen as an examination by the analyst of a stretch of discourse between speaker and hearer(s), and not just assessed by looking at speaker intention within a single utterance. Expanding the focus in this way enables both unintentional and unsuccessful humour to be included. On occasions, whilst speakers may not have intended to be humorous, hearer(s) may find the speaker(s) actions to be amusing, and they can invoke humour, often initially through laughter, to signal this. Similarly, if a speaker has intended something to be humorous and hearers do not participate, then it is the hearer(s) who can be viewed as refusing to acknowledge that humour has taken place. Unsuccessful and failed humour can reveal much about the power relationships that are being enacted within workplace interactions, and these tactics can often (though not always) be used as strategies of resistance/subversion to those who occupy superior positions on the institutional hierarchy.

In this study, humour is defined as follows:

> Instances where participant(s) attempt to signal amusement to one another, based on the analyst's assessment of interlocutors' paralinguistic, prosodic and discoursal clues. Humour can be a result of either intentional or unintentional humorous action, and can be classified as either successful or unsuccessful. (Adapted from Holmes 2000b)

Humour can be produced individually or jointly. Following Holmes (2006b), the category of *conjoint* humour is used to account for instances where more than one participant is engaged in producing humour. This includes coining a continuum with a *maximally* collaborative floor at one end and a *minimally* collaborative floor at the other, viewed in light of Coates's (1988, 1996) distinctions of an OAT floor at the minimally collaborative end, and an ATN floor at the maximally collaborative end. Instances that occur in the midpoints of this continuum are identified as *mixed* examples. Instances of conjoint humour are classified according to the participant who initiates and then 'seeds' the humour: this participant will begin a humorous sequence, which then progresses to become 'an extended jointly constructed humorous interaction' (Holmes et al. 2001: 98).

As highlighted earlier, humour is multifunctional. It is frequently used to maintain good working relations in the workplace, though it can also be used as a strategic device to invoke power to produce challenges and subvert existing power relations (Holmes 2000b; Holmes and Stubbe 2003b). Part of the power of humour resides in the fact that it is indirect and ambiguous (Crawford 1995). It can operate rather like a safety net, as participants can always deny that they were being serious if challenged by receiver(s). Holmes (2000b) draws upon Brown and Levinson's positive and negative politeness strategies and Pateman's (1980) 'repressive' power to characterize how humour can be used to maintain good working relationships. In contrast, she characterizes contestive humour, later termed subversive humour (Holmes and Marra 2002), to refer to instances where subordinates use humour to challenge their superiors. Whilst the functional categories of humour that I use in my study are influenced by Holmes's work, there are some key differences.

As an alternative to Brown and Levinson's positive and negative politeness categorizations, I define the category of humour as a strategy to create/maintain solidarity and collegiality. This includes humour being used to share criticisms of outsiders and others (Holmes 2000b), for self-deprecation, including embarrassment (Coates 1996; Kotthoff 2000) and apologetic sentiments (Holmes 2000b), as a tension releaser (Pizzini 1991; Holmes 2000b) and as an aggression diffuser (Linstead 1988). It also includes supportive humour signalled by hearer laughter (Coates 1996). Whilst I do use the category of 'repressive' humour, I define this in a broader sense than Holmes (2000b) in order to foreground the unequal power relationships between superiors and subordinates, particularly in the specific context of formal business meetings. Holmes's definition refers to instances where superiors pay attention to subordinates' face needs by disguising a less acceptable message such as directives and criticisms through humour. However, I would argue that, even when there is no obvious attempt to gain compliance or to criticize, whilst superiors are using humour on the surface to enact solidarity and collegiality, these instances should also be identified as repressive, as superiors are still engaged in performing the overall goals of the organization, and are thus repressively enacting their power. As Mills (2003: 59) points out, work following Brown and Levinson, including Holmes (2000b), can mask the ways in which politeness is being used strategically, particularly in institutional contexts.

I utilize Holmes and Marra's (2002) 'subversive' humour category to account for challenges from subordinates to superiors. Using humour in this manner enables socially risky opinions to be expressed, under the guise that the speaker is not being serious (Crawford 1995). Holmes and Marra (2002: 72–74) argue that subversive humour can consist of challenging/subverting the power and status of influential individuals in companies, or the 'relevant values, attitudes and goals' of a particular group/organization (2002: 73), or it can refer to questioning at a 'societal level', by 'questioning the ideology of the business community' and wider 'institutional or social values' (2002: 72–74). These levels are useful distinctions to bear in mind when conducting the analysis. Finally, I have coined a further category, rivalrous humour, to account for instances when FAAs between status equals function as protests/criticisms/challenges, disguised through the tactical use of humour. Humour enables socially risky opinions to be expressed about status equals, being utilized as a shielding device. It is important to point out that the multifunctionality of humour can co-occur within particular stretches of talk, and on occasions, humour may well be fulfilling more than one of these functions simultaneously. Again this stresses the importance of a close textual analysis within the particular CofPs under study.

To summarize, the analytical categories of humour that are applied to the data in this study are:

- humour to create/maintain solidarity and collegiality
- repressive humour
- subversive humour
- rivalrous humour

The first two categories, humour as a solidarity-building device, and repressive humour can be seen as enacting a stereotypically feminine style, with both invoking co-operative strategies of politeness in order to pay attention to interlocutors' face needs. However, if humour is being enacted as a device to challenge those in positions of power, that is, as part of the subversive or rivalrous category, it can be aligned with a more masculine, competitive style. However, these delineations are not quite as straightforward as they are with other linguistic practices, due to humour being such an ambiguous, indirect device. As Holmes and Schnurr (2005: 130) point out, arguably humour can always be viewed in a somewhat positive light, having a 'softening effect on even the most corrosive comment'. However, as they go on to stress, there is a substantial difference between humour being used supportively/as a strategy of mitigation to pay attention to face needs and humour being used to challenge and undermine. Therefore, the stereotypical patterns of masculine competitiveness and feminine collaboration and support can still be mapped here.

Small talk

Like humour, small talk has also been traditionally perceived as a non-serious mode of discourse (Coupland 2000). Indeed, small talk has much in common with humour, being a multifunctional device that also plays a range of integral roles in workplace interaction. The years of lambasting that small talk has suffered as a trivial or superfluous mode of talk have been discredited with recent commentaries and investigations on small talk in the workplace (Coupland 2000; Holmes 2000d, 2006a; McCarthy 2000; Holmes and Stubbe 2003b, Koester 2006). As Candlin (2000: xx) points out, small talk is now firmly on the 'interactive sociolinguistic agenda'. However, whilst attitudes have changed within sociolinguistics, small talk is still negatively perceived within popular culture (Holmes and

Stubbe 2003b). Indeed, when talking to workplace practitioners, I have previously recommended that small talk is replaced with Fletcher's (1999) term *relational practice*, which Holmes and Marra (2004) use as an umbrella term, subsuming small talk into the category of 'creating team' within workplaces (see Mullany 2006b for further discussion).

Small talk as stereotypically feminine gendered discourse is further emphasized by Holmes and Stubbe's (2003b: 106) view that overall, small talk functions to 'nurture or develop social relationships'. Holmes (2000d: 58) directly coins small talk as a means of 'constructing an identity which is perceived as predominately "feminine" in western cultures', along with 'a popular conception that 'many women mix business with talk about their personal lives and expect other women to do so'. Furthermore, Coupland (2000) argues that part of the reason why small talk has been evaluated for so long as small and trivial is due to its ideological association with women. Interestingly, to illustrate this point further, Holmes and Stubbe (2003a) observe that whilst gender is not explicitly cited as a focus of Coupland's (2000) collection it is overwhelmingly dominated by the interactions of women, and it also focuses on numerous domains that are most commonly associated with women, such as supermarkets and hairdressers.

Coupland (2000) makes the crucial point that, whilst one of the primary functions of small talk is its relational, affective role, in professional settings it also fulfils a range of transactional goals. She goes further in pointing out that small talk plays a fundamental role in workplace interaction and thus 'cannot be segregated from the "mainstream" concerns of talk at work' (2000: 6). Candlin (2000) also makes the point that the distinction between small talk operating as either relational or transactional talk is very difficult to ascribe in professional, institutional contexts. He argues that such ambiguity can be accorded with the 'multi-disciplinary goals of much professional activity' (2000: xv). Holmes (2000d) defines small talk on a continuum, and this neatly reflects Candlin's (2000: xv) observation that small talk is located within 'the pragmatic space between and among the transactional and relational functions of talk'. Holmes's continuum, illustrated in Diagram 4.1, is a useful tool and is thus adopted as an analytical framework for identifying small talk in my study.

Holmes provides further criteria for the parameters of this continuum, illustrated in Diagram 4.2. These analytical tools are very useful when applied through an ethnographic, CofP framework. Within CofPs, an overarching examination of context will include the topic and relative informativeness of talk, which will enable an assessment of whether the interaction is more transactional or social. Holmes points out that talk

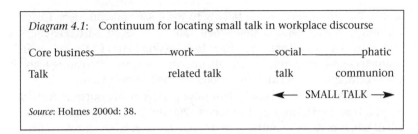

Diagram 4.1:   Continuum for locating small talk in workplace discourse

Core business————————work————————social————————phatic

Talk   related talk   talk   communion

←— SMALL TALK —→

Source: Holmes 2000d: 38.

Diagram 4.2:   Criteria for distinguishing business talk from phatic communion

CORE BUSINESS TALK————————————————PHATIC COMMUNION
Relevant 'on-topic' talk   Atopical talk
Maximally informative   Minimally informative
Context-bound   Context-free
Transactional   Social

Source: Holmes 2000d: 37.

shifts and drifts along the continuum during workplace interaction. Conceptualizing small talk on a continuum should make clear that the analytical aim is not to look for a categorical decision as to whether talk is transactional or affective. As Holmes and Stubbe (2003b: 89) point out, from a social constructionist perspective, within *all* talk participants are 'unavoidably involved in constructing, maintaining or modifying the interpersonal relationship between themselves and their addressee(s)'. On an interrelated point, Candlin (2000: xvi) argues that researchers should not be looking to identify whether small talk is a deviation from transactional talk. Instead, the crucial point is to acknowledge that relational talk 'is centrally contingent to professional practice'. Holmes (2000d: 43) observes that the fluidity between business talk and small talk provides evidence of Fairclough's (1992) conversationalization of public discourse (see Chapter 2), with the different 'lifeworlds' of work and leisure clearly overlapping (see also Koester 2006).

Holmes (2000d) and Holmes and Stubbe (2003b) argue that small talk generally occurs at the boundaries of interactions, including the commencement and termination of meetings. Small talk can also be used to re-establish relationships if colleagues have been away from work, with small talk acting as a bridge-builder to more task-oriented talk. As well as occurring at meeting boundaries, Holmes (2000d), drawing on Coupland et al.'s (1992) study, points out that small talk can also regularly occur within the main body of meeting discourse. She observes that at certain points during meetings interactants 'regularly digressed from the topic, and sometimes social discourse displaced task-oriented or work discourse' (2000d: 44). This may include gossip, with participants introducing irrelevant details about people whose names are brought up in the process of work-related talk.

As with humour, Holmes (2000d: 48–49) draws on Brown and Levinson's (1987) concepts of politeness to provide a theoretical grounding to elucidate the functions of small talk. She argues that 'small talk might be considered a core example of positively polite talk ... small talk typically serves to maintain or renew social relationships'. In light of the critique given to Brown and Levinson's politeness theory in favour of a CofP approach to politeness, and my rejection of their positive–negative distinction, any reference to positive politeness is abandoned, and instead, small talk can be identified as an important strategy which creates/maintains solidarity and collegiality. However, as Candlin (2000: xix) points out, it is important to be aware that 'surface interactive cooperativeness' in a Gricean manner does not mean that there is co-operation at a deeper level. Indeed, it is essential to realize that 'entrenched and often institutionalised equilibriums of power may easily outlive the smooth surface co-construction of an interaction'. This point is also made by Mills (2003).

In response to this and further echoing the humour model, small talk can also be analysed as fulfilling a 'repressive' function, being used as a surface expression of co-operativeness in order to disguise the unequal power relationship with their subordinates, and this can include the strategic use of small talk to manage and control encounters. It is the superior who is in charge of the amount, type and positioning of small talk that occurs in an encounter, and it can be used strategically by a superior to bring an encounter to an end. It can also be utilized by superiors to 'ease the transition to work-related topics' (Holmes 2000d: 52).

Furthermore, Holmes (2000d: 54) also observes that small talk can be used by subordinates as a strategy of 'resistance' with their superiors. However, Holmes only uses two oft-cited examples of data to illustrate small talk fulfilling this 'resistant' function, and both of these occur in dyadic, informal, non-meeting interactions on topics which are personal to the subordinates' lives outside of the workplace (Holmes 2000d: 54–56; Holmes and Stubbe 2003b: 104–105). It thus seems likely that small talk fulfilling this resistant function would not be expected in formal business meetings with a set agenda and multiple participants, though it is perhaps possible that it may function in this manner in highly integrated, well-established CofPs. Small talk clearly lacks the power of humour. Superiors always have the power to bring a period of small talk to an end, and it is far more easily dismissed and dealt with by superiors.

Bringing together an analysis of all of these linguistic practices from the perspective of gendered speech styles will enable a thorough examination of managerial interaction to be given. By taking a CofP approach to conceptualizing (im)politeness, the linguistic practices outlined here are viewed through a recent innovative development within pragmatics, and it is the intention that this will produce a thorough, context-specific analysis. The data analysis will now take place in the next three chapters. In Chapters 5 and 6 the analysis focuses primarily on how managers enact their identities in their workplace CofPs, examining the stereotypically gendered speech styles outlined in this chapter, as part of a fine-grained, CofP, context-sensitive analysis. In Chapter 7 these findings are assessed from within the perspective of broader gendered discourses. This includes an assessment of evidence of the dominant ideology of gender differences in language use, as well as evidence of other broader gendered discourses, maintained by gender ideologies, that are in evidence in the workplaces under study. Overall assessments of gender inequalities and practical suggestions for the future based on these results are then given in Chapter 8.

5
The Retail Company

Meeting data

In the retail company, the managerial meetings of two departmental CofPs, the Technical Department and the Product Department, are examined. The third meeting is taken from a company-wide CofP, the Sales Group. All three meetings are chaired by an upper-middle management level employee. The Technical Department is run by a male manager. The Product Department and the Sales Group are run by the same female manager. As pointed out in Chapter 3, having the same person in charge of two CofPs provides the opportunity for comparisons to be made between how identities are enacted in different CofP meeting encounters. Furthermore, having two different departmental CofPs within the retail company enables comparisons to be made between them. This chapter will commence with an examination of the departmental CofP meetings. These encounters both have the primary function of planning for the department's performance over the next week. The Chairs are direct superiors of all participants and are responsible for disseminating weekly information updates to middle/lower-middle managers. Chairs will report back on previous performances/issues concerning the department, and decisions will be taken to solve new tasks/problems. These meetings may also give the opportunity for lower-level managers to update their boss/colleagues on any new issues that may have arisen.

The Technical Department

The Technical Department consists of three male managers and one female manager, summarized in Table 5.1. This meeting commenced

Table 5.1:   Technical Department members

Gender/number	Name	Professional status
MC	Steve	Upper-Middle Manager (Chair)
F1	Sue	Middle Manager
M2	Mike	Lower-level Manager
M3	Matt	Lower-level Manager

at 11am on a Monday morning. On the day of recording, I was shadowing Sue. During informal talk prior to the encounter, she informed me that Steve had been on holiday for the past two weeks. As his deputy, she had taken on his role during this time. From a CofP perspective, it is possible to classify Steve, Sue and Mike as *core* members. Matt was a temporary appointment, soon to move on to another of the company's outlets. Both Mike and Matt were 12 minutes late, so a one-on-one encounter between Steve and Sue constituted the first part of the meeting. Afterwards, I continued shadowing Sue and we went for lunch in the canteen, where we talked informally about the meeting and the Technical Department in general.

Steve uses stereotypically feminine small talk to open the meeting:

Example 1

Sue enters the meeting room

1. Steve: Sue
2. Sue: Hi Steve
3. Steve: Back from hols [(smiles) (-)] had a fantastic time
4. Sue: [((laughs))]
5. Steve: err just wanted to catch up and I've got a list of things
6.   here that I'll just (.) fly past you [(-)   ] and just you know
7. Sue: [yeah]
8. Steve: sort them through (.) erm the batch runs

It is well established that small talk frequently occurs at boundary points in interactions, such as meeting openings, as highlighted in Chapter 4. Small talk can be identified as a bridge-builder here, with Steve re-establishing collegial relations with Sue following his holiday. After conventional first name greeting, Steve briefly invokes small talk, in conjunction with humour, signalled by his smile and Sue's laughter, due to his use of the abbreviated term 'hols'. He divulges personal information, evaluating his holiday, and then after a hesitation he sets out the structure of the meeting (line 5). Steve can thus be seen as using small talk and humour repressively here to minimize the power relationship between himself and Sue, re-establishing collegiality after a period of absence, as well as acting as a link into commencing meeting talk 'proper'. Steve skilfully moves from small talk to business talk to engage in agenda-setting. He does this in a non-authoritarian, informal manner. Although he had come up with an official printed agenda for the meeting, he refers to this rather informally as a 'list' that he will 'fly past' Sue, using 'just' as a minimizer and 'you know' as a hedge to further mitigate his enactment of power. Sue signals her compliance with Steve at line 7.

The other example of stereotypically feminine small talk that occurs in this meeting is also initiated by Steve at another boundary point, when latecomers Matt and Mike enter:

Example 2

Mike and Matt enter the meeting room

```
 1. Steve:   Hi Mike [hi Matt] [it's alright no problem]
 2. Mike:            [sorry    ]
 3. Matt:                      [er sorry we're late    ]
 4. Sue:     Hello
 5. Mike:    Hello
 6. Steve:   Okay so we're talk- so yeah (-) we're ta-
 7.          fantastic (-) %okay% (-) Nigel Nick
 8.          we're just gonna got through err you know
 9.          sort of I'm back (.) as you know and I'm here
10. Mike:    you're ba[ck    ]
11. Steve:            [ermm] from hols great time [(-)    ]
12. Mike:                                         [good]
13. Steve:   great time erm just a few things that I want to
14.          go (.) through
15. Mike:    yeah
16. Steve:   Errr (-) so batch running
```

Steve greets Mike and Matt individually using their first names with a conventional phatic token. They both apologize for their lateness and Steve immediately stresses that this is okay, overlapping Matt's apology. Again, this appears to signal Steve's non-authoritarian, conciliatory approach to departmental meetings. Steve starts to bring Mike and Matt up-to-date with what he and Sue were talking about, but after two false starts he instead chooses to express his approval of their arrival. He then directly addresses them again and attempts to set out his meeting agenda. He hesitates, this time uttering collective 'we', minimizer 'just' and two pragmatic particles, 'you know' and 'sort of', functioning as hedges. These lead him into small talk, which re-establishes their relationship following Steve's absence. Steve again directly mentions his holiday and that he had a good time, which is positively evaluated by Mike (line 12). At line 14 he finally completes his agenda-setting, and then changes the structure of the meeting to accommodate the latecomers. He starts to go through the items he has gone through with Sue, again starting with 'batch runs'.

There are 25 directives in total in this meeting, and Steve issues 22 of these (88 per cent), as would be expected by his superior managerial role. All of Steve's directives are issued using stereotypically feminine mitigation strategies, and he combines a wide variety of mitigation tactics to pay close attention to the face needs of his subordinates. His mitigation strategies include indirectness through questions and statements, 'let's', plural inclusive pronoun 'we' and 'need' statements, minimizers and modals as hedges. Steve's use of directives is exemplified when discussing a departmental induction, a key topic in the meeting.

The induction day

Steve wants his department to run their own recruitment induction day, which is something that the Product Department have already done. Instead of commanding his subordinates to do this, he instead uses the following wide range of mitigation tactics:

Example 3

Steve wants his department to run an induction day

1. Steve: Do you feel that (-) we need to do perhaps something
2.   like (-) the Product Department did?
3. Mike: Set a date to sort it out
4. Steve: Cos as Sue quite rightly pointed out (.) all it's all been
5.   done for us and the things etc. Why don't we take advantage
6.   of that? (.) Sue's offered her support with perhaps John? (-)
7.   er you know perhaps to run that (.) why don't we just set a
8.   date now?
9. Matt: Yeah
10. Steve: And say right okay 'let's do it'
11. Sue: Just get everybody in
12. Matt: Yeah

Steve starts off by using an interrogative, requesting that his subordinates express their opinions on the idea of running their own induction day. As part of this he uses hedging devices 'perhaps', 'like', and 'we' as part of a 'need' statement to express joint action and responsibility.

Mike's response suggests compliance with the idea (line 3). Steve goes on to provide justifications for his 'suggestion'. The directive is again formulated as a request with collective pronouns (lines 5–8) along with hedges ('you know', 'perhaps'), and 'just' as further mitigation tactics. Steve will play no part in the departmental induction day, which the meeting participants agree to, but his inclusive and collective language strongly indicates that he will be involved. He includes his subordinates, superficially at least, in the decision-making process and gains their compliance. Steve's mitigated directives can thus be classified as examples of repressive discourse, as he attempts to minimize the status differences that exist between himself and his subordinates, displaying power in a covert, rather than overt manner.

The only other participant to issue directives in this meeting is Sue, the next most senior person in the CofP. She issues a directive to Steve in the one-to-one situation, one to subordinates Mike and Matt, and one to all participants. All of Sue's directives are mitigated, and can be accorded with a stereotypically feminine speech style. The directive that Sue issues to the whole group also occurs on the topic of the induction day:

Example 4

The participants have agreed to run their own induction day

```
 1. Sue:    I'd kind of like to keep it sort of like within us
 2.         (xxx) because (.) if we've got sixteen people to do
 3.         an induction with (-) if the rest of the store hears
 4.         we're doing an induction they'll want to be wanting
 5.         to put dribs and drabs of people in, which will make
 6.         it too many people really [sixteen's a number]
 7. Steve:                            [yeah              ]
 8. Matt:                            [then sixteen's     ] sixteen's
 9.         a pretty big number to do
10. Steve:  Yeah
11. Sue:    We'll have to be a little bit secretive about it
```

Sue heavily mitigates her directive at line 1, using modality and pragmatic particles ('kind of', 'like' and 'sort of') as hedges. She provides a justification for her viewpoint, placing 'we' versus 'they' (the rest of the store). She gains support from Steve (line 7) and then from Matt (lines 8–9), who overlaps Steve's supportive minimal response to engage in supportive simultaneous talk, collaboratively engaging in the joint production of discourse by completing Sue's utterance. Steve agrees again (line 10), and Sue re-issues her directive, this time mitigated with minimizers 'little' and 'bit', along with the use of collective 'we' to invoke in-group identity. What Sue is suggesting, not sharing their induction with other departments, goes against company culture, and she may expect some resistance to her directive, particularly as she is asking them potentially to lie. Immediately after line 11, Mike invokes humour as a tension releaser, which turns into an episode of supportive conjoint humour:

Example 5

1. Mike: Oh you devious thing
2. Sue: I know ((laughs))
3.   ((laughter from all))
4. Matt: You devious thing
5. Sue: ((in a joking tone)) ooooohhhhhh
6. Mike: No I agree with that [(-)   ] we would struggle
7. Steve: [yeah]
8. Matt: Yeah

This humorous stretch of discourse signals that a potentially controversial issue has been agreed upon, and that members will comply with Sue's directive. Mike and Matt produce an instance of conjoint humour, best classified as a 'mixed' example on Holmes's (2006b) conjoint humour scale. The conversational floor is OAT, but the repetition of utterances (lines 1 and 4) is typical of supportive, collaborative talk. This episode confirms agreement with Sue, emphasizing solidarity/collegiality with her after her issuance of a potentially controversial directive. They use the stereotypically masculine humorous style of banter (Mills 2003), characterized by jocular abuse. The banter functions to signal solidarity and collegiality with Sue, teasing her by terming her a 'devious thing'. As Holmes (2000b) points out, jocular abuse is often used to signal solidarity between status equals who have good working relationships. Sue agrees, laughs and makes a humorous noise after Matt repeats Mike's utterance, signalling that she is aware they are not being serious. Both Mike and Matt agree with Sue's point and therefore do not appear to be challenging her. They can instead by perceived as skilfully negotiating a potentially conflictive situation, drawing on humour as a resource to express their co-operation.

The departmental vision

Another key topic in the meeting is a problem-solving episode where the team have to decide upon how they are going to display the new departmental vision to their subordinates on the shop floor. The following episode includes the only example of Steve issuing criticism in a meeting, when evaluating a potential solution put forward by Mike:

Example 6

Participants are discussing how to display their new departmental vision

1. Mike: You swipe that and that's got to be there for
2.   (-) check in and then you've got the top part
3.   on the top
4. Steve: That might be a bit too small
5. Mike: Bit small though [innit   ]
6. Steve: [It's a bit] small
7. Matt: Unless you stick something over the photo cos
8.   mine's terrible
9. Sue: ((laughs))
10. Steve: I was just wondering if we could do something on the back?

Steve pays close attention to Mike's face needs when criticizing his idea, using the stereotypically feminine mitigation strategies of hedging ('might') and minimizing ('bit'). Mike immediately signals that, not only does he think Steve's criticism is justified, he also agrees. He repeats an elliptical version of Steve's words, along with the informal, colloquial tag 'innit'. In line 6, Steve overlaps Mike, repeating his criticism, with 'bit' as a minimizer, echoing Mike and confirming rejection of the idea.

Immediately after Steve's criticism, Matt takes the floor and invokes humour. Matt's comment that his photo is 'terrible' is self-deprecating, and functions to emphasize collegiality and solidarity amongst the group after Mike has been criticized. Sue laughs in response. Steve then takes the conversational floor, and issues another suggestion in a heavily hedged manner.

The discussion of how to display the vision continues, and Steve can be witnessed using humour, arguably to diffuse any potential tension that may exist due to difficulties the group are having in coming to a decision:

Example 7

The team are discussing displaying the department's vision on plastic cards

1. Mike: They'd have another one
2. Steve: They'll have another one around their neck
3. Sue: ((laughs))

Steve's humour is signalled by Sue's laughter as a contextualization cue. It functions repressively, being used to support his team's ideas so that they come to a solution. When the group comes to a decision, Steve expresses his approval of them as a whole:

Example 8

The participants have agreed on how to display the new 'vision'

1. Steve: Fantastic I knew we'd come up with a solution (-) great
2. Sue: If in between time anybody wants any sticky back (-)
3.   I can print some more
4. Steve: good (.) great (.) fantastic (.) okay

Steve directly expresses his approval, using the evaluative adjectives 'fantastic' and 'great' (line 1). He then goes on to express solidarity and collegiality, directly stating his belief in the competence of the group that he 'knew' they would come up with a solution. By using personal pronoun 'I', Steve firmly indicates that he has faith in his department's skills and abilities, and by using 'we' in close succession he indicates his assessment of their collective performance as a non-hierarchical team. He re-emphasizes his approval following Sue's co-operative offer, issuing a series of three successive adjectives.

The country-wide conference

The remaining instances of humour in this meeting are initiated by Steve. He is responsible for three instances, one of which is conjoint. This conjoint example occurs when he is informing his subordinates of the national conference that he needs to attend. His initiation of conjoint humour can be classified as being primarily towards the minimally collaborative end of the conjoint humour scale, with Steve, Mike and Matt all joining in to contribute witty one-liners:

Example 9

Steve is informing his subordinates of a country-wide conference that he will attend

1. Steve: Simon Jones will be there so that's something
2.   to look forward to
3. Mike: So much better to know they'll be there
4. Steve: ((laughs)) they didn't tell you that they're coming
5. Matt: [No they didn't did they]
6. Steve: [No no no   ] no
7. Mike: We got stitched up for the evening (-) and I don't know
8.   what they've done to you yet
9. Steve: ((laughing)) Oh well I'm waiting to find out actually
10. Sue: ((laughs))

Steve invokes subversive humour with his sarcastic comment that his country-wide conference meeting with Simon Jones will be 'something to look forward to', thus functioning as a criticism of a member of senior management. It is well known within this CofP that Steve does not get on well with Simon Jones. As Steve appears to have sanctioned criticism, Mike joins in, criticizing the senior managers for not letting him know they were going to be attending an event. Steve indicates that he finds Mike's comments humorous by laughing, and then adds to the humorous episode (line 4). Matt and Steve then engage in supportive simultaneous talk, jointly agreeing with each other. Mike continues the humorous sequence by engaging in banter with Steve (lines 7–8), and Steve follows this up with a quip of his own (line 9). Sue then signals her amusement. This example fulfils a dual function: by being sarcastic about a future meeting with his superiors, Steve can be seen as invoking subversive humour here as a guise to express his displeasure that he has to go to a country-wide managerial meeting. However, this example also fulfils a repressive function, particularly as Simon Jones is not present. Steve can be seen as minimizing status differences to build solidarity with his subordinates by placing social distance between himself and senior management. Steve, Mike and Matt thus utilize stereotypically masculine strategies here by engaging in subversive humour through banter and one-liners.

Endings

After Steve reaches the end of his agenda, he carefully attempts to ensure that everything that needs to be brought up has been covered:

Example 10

Steve had finished his last agenda item

1. Steve: Okay (-) errr is there anything else? (-) Mike? (.)
2. Mike: No
3. Steve: Nothing
4. Mike: No everything's been covered
5. Steve: Okay (-) Sue?
6. Sue: No
7. Steve: No (-) Matt?
8. Matt: No
9. Steve: No (-) you're alright?
10. Matt: Yeah fine

When there is a pause after Steve's initial request for 'anything else', he begins to address each member individually to ensure there is nothing else that they want to bring up. He directly asks each member, using their first names, and once he gains confirmation he reiterates all of their responses, functioning as an additional mechanism to ensure finally there's nothing that any member may want to bring up.

Steve is the only participant within the meeting to express approval, as would be expected by his role. In addition to Examples 2 and 8, Steve also issues his approval of Mike and Sue, using evaluative adjectives 'excellent' and 'great' to approve their actions when they are reporting back upon completed tasks. At the close of the meeting, Steve expresses his approval once more:

Example 11

1.	Steve:	Thank you very much for looking after the ship while I've been
2.		away especially to Sue (-) thank you very much errr (-) it was
3.		great coming back you know no issues or anything and that's
4.		all down to you and the team so thank you very much (-) okay?
5.	Matt:	yeah
6.	Mike:	yeah
7.	Sue:	Thank you

Steve ensures Sue, in particular, is given credit for her performance when covering his role, twice thanking her (lines 1–2). He then expresses his approval of her ability to fulfil his role, stating how this is because of the abilities and skills of her and the team as a whole. By drawing on the stereotypically feminine style of expressing approval, Steve is helping to strengthen the feelings of collegiality and solidarity in his department. Using this tactic at the end of a meeting works to finish on a positive note, with Steve acknowledging again that he has confidence in his departmental team. At the end of line 4, Steve's use of 'okay' as a discourse marker signals that he is closing the meeting, but this also simultaneously functions as a question to check one more time that his subordinates do not want to take the floor to add anything else.

Summary

Overall, Chair Steve can be witnessed performing his managerial identity in the Technical Department meeting by drawing upon a range of stereotypically feminine strategies to enact power and authority. He issues directives with a wide range of mitigation strategies, as well as using mitigation when criticizing Mike – the only example of criticism in the meeting. He pays attention to his subordinates' face needs by setting the agenda in a non-authoritarian manner, and he accepts Mike and Matt's apologies for lateness without any reprimand. He uses humour and small talk strategically to reduce social distance between himself and his subordinates, functioning repressively to express solidarity and collegiality (superficially at least) with his team, including using humour as a tension releaser. By directly expressing approval, Steve demonstrates to his subordinates that he recognizes and appreciates their achievements. He also ensures all members are offered two opportunities to take the conversational floor before he closes the meeting. Steve does draw upon a more stereotypically masculine style when engaging in subversive humour, using sarcasm, directed at his overall boss at a country-wide level, as well as engaging in banter with Mike (Example 9). However, as Simon Jones is not present at the meeting, this subversive humorous episode also fulfils the function of reducing status differences in order to enhance a sense of solidarity with his immediate team, as opposed to aligning himself with senior management.

Sue also uses very similar stereotypically feminine strategies when performing her managerial identity in order to enact authority. Like Steve, she mitigates all directives. She collaboratively joins in with conjoint humour, as well as laughing supportively during all humorous episodes. Mike and Matt use stereotypically masculine banter and one-liners, but they do so in a manner that fulfils the primary function of enhancing solidarity with fellow CofP members. Matt also uses the stereotypically feminine styles of self-deprecating humour and supportive simultaneous talk to signal co-operation and solidarity with all other group members. Humour is used by Mike, Matt and Steve to release tension, re-affirming solidarity and collegiality after potentially problematic periods. In terms of linguistic politeness, members appear to pay close attention to each others' face needs. Those who occupy more powerful positions on the institutional hierarchy focus on reducing social distance in order to emphasize solidarity and collegiality, enacting power and authority covertly. Other members use linguistic strategies to enhance solidarity and collegiality amongst the group.

To conclude, there is much evidence of male managers here breaking the stereotypical expectations for their gender by drawing on a range of stereotypically feminine styles, as well as Sue also favouring stereotypically feminine styles. In Chapter 7, the broader overarching gendered discourses within which this CofP operates will be analysed. This includes examining evaluations and assessments of managers in this CofP, drawing in particular on interview data with Sue, as well as on informal talk with Steve.

The Product Department

The Product Department consists of four female managers and two male managers, summarized in Table 5.2. This meeting took place on Wednesday afternoon from 2.30–4.00pm. I had been shadowing Karen on the day of recording. She informed me that there would be two new trainee managers present for the first time, Kirsty and Eddie, who can be classified as peripheral CofP members. She also informed me that Mary and Tony were her status equals and had been at the same middle-management level as Karen for approximately the same amount of time (12 months). The Product Department meeting commenced on time with all participants present. Amy was the last participant to arrive at the meeting, and opens the encounter as follows:

Example 12

Amy sits down at the meeting table

1. Amy: Right (.) there's a lot to get through today so (.)
2.   I'll start off with figures

There is no small talk here, and Amy directly announces how much work they have to do without any mitigation. She also stresses her own authority as Chair and superior of all present, particularly through the use of 'I'. Amy can thus be seen using a stereotypically masculine style here, assertively and authoritatively opening the meeting and launching straight into task-orientated talk.

There are 48 directives issued in this meeting. Amy issues 45 of these (93.7 per cent). The majority of Amy's directives (43 out of 45) are mitigated. As with Steve, Amy uses a wide variety of stereotypically feminine styles to do this, including questions instead of commands, 'we' and 'let's' indicating collective responsibility, 'we' and 'just' as part of 'need' statements, conditional 'if', a range of hedging techniques, rationalizations

Table 5.2:   Product Department members

Gender/number	Name	Professional status
FC	Amy	Upper-Middle Manager (Chair)
F2	Karen	Middle Manager
F3	Mary	Middle Manager
F4	Kirsty	Lower-level (Trainee) Manager
M1	Tony	Middle Manager
M2	Eddie	Lower-level (Trainee) Manager

and justifications, as well as humour to minimize status differences (see also Mullany 2004). An illustration of Amy's directives can be seen in Example 13, where Amy is talking on the topic of stock ordering (see also Example 21, lines 19–22):

Example 13

Amy has detailed a problem with ordering too much stock

1. Amy: There's definitely work we can do (.) we we're not
2.   the bad example in the store [(-)   ] but only by keeping
3. Tony: [mhm]
4. Amy: our eye on it will we re[main] a good example in those
5. Mary: [mm]
6. Amy: departments which is (.) you know important isn't it
7. Karen: mm

Amy uses pronoun 'we' four times here (lines 1 and 4) to stress the team's collective responsibility, along with 'our' to modify her metaphorical use of singular noun 'eye', a further attempt to strengthen the group's sense of identity as a cohesive unit. By stating that they have a singular 'eye', arguably she implies that all members view things through the same lens. In line 6 she mitigates the directive further with the hedge 'you know', and provides a justification for her directive, followed by a tag question, checking for compliance, which Karen issues. Amy can thus be seen to be superficially minimizing status differences to gain the compliance of her subordinates covertly, in a supportive and collective manner.

However, it is important to point out that Amy's mitigated directive also co-functions as an indirect warning to her subordinates, not to become 'the bad example'. Warnings are rare speech acts in all six CofPs, but Amy issues two in this meeting. The other example co-occurs with one of her unmitigated directives:

Example 14

Amy is talking about forfeits departmental managers have to perform if they fill out absence rotas incorrectly

1. Amy: When I got them in {departmental name} I gave
2.   them back to the managers (.) who'd let me down
3.   so they ended up doing the forfeits ((smile voice))
4.   so be warned
5.   ((laughter from all subordinates))

6. Amy: Don't do it
7. Mary: hh. (-)

The direct imperative is given at line 6, after Amy has issued a warning, uttered as a direct, performative speech act (line 4), mitigated only by humour in the form of a smile voice. Amy personalizes the 'offence' using 'me' to strengthen her warning ('let *me* down'), and then openly states her delegation of responsibility should the department be punished. The bald, on-record directive acts as a threat after the warning has been given. As someone who has legitimate power to utter such warnings and unmitigated directives in his CofP, Amy's discourse should not necessarily be interpreted as impolite, though she is paying far less attention to the face needs of her subordinates than she has done when uttering previous directives, thus strengthening the overall force of her message. There is thus clear evidence of Amy using an assertive, stereotypically masculine speech style here. Mary's exhaling potentially signals resistance to Amy's warning, but this is ambiguous, and does not result in a response from Amy, who swiftly moves on to the next topic.

The three other directives in this meeting are issued by Karen, Mary and Tony, and are directed at each other. All of these are mitigated. Eddie and Kirsty do not issue any directives, as would be expected due to their lack of knowledge, experience and status.

The wrong information and a social faux pas

There are three examples of criticism and two challenges by Amy in this meeting. Whilst all of Amy's criticisms are mitigated (see Example 17), her challenges are both issued without any mitigation. One is directed at Karen when she provides the wrong information to new CofP members Kirsty and Eddie (Example 15), whilst the other is directed at Mary when she has committed the social faux pas of yawning at the meeting table (Example 16):

Example 15

Amy is explaining departmental policy to Kirsty and Eddie

1. Amy: we're going to be carrying it for more than fifteen weeks=
2. Karen: =yeah it's ten weeks for stock and it will be calculated
3.   on how many sales within five weeks
4. Amy: No it's longer than that Karen
5. Karen: Oh (.) right
6. Amy: It's longer

Amy issues a direct challenge to the utterance Karen has attempted to latch supportively onto Amy's utterance (line 4), negatively evaluating her by directly stating that she is wrong, thus performing her challenge in a stereotypically assertive, masculine manner. Karen's reply is rather ambiguous, and Amy takes the floor to reiterate her point:

Example 16

Amy is running through the staff rota to confirm Tony's hours

1. Amy: When I came back in at lunchtime today (-) so erm (-)
2. Tony: (xxxx xxxx) evening
3. Amy: No (-) no your not erm (-)
4. Mary: ((yawning)) oh excuse me ((laughs))
5.   ((laughter from many))
6. Amy: What are you laughing at?
7. Mary: I've been taped yawning sorry about that
8.   ((laughter from many))
9. Amy: It's really boring this meeting is it?
10. Mary: No I just need some food (-)
11. Karen: I I (.) It's not (.) but we haven't got a duty manager

Whilst Amy is attempting to finalise the staff rota, Mary yawned. Amy did not notice, but when laughter begins (line 5) Amy does not know why. She appears to interpret this as a potential criticism, signalled by the accusation she levels in the syntactic form of a question (line 6). Mary invokes humour, laughing to hide her embarrassment, and all other subordinates join in with her laughter. The fact that Mary has yawned during the meeting is the source of amusement for all apart from Amy. Her displeasure at Mary's action is illustrated in line 9 with a challenging tag question, where she directly asks Mary whether she thinks the meeting is 'boring'. By uttering this challenge and not participating in the laughter, Amy signals that she has perceived Mary's acts to be inappropriate. It is thus possible to see Amy's challenging question functioning as an accusation of impoliteness directed at Mary. By yawning, Mary can be seen to have committed an impolite act, and thus gone beyond the boundaries of acceptable behaviour in this CofP. The presence of the tape recorder has not helped, as part of the humour comes from Mary being recorded yawning. However, this example provides a useful illustration of Amy competitively and assertively challenging Mary, thus using traits stereotypically associated with a masculine interactional style.

A problem with sales?

It is interesting to compare the 'yawning' example directly with another stretch of discourse where Amy uses the same accusatory question 'What are you laughing at?' to criticize Tony's laughter. However, on this occasion, Amy mitigates the illocutionary force of her question with humour:

Example 17

Amy is announcing the department's sales figures

1. Amy:	Looking at where we are at year to date then	
2.	there's a few more surprises in store really erm	
3.	I came into product in week ten so I've had	
4.	[a look at the picture from week nine to now]	
5. Tony:	[((raises his eyebrows and starts to laugh))	]
6. Amy:	((smile voice)) What are you laughing at?	
7.	[((laughs))	]
8. Tony:	[rabbits from a hat]	
9. Amy:	There's no sur[prise	]
10. Tony:	[just wondering)] [((laughs))]	
11. Karen:	[((laughs))]	
12. Amy:	Yeah we're doing really well actually	
13. Tony:	Hurray	

Amy has missed Tony raising his eyebrows and is unsure why he is laughing. However, unlike Example 19, Amy uses a smile voice and laughs herself, invoking repressive humour to criticize Tony's laughter. Amy's accusatory question indicates that she wants to know what Tony did/said, to check that he was not acting in an impolite manner. Indeed, Tony's paralinguistic and linguistic acts can be interpreted as subversive, hidden through the guise of humour. He continues this with the humorous utterance 'rabbits from a hat'. Amy then steps in to diffuse the situation as it becomes clear that Tony is surprised by Amy's reporting of the sales figures. Before the meeting officially commenced (and before Amy arrived), Tony stated that he was pleased with the previous week's sales in informal talk with Karen. Tony can thus be seen to interpret Amy's use of 'surprises' as a preamble to a negative report. At line 9, Amy backtracks and denies that there is a 'surprise', and follows this up with an expression of approval of the department, then positively evaluated by Tony. At the end of Amy's reporting of the sales figures, the core group, encouraged by Amy, collectively express their own approval of themselves:

Example 18

Amy is completing her weekly run through the sales figures

1. Amy:	Overall the department's gone from plus six to
2.	plus ten point one
3. Mary:	Ahah
4. Karen:	((claps)) hurray
5. Tony:	Hurray

6. Mary: ((laughs))
7. Amy: Brilliant isn't it
8. Tony: Yeah that's [great yeah   ]
9. Amy: [absolutely fan]tastic so I'm really thrilled
10.   with that one
11. Karen: We're excellent

After Amy informs the group of their performance (lines 1–2), core members Mary, Karen and Tony all express their pleasure at the results (lines 3–6). Amy then confirms her approval, intensifying this by using 'brilliant', 'absolutely fantastic' and 'thrilled'. Karen then collectively praises the group, declaring that 'we're excellent' (line 11). Allowing her subordinates to express approval of themselves decreases hierarchy between Amy and her department, strengthening a feeling of in-group solidarity and collegiality. This overall positive evaluation on the topic of sales figures may also help to counter any negativity that Tony may have perceived earlier. Amy expresses approval of her subordinates' abilities, skills and their performance on 10 occasions in this meeting in total. She expresses approval of all core members of her CofP, (four times to Karen, twice to Mary and twice to Tony), and twice to the CofP as a whole. She does this using the evaluative adjectives 'fantastic', 'fabulous', 'great', 'brilliant' and the phrase 'good stuff'.

New recruits and a 'spot the baby' competition

Interestingly, *all* instances of stereotypically feminine small talk are accompanied by humour in this meeting. There are nine recorded examples of small talk overall. All but one occur within the main body of meeting discourse. Amy is responsible for the most occurrences, (six instances), Karen is responsible for two instances and Mary for one instance. As with humour, Amy's instances function repressively, to minimize status differences in order to strengthen solidarity and collegiality with her team. Karen and Mary's instances all fulfil the function of enhancing solidarity and collegiality.

Example 19 illustrates humour co-occurring with small talk, with Amy making a smooth transition from business talk to social talk and then back to business talk, informing meeting participants about new recruits to the company:

Example 19

Amy is giving details about new part-time recruits

1. Amy: We need to look at what hours we've got for him and
2. Amy: then Andrew (-) who's [((laughs))] he's gonna be a
3. Mary: [((laughs))]

112 *Gendered Discourse in the Professional Workplace*

4. Amy: favourite of ours
5. Amy: [I think he's really sweet   ] lit- little lad who wants to
6. Mary: [absolutely (xxx) cracking lad]
7. Amy: be a policeman erm he again wants evenings and weekends
8. Amy: so I'm gonna offer him and then an older guy called Samuel

When Amy begins to introduce Andrew, she invokes repressive humour, signalled by laughter, which Mary simultaneously issues, emphasizing her support for Amy's perspective. Amy then moves from task-oriented talk to small talk by engaging in 'gossip' about Andrew. The conversational floor changes to an ATN floor (lines 5–6), as Mary also joins in, overlapping Amy's turn with supportive simultaneous talk. In lines 2, 4–5 and 7 Amy presents the meeting with her own personal evaluation of Andrew, including use of stereotypically feminine evaluative adjectives 'sweet' and diminutive 'little'. After informing the meeting of Andrew's desire to be a policeman, Amy moves swiftly along the small talk continuum, from additional 'gossip' back to business talk.

The next extract of humour and small talk co-occurring is much longer, illustrating that on some occasions, Amy allows small talk in the main body of meeting discourse to continue for lengthy periods. This example is initiated by Karen, and is on the topic of a 'spot the baby' competition that the company has organized. All core CofP members take part, fulfilling the primary function of enhancing solidarity/collegiality amongst the group. Conjoint humour is also prevalent:

Example 20
Amy is informing her team of a company 'spot the baby' competition
 1. Amy: so if you can bring in photos of yourself as a child (.)
 2.   [then we're going to have]
 3. Karen: [((laughs)) Stuart   ] made my rin- made me ring my mum
 4. Mary: [mm   ]
 5. Karen: from the office on ((laughing)) Monday (to stop by)
 6.   cos he knew I was seeing on [Tuesday   ]
 7. Mary: [((laughs))]
 8. Mary: [He did yeah [((laughs))   ]
 9. Amy: [we did this as a section managers] team and
10. Amy: everybody guessed me straight
11.   [away so I thought well you know I've obviously]
12.   [((laughter from all))   ]
13. Amy: retained my youth [ful looks   ]
14.   [((laughter from all))]
15. Karen: [there were] a whole stack as well yester[day she just]

16. Amy: [yeah   ]   [did she?   ]
17. Karen: like like reminicising for [(xxx)
18.   [((laughter from many))
19. Karen: [((laughing) it will be in there (xxx xxx)]
20. Tony: [You haven't got any bathtime ones   ] in there
21. Karen: No I took out all [the rude] naked ones ((laughs))] (.)
22. Amy: [((laughs))]
23. Karen: ['mom I only needed one' ((laughs))]
24. Amy: [there's also a lovely feature   ] on there

At line 2, Amy attempts to move the topic from the spot the baby competition to the next piece of information that she needs to disseminate about the company's newsletter. However, at this TRP Karen also simultaneously takes the floor and embarks upon a vignette detailing how Stuart, the colleague running the competition, made her ring her mum from work. Whilst Amy had already moved on to the next item, she cedes the floor to Karen, without any reprimand. Karen invokes humour by laughing, and Mary signals her amusement and support for the story (lines 7–8). At line 9, Amy has the option of bringing talk back to the next item, to which she had already given the preamble. However, instead, she overlaps with Mary's utterance and laughter to continue both the small talk and the humour, disclosing details of what happened at a section manager's event, a further example of Amy reducing the status between herself and her subordinates. All members laugh in response, including Amy.

Amy supportively overlaps Karen (line 16), including issuing a facilitative tag question, giving Karen license to finish her humorous small talk. At line 18, amusement at Karen's story is again indicated by laughter, and then Tony and Karen engage in overlapping supportive simultaneous talk (lines 19–20). Amy signals support and amusement again (line 22). Karen and Amy's talk then overlaps once more, and on this occasion Amy signals the end of small talk by moving back to the earlier information she had begun to mention. She reformulates this using the stereotypically feminine adjective 'lovely'. The conjoint humour here is towards the maximally collaborative end of the continuum due to the frequent occurrence of supportive simultaneous talk, signalling an ATN, collaborative conversational floor. Amy demonstrates that not only is she willing to let her subordinates introduce small talk into the meeting, she is also willing to let this continue, both by joining in herself and by actively supporting them. In examples 19 and 20 it is possible to see both the transactional and affective roles that humour and small talk fulfil in this CofP.

There are 52 instances of humour overall in the Product meeting. Amy is responsible for the most (19 instances), followed by Mary (15 instances) and Karen (12 instances). Tony is responsible for six instances. Unsurprisingly, peripheral CofP members Eddie and Kirsty do not initiate any humorous instances. There are four instances of conjoint humour in total, all are initiated by women managers (one by Amy, one by Mary and two by Karen, one of which is illustrated above). Amy's instances all function repressively, to reduce status differences (superficially at least) and enact solidarity and collegiality with her subordinates. All instances of humour by status equals fulfil the function of maintaining solidarity and collegiality, with the exception of Tony's subversive instance (Example 17).

Endings

Like Steve in the Technical Department meeting, after Amy has reached the end of her agenda items, she opens the floor to all. There are distinct similarities here between the manner in which she ensures all participants have been given the opportunity to take the floor, and Steve's tactics in Example 10, with Amy directly allocating the turn-taking system to each individual manager:

Example 21

1.	Amy:	Okay (-) anything from any of you? Tony?
2.	Tony:	yeah ermmm (-) talking about commercial
	[...]	
3.	Amy:	Okay (-) is that it Tony?
4.	Tony:	yeah
5.	Amy:	Karen anything from you?
6.	Karen:	Ermmm from the recruitment evening
	[...]	
7.	Amy:	Was that it from you Karen?
8.	Karen:	Yes yeah
9.	Amy:	Okay fab (-) Anything Eddie?
10.	Eddie:	No not today
11.	Amy:	No
12.		((laughter from many))
13.	Amy:	How are you feeling?
14.	Eddie:	Alright yeah, I've been round with Bobbie this morning
15.	Amy:	Good (-) okay (-) Kirsty?
16.	Kirsty:	nothing
17.	Amy:	Yeah you're feeling okay?
18.	Kirsty:	Yeah
19.	Amy:	Erm I was just gonna say what you just need to remember

20.   is there's all of us (.) so if there's anything just shout up
21.   you know (.) we all have a pretty good idea what's going on
22.   so you know just just a- ask the question (-) Mary?
23. Mary: Two things
[...]
24. Amy: Is that everything Mary?
25. Mary: Yeah

Just like Steve, Amy uses all participants' first names and goes around each individual to check if they have anything else to report. All core participants do have information that they bring up. Once they have finished, Amy double checks they have completed their turn, again using first names within interrogative form. When checking with new peripheral CofP members Eddie and Kirsty, Amy asks both of them personal questions, (lines 13 and 17) on how they are 'feeling', thus briefly engaging in stereotypically feminine phatic talk about emotions to ensure that her new subordinates are okay. She then follows this up with the heavily mitigated directive, telling them to ask one of the team if they are not sure of anything. She uses 'just' as a minimizer five times along with hedge 'you know' twice, conditional 'if' and 'we', 'us' and 'all' to emphasize group solidarity and shared responsibility. As well as repressively giving Eddie and Kirsty referential information and repressively delegating her core group members to help their new colleagues, this also fulfils the affective goal of demonstrating the faith she has in the abilities of her core team, evaluating them as being helpful and co-operative work colleagues, simultaneously reducing her overall power and authority as being the sole person who holds the knowledge that they need to learn.

Example 22 illustrates how Amy closes the meeting:

Example 22

1. Amy: yeah (-) okay that's it (.) unless there's anything else
2.   anybody? (-) no (.) okay

Similar to Steve, Amy gives all subordinates one final chance to take the floor, gives time for responses, and then reiterates that there is nothing else by uttering 'no'. She then uses 'okay' as a discourse marker to signal the official termination of the meeting.

Summary

Overall, Amy uses a range of stereotypically feminine interactional strategies in her departmental CofP, including various mitigation techniques for directives and criticisms, expressions of approval, and the utilization of humour and small talk as repressive devices to minimize status differences and invoke a sense of solidarity and collegiality within her team. She prolongs small talk within the main body of meeting discourse, and uses supportive simultaneous talk to collaborate with and encourage her subordinates. She ensures that all participants are directly offered the conversational floor, checking and double checking at the meeting's termination that they have all had the opportunity to bring up their own topics. She also directly enquires about the emotional well-being of her new team members. However, Amy can also be witnessed using stereotypically masculine strategies on some occasions, including an authoritarian, assertive stance at the beginning of the meeting, unmitigated directives and challenges, as well as warnings, albeit her warnings are mitigated to some extent.

The other CofP members in the Product Department draw upon a range of stereotypically feminine strategies. The only exceptions are Tony's use of the stereotypically masculine style of subversive humour to challenge Amy's reporting of the sales figures, which turns out to be a misinterpretation, and Mary's yawn. This episode of impoliteness enables the boundaries of polite and impolite behaviour to be observed. Whilst Mary tried to hide her embarrassment by laughing and providing an explanation of why she is tired, Amy's confrontational response firmly indicates that she has perceived Mary's actions to be impolite.

To conclude, whilst Amy draws upon a range of stereotypically feminine strategies in this encounter, there are exceptions to this, and she can also be seen to be breaking the stereotypical expectations for her gender. The manner in which Amy is evaluated, along with the manner in which she evaluates herself is analysed in Chapter 7, and will be viewed in conjunction with these findings. Interviews took place with Amy and Karen from this CofP. Many other interviewees within the company also discuss Amy's managerial style and provide evaluations of her based on her gender identity. Amy had already been in charge of two other departments before she took control of the Product Department, so a number of other lower-level managers had also experienced Amy as their direct superior. These data, along with other data from the multi-method approach, provide a wealth of opportunity for investigating the wider gendered discourses within which Amy and her CofP members operate. The gendered discourses that are examined in relation to Amy and to this CofP will also be analysed in conjunction with the findings of the next meeting, where Amy also has ultimate power and authority, but on this occasion within a company-wide CofP.

The Sales Group

Unlike the departmental meetings, in the Sales Group, there are also three other upper-middle level managers who are members, as well as Amy. The rest of the group consists of a range of members who also additionally belong to their own departmental CofPs. Members of this CofP are those whose roles are directly related to sales. The primary purpose of the Sales Group meeting is for all members to report back on their sales figures from the previous week. The upper-middle managers give overall figures, and middle managers then report back individually on their particular sections. It is the upper-middle managers' role (including Amy's) to evaluate the previous week's figures, plan the week ahead and resolve any issues that may have arisen. The meeting is designed to fulfil both retrospective and planning functions, and task-orientated problem-solving may also take place. Announcements looking ahead to the forthcoming week are made, and occasionally problems that have arisen will be discussed. The Sales Group is an almost equal mix of female and male managers (six females, five males), as summarized in Table 5.3.

The Sales Group meeting is held at 8 am every Tuesday morning and always takes place on the shop floor. On this occasion, it ran for 45 minutes. I had been shadowing Amy on the previous day, and had met up with her half an hour before the meeting commenced. Amy

Table 5.3:   Sales Group members

Gender/number	Name	Professional status
FC	Amy	Upper-Middle Manager (Chair)
F2	Kelly	Upper-Middle Manager
F3	Janet	Middle Manager
F4	Karen	Middle Manager
F5	Sara	Middle Manager
F6	Sybil	Middle Manager
M1	Gary	Upper-Middle Manager
M2	Jack	Middle Manager
M3	Billy	Middle Manager
M4	James	Upper-Middle Manager
M5	Paul	Middle Manager

briefed me beforehand on the topics she would cover and the pattern the meeting always took: she gives each participant the floor to report on their sales figures, the figures are evaluated, and then any other problems/issues are discussed. Amy opens the meeting as follows:

Example 23

1. Amy: Okay (-) so time to start (.) Gary
2. Gary: Yeah (-) erm we had a reasonably good week last week

Amy thus opens the meeting in a similar way to her departmental CofP meeting, performing her managerial identity by drawing on a stereotypically masculine style. She does not use any phatic tokens, instead simply using 'okay' and 'so' as discourse markers. She then directly and assertively states that it's 'time to start' and immediately allocates Gary the first turn, just by stating his name. Gary complies and takes the floor. Amy uses this direct pattern of individuals' first names only throughout the rest of the meeting to signal to individuals that it's their turn to take the floor to report on their figures (see Example 24, line 3).

There are 20 directives issued in total. Amy is responsible for 16 of these (84.2 per cent), and all are mitigated. She uses very similar stereotypically feminine strategies to mitigate her directives as those she used in the Product meeting, including conventional hedging devices, minimizers, modals and inclusive pronouns, justifications and rationalizations, as typified when she is discussing clearance stock:

Example 24

Amy is discussing clearance stock

1. Amy: We've still got twenty-two percent left (-) erm I think we need
2.   now just to double check our (-) stock figures and make sure
3.   that everything that we have got is out (-) Billy

Amy utters a justification as a preamble, and then uses 'we' four times, including as part of a need statement, along with 'I think' as a hedge and minimizer 'just'. Of the remaining four directives in the meeting, upper-middle manager Gary is responsible for uttering two of these and his status equal James utters one, as would be expected by their role. Middle manager Paul also issues a directive. This is heavily mitigated and is in the turn allocated to him by Amy. Paul and James mitigate their directives using minimizers, inclusive pronouns and conditionals. Similarly, upper-middle manager Gary uses a range of mitigating strategies when uttering his first directive:

Example 25

Gary has expressed concern about low levels of stock

1. Amy: We took more than that after being closed for three hours
2. Gary: So it's a little bit of a something we may need to think
3.   about this week
4. Amy: Yeah
5. Karen: Yeah

Gary uses a combination of stereotypically feminine styles here, minimizers 'little' and 'bit', followed by the non-specific pronoun 'something', inclusive pronoun 'we' and modal 'may' as part of a need statement to minimize his command. Amy and Karen immediately agree. In contrast, Gary's second directive is an aggravated, bald, on-record imperative issued to Sybil. This occurs during a stretch of discourse where upper-middle manager Kelly has the floor:

Example 26

Kelly is explaining that the shop floor is getting a new lighting system.
Sybil and Sara are whispering during lines 1–2.

1. Kelly: Next week we're going to be installing (.) the new lighting
2.   in the store we're going to go in the left side cos starting
3.   on the right side they'll be well up to deal with the job
4. Sybil: What's this changing?
5. Kelly: Sorry?
6. Sybil: What's this changing?
7. Kelly: We've got a new one through
8.   [systems and   ]
9. Gary: [go and have a look] in the showroom you'll see in the
10. Gary: showroom there's a new lighting system
11. Amy: What times are they working Kelly?

At line 4 Sybil asks Kelly for confirmation of what is changing, indicating that she missed the first part of her utterance (lines 1–2). Sybil had been whispering to Sara at this time, and Gary had been glaring at them in a manner which suggested his disapproval. At line 5, Kelly's side sequence requests that Sybil repeats her question. Kelly begins to answer this, but Gary disruptively interrupts and reformulates her declarative about the new lighting system in the form of an aggravated, bald, on-record imperative to Sybil. As Sybil's immediate superior, Gary commands Sybil to go and look in the showroom. He thus draws upon a range of stereotypically masculine speech styles here, using a direct, unmitigated strategy which strengthens hierarchical differences, as well as disruptively interrupting Kelly. The aggravated nature of Gary's direct directive indicates that Sybil has broken politeness norms, being impolite by whispering and then expecting the floor holder, a superior, to stop and repeat information that she should have heard in the first place. Gary can thus be seen as reprimanding Sybil here. Amy then takes the floor.

'I'm only pulling your leg'

Unlike in her departmental meeting, Amy does not issue any warnings or challenges in the Sales Group meeting. However, there are two examples of criticism giving, and both of these are issued by Amy. One is a mitigated criticism to status equal Kelly regarding suggested modifications Amy has to an idea Kelly has had. The second is also aimed at another of Amy's status equals, James. Whilst Amy does mitigate her criticism of James, she does this using humour functioning in a rivalrous manner, invoked by the use of stereotypically masculine strategies of banter and jocular abuse:

Example 27

James has just detailed that his department has had the most successful sales week

```
 1. Amy:    ((smile voice)) is that why you came to
 2.         [the meeting?   ]
 3. James:  [I'm sitting here] next to three (xxx) and
 4.         business is dealt by the three thirty-eight
 5.         thank you very much erm=
 6. Amy:    =you don't come all these weeks when
 7.         it's down and then when it's up he's here
 8.         ((laughter from many))
 9. James:  I've been quite stretched (xxx) (-)
10. Amy:    I know you have I'm only pulling your leg James
```

Lines 1–2 and 6–7 illustrate Amy using banter, followed by jocular abuse, to criticize James for not attending the Sales Group meeting in previous weeks. In lines 1–2 she issues an FAA in interrogative form, asking him if the only reason he came today was because his team had performed well for the first time in weeks, using a smile voice. She continues her critique with jocular abuse, accusing him of attempting to avoid criticism, only attending when he knew he would receive praise. Amy's change of pronoun from 'you' to 'he' (line 7) signals an attempt to place some distance between James and the rest of the group. Amy's accusation is found to be amusing by many members. However, following James's responses where he defends himself, Amy uses the idiomatic expression 'I'm only pulling your leg', to overtly state that she was only joking, suggesting that James has misinterpreted her intentions if he is taking her seriously. This is an excellent example of the ambiguity of humour, and how participants can deny the force of an unfavourable message. Even by idiomatically stating that she was using humour, and thus by implication that James shouldn't take her seriously, the critical force of Amy's message remains.

There are 13 instances of humour overall in this meeting. In contrast to the Product meeting, only one of these is initiated by Amy, the rivalrous instance cited above. Out of the other upper-middle managers, four examples are initiated by Gary and two are initiated by James. These are all examples of repressive humour, being used to reduce status differences and enhance a sense of collegiality and solidarity within the group. The other remaining instances function to maintain solidarity/ collegiality, and are initiated by Janet, Paul (two instances each), Karen and Sybil (one instance each).

The boxes staff

Only one example of humour is conjoint in this meeting. This is initiated by Gary on the topic of a particular section of his department, the 'boxes' staff. This is a very brief example, and Amy does not take part. It can be seen to contrast with the lengthy, extended instances that occurred in the Product meeting in conjunction with small talk:

Example 28

Gary has the floor to disseminate his department's weekly sales figures

1. Gary: people that have performed really well department wise
2. Gary: was er ((laughing)) I have to say [((laughs))   ]
3. Paul: [oh not boxes]
4. Gary: oh (.) boxes
5.   ((laughter from many))

Gary invokes humour here derived from the fact that every week the 'boxes' staff in his department perform better than his staff in other sections. Gary signals humour through the contextualization cue of laughter in line 2, and this gives Paul enough indication that he can simultaneously complete Gary's utterance while he is laughing. Gary then builds on this, and the prosody he uses in line 4 indicates that he is jokingly attempting to be surprised by uttering 'oh' and then repeating 'boxes'. Although this example is short and involves only two participants, it can be classified towards the maximally collaborative end of the conjoint scale due to collaborative speech through supportive overlaps and repetition of utterances. Interestingly, there are no recorded examples of small talk in this meeting, either with or without humour, again providing a contrast with the Product Department meeting where Amy introduces, encourages and prolongs small talk in conjunction with humour. Karen was also responsible for initiating small talk in the departmental meeting, but does not issue any instances in the Sales Group meeting.

Approving and ending

Amy is the only participant to express approval in this encounter, which accords with her role as Chair, and as the manager with ultimate control of the Sales Group. She does so on seven occasions, once to the group as a whole, to her status equals Kelly (three occasions), once to Gary and once each to subordinates Janet and Paul. Amy uses exactly the same strategies to express approval here as she did in her departmental CofP, either 'fabulous' (or its abbreviated form 'fab'), 'fantastic', 'good', 'great' and excellent'. Indeed, Amy uses her expression of approval of the group as a whole to also fulfil the function of ending the meeting overall:

Example 29

Amy is talking on the final meeting topic

1. Amy: that would be good (-) okay?
2. Sybil: mhm
3. Amy: Fab

By concluding the meeting in this positive manner, Amy positively evaluates the encounter as a whole, strongly suggesting that participants should feel pleased with their performance and should also view the encounter positively.

   In overall summary, as with the Product meeting, there is evidence of Amy utilizing a range of stereotypically feminine speech styles, but on occasions she also draws upon stereotypically masculine styles. She mitigates all directives in this encounter, and expresses approval at strategic points in the interaction. However, she opens the meeting in an assertive, direct manner, and uses a very direct, elliptical method for allocating the floor to individuals throughout. She also uses the stereotypically masculine styles of banter and jocular abuse as part of rivalrous humour to criticize her status equal James.

By comparing the two CofPs, evidence of Amy using the same stereo-typically feminine strategies to express approval and mitigate her directives is seen. However, there is also evidence of Amy changing the manner in which she performs her identities within the two different CofPs. It is notable that there is no stereotypically feminine small talk in the Sales Group meeting initiated by Amy or any other participant, along with no examples of repressive humour by her as an attempt to reduce status differences. Arguably, in the Sales Group meeting, Amy appears to maintain a key focus on the 'serious', task-orientated aspects of the meeting; the only time she does invoke humour is in a stereotypically masculine style, as a guise to criticize one of her status equals.

Crucial, fine-grained contextual detail from these CofPs, gained via ethnographic observation, can be put forward as key factors to explain the differences in the strategies that Amy employs in the two different CofP meetings. As the Sales meeting took place at 8 am, Amy explained to me both before and after the meeting that she is very conscious of time and the fact that participants need to get on with daily tasks before store opening. She thus aims to keep the encounter as 'work-focused' as possible, and participants appear to comply with this by not initiating any small talk themselves. Indeed, Amy stated that she deliberately holds this meeting on the shop floor as a tactic to ensure that it does not run over.

In conjunction with these factors, the different role responsibilities that Amy has within the two CofPs are also justifiable reasons for the differences in the manner in which she enacts her managerial identity, confirmed again during informal and interview talk with her. In her departmental CofP, Amy is responsible for the 'welfare, knowledge, motivation and development' of her subordinates, (quoting Amy directly from her interview data), as well as having sole responsibility to ensure that the department works effectively and efficiently as a team. The strategies Amy uses, particularly with humour and small talk, can thus be interpreted as enhancing such aims. On the other hand, in the Sales Group, her role is more of an overseer as opposed to being directly responsible for the welfare, knowledge and development of every team member. Whilst she does have ultimate responsibility for decision-making and motivation in the Sales Group, these responsibilities are shared between her and the other three upper-middle management members of this CofP.

The majority of other CofP members show evidence of stereotypically feminine speech styles in the Sales Group meeting, mitigating directives and using humour to maintain solidarity/collegiality. However, there is an example of Gary utilizing both stereotypically masculine and stereotypically feminine strategies with his issuance of directives, in response to Sybil's impoliteness towards Kelly, where she ignores her superior's face needs by whispering whilst Kelly was speaking.

As highlighted in the summary of the Product Department meeting, there are many opinions and evaluations of Amy in the retail company data, including her own, regarding the enactment of her gender and professional identities as well as the assessment and evaluations of other members of this CofP on gender grounds. All of these data will be fully explored in Chapter 7.

6
The Manufacturing Company

Meeting data

Out of the three CofP meetings to be analysed from the manufacturing company, one is a departmental CofP, whist the other two are meetings from larger, company-wide CofPs, comprising members from across four of the company's departments. The departmental CofP meeting is of the Services Department, and is chaired by one of the company's two female directors. The wider CofP meetings of the Product Review Team and the Business Control Team are both chaired by males. The Product Review Team Chair is also one of the company's eight male directors. The Business Control Team meeting is supposed to be chaired by another male director. However, he gives his apologies at the last minute and instead nominates a middle-management level male to take his place. All three meetings are regular encounters. The Services Department and the Product Review Team hold monthly meetings, whilst the Business Control Team holds meetings on a weekly basis.

Approximately two months before I began this fieldwork, the manufacturing company underwent considerable re-structuring: as a result, all of these CofPs are fairly new. Whilst all participants have been managers within the company for at least two years and tend to know each other well, having previously been part of differently structured CofPs, the three CofPs examined in this chapter are in the fairly early stages of development.

The Services Department

There are 11 members of the Services Department, six females and five males. One female member is the Chair's personal assistant and departmental secretary for the CofP, leaving an equal number of female and male managers. After the company's restructure, the Services Department is composed of two sections, supply and engineering. Whilst all supply section members were part of Carrie's old departmental CofP, called the Distribution Department, the engineering members are new. Supply members could thus be perceived as more established members of the CofP than their engineering counterparts, although the remit of the CofP is different. All members' details are summarized in Table 6.1.

The monthly Services Department meeting is both a retrospective and planning meeting, with Carrie being responsible for reporting back and disseminating updates. She then allocates a turn to each subordinate to report on their 'whereabouts' over the next month, and finally opens the floor to all members to give the opportunity to bring forward any problems/issues that may have arisen, as well as enabling them to seek clarification on any issues already brought up. This meeting may therefore also include problem-solving. The encounter commenced at 9 a.m. on a Monday morning in the open plan Services office, and ran for 45 minutes. I had been given a tour of the Services Department when shadowing secretary Jackie on a previous visit, and had observed a number of CofP members engaging in their professional roles. I accompanied Chair Carrie to the meeting, and she outlined the pattern the meeting would take beforehand. After the meeting, we spent half an hour engaging in informal talk and she gave her assessment of what had taken place. Carrie opens the meeting in the following manner:

Example 1

1. Carrie: Morning everyone (.) hope you all had a good weekend (.)
2.   okay we'll get going then with my report (.) sizing survey

Carrie engages briefly in stereotypically feminine small talk, using conventional phatic tokens to re-establish contact with her subordinates after the weekend. She then signals the 'official' start of the meeting with the discourse marker 'okay', using collective 'we' as part of a brief agenda-setting, informing members that the meeting will begin with her report. She then moves on to the first topic.

There are 42 directives issued overall in the Services meeting, and Carrie is responsible for issuing 37 (88.1 per cent) of these, as would be expected by her role as Chair and direct superior of all present. The majority of her directives are mitigated. She draws upon a range of

Table 6.1: Services Department members

Gender/number	Name	Professional status and departmental sub-section
FC	Carrie	Company Director (Chair)
F2	Jill	Lower-Middle Manager: Supply
F3	Jane	Middle Manager: Supply
F4	Jackie	Departmental Secretary and Carrie's Personal Assistant
F5	Phyllis	Middle Manager: Supply
F6	Joan	Lower-Middle Manager: Engineering
M1	Jim	Middle Manager: Engineering
M2	Phil	Middle Manager: Supply
M3	Robert	Lower-Middle Manager: Supply
M4	Doug	Middle Manager: Engineering
M5	Arthur	Upper-Middle Manager: Engineering

stereotypically feminine styles, very similar to the mitigation devices used by Steve and Amy in the retail company, such as the following, when discussing the company's new computer system:

Example 2

1. Carrie: You just need to sort of sink yourselves in and if you want
2. information go to sort of the nearest person that's doing a regular
3. search to trawl it for you for a little go on there (-) now

In Example 2, Carrie uses minimizer 'just', 'sort of' as a hedge twice, conditional 'if' and 'little' to mitigate her directive for members' computer training.

One warning is issued in this meeting, and it co-occurs with a directive mitigated with humour and conditional 'if':

Example 3

Carrie is informing the group of the time they need to leave work on Christmas Eve

1. Carrie: One o'clock will be the time (.) and that way
2. ((smile voice)) if you go to the pub then you're
3. not welcome back
4. ((laughter from many))

Carrie invokes humour using a smile voice. Her humour functions to disguise the directive and warns subordinates that they must leave at one o'clock as the company is going to close for the afternoon. Many participants signal their amusement at Carrie's utterance.

Despite the majority of Carrie's directives being mitigated, seven of her 37 examples are unmitigated, on-record directives thus issued in a stereotypically masculine style, as in the following example, where she is disseminating new product information:

Example 4

1. Carrie: Anything to do with those sizing issues give them to
2.   Simon or Leah (.) the next thing

Carrie issues a bald, unmitigated directive, pausing briefly and then moving on to the next issue on her list of items to disseminate.

'Hold on a minute'

Two of Carrie's unmitigated directives are aggravated. One of these co-occurs with a direct, unmitigated challenge, issued by Carrie to deliberately attack the face needs of Phyllis:

Example 5

Jackie and Jane are discussing storage space in the department

1. Jackie: Also they've moved the [(xxx xxx xxx xxx xxx)   ]
2. Phyllis: [subscription to magazines]
3. Phyllis: [the magazines]
4. Jane: [we could   ] take them over there and the new
5.   ones could go in to Sharon and ask
6. Jane: [(her to   ]
7. Phyllis: [either they] are [lost or   ]
8. Carrie: [hold on a minute] wait till they're done
9. Jane: Well at the moment they're over there

Prior to this stretch of discourse, Carrie and Jane have been discussing storage space. At line 1, Jackie takes the floor to discuss this. Phyllis uses a stereotypically masculine style by disruptively interrupting Jackie, introducing a new topic, but neither participant cedes the floor. Phyllis persists in talking over Jane and Jackie's interaction. At line 8, Carrie issues an aggravated directive in the form of an FAA to Phyllis, telling her to 'hold on a minute' and 'wait' until Jackie and Jane have finished. Phyllis has attempted to take the floor on a different topic without any authorization. Arguably, from Carrie's reaction, it appears that Phyllis's actions can be interpreted as breaking the norms and conventions of linguistic politeness in this CofP. Carrie draws upon a stereotypically masculine speech style, issuing an aggravated directive to challenge

Phyllis's actions. Phyllis immediately complies and Jane re-takes the floor. The other instance where Carrie issues an aggravated directive co-occurs with bald, on-record criticism and is part of a longer period of tension between Carrie and Phil (see later).

Overall, in the majority of cases, Carrie issues her directives in a repressive manner, paying attention to her subordinates' face needs by minimizing status differences between them and issuing directives using a range of mitigation techniques. However, like Amy in her departmental meeting there are some examples of Carrie also using stereotypically masculine styles to issue directives to her subordinates, thus enacting authority oppressively. Three other participants issue directives in the meeting. Jane and Phyllis issue two mitigated directives to their status equals. Interestingly, the other person to issue a directive is Jackie, the CofP secretary.

Secretaries gaining power

Jackie's directive is issued to all CofP members. It neatly illustrates the negotiable nature of power highlighted in Chapters 2 and 4, with the role that secretaries perform and the knowledge and resources they have access to enabling them to enact power over their managerial superiors, albeit briefly. Jackie issues her directive as follows:

Example 6

Carrie is discussing the group's travel plans for the next month

1. Carrie: In January most of you are [going out   ]
2. Arthur: [%(xxx xxx)%]
3. Jackie: [can   ] I just say that if you've got your
4. Arthur: [%(xxx)%]
5.   flight plans on way to me next week you need
6.   to get them to me by Tuesday
7. Carrie: Okay

Jackie overlaps Arthur's indecipherable utterance to gain the floor at line 3 and issues her directive, using modal 'can', minimizer 'just' and conditional 'if', along with the metadiscoursal 'say' to clearly signal that she is going to take the conversational floor, with 'just' indicating that this will only be for a short period of time. Carrie supportively indicates compliance and agreement by uttering 'okay', arguably in response on behalf of all.

There are two examples of Carrie expressing approval in the meeting, once to Jim and once to Jane. On both occasions, Jim and Jane have suggested solutions to problems that have arisen. Carrie informs Jim that his idea to discuss a stock problem with another colleague 'will be good', and she uses exactly the same construction to express her praise of an idea Jane has had to solve a distribution problem. Carrie thus draws upon stereotypically feminine speech strategies to approve the problem-solving abilities of two of her subordinates.

Carrie and Phil

There are eight examples of criticism in this meeting, and they all take place between Carrie and Phil. Of these instances, Carrie is responsible for just two instances, one of which is mitigated, whereas Phil is responsible for issuing six direct, unmitigated criticisms of Carrie. Furthermore, unlike in any other meetings so far, there is evidence of a subordinate issuing challenges to a superior, with Phil twice challenging Carrie, thus enacting a range of subversive strategies that question her authority. These hostile exchanges run throughout the meeting, with Phil acting in a competitive, dominant and thus stereotypically masculine manner to his superior, directly criticizing and challenging her. Ethnographic information gained during informal talk with Carrie after the meeting enhanced my understanding of this situation. At the time of recording, Phil was being investigated on a disciplinary charge by the company's executive, of which Carrie is a member. Later that day, Carrie and all other directors conducted a disciplinary hearing with Phil. When I returned to the company a week later, Carrie informed me that Phil had decided to hand in his resignation. Phil's hostility throughout the meeting is also signalled through his negative body language. He sat slumped in his chair with his arms crossed throughout. He hadn't brought any materials along, whereas all other participants had brought diaries and other relevant documentation with them.

In Example 7, Phil negatively evaluates Carrie, contesting her authority by issuing an unmitigated criticism followed by an unmitigated challenge, on the magazine topic that Phyllis has now brought up:

Example 7

The group have been discussing the circulation of magazines

1. Jane: Even if they go on [circulation (.) that (xxx)   ] to be
2. Carrie: [well I get quite a few don't I]
3. Jackie: Yeah cos they come through for you
4. Phil: But she doesn't pass them on

5. Carrie: I do ((laughs))
6. Phil: Well I don't get them
7.   ((laughter from women managers))
8. Jane: Yeah but that's not what I'm saying

Phil directly criticizes Carrie for being responsible for the lack of magazine circulation (line 4). He intensifies his criticism, using the third person pronoun 'she', acting as a form of impersonalization. Phil can be interpreted as breaking politeness norms and conventions, directly challenging Carrie with this FAA, thus engaging in subversive discourse. Carrie immediately issues a bald denial, signalling that she perceives Phil's challenge to be impolite, and thus defends herself in response. She then follows this up by laughing, indicating that she is attempting to invoke humour to reduce tension.

Phil then implies that Carrie is lying by directly stating that he does not receive any magazines. All women managers in the group laugh at this point, signalling that they are attempting to release increasing tension which has developed. Jane then takes the floor again and arguably distances herself from Phil, as well as functioning as an indirect criticism of him for shifting her topic away from the point she was trying to make.

The other challenge Phil issues to Carrie is on the topic of conference attendance, where he informs her that one of the ideas she has had is 'ridiculous':

Example 8

Carrie has arranged for a company director to give her team a presentation to save them from travelling to a conference which Phil wants to attend

1. Phil: The thing about this is it's for {conference name} and not preview
2. Carrie: You won't get that yet
3. Phil: I thought that's what they were presenting down in London
4. Carrie: I hope not
5. Phil: That's ridiculous
6. Carrie: Okay well he'd better do that then with us (.) you've had already a
7.   précis of that though haven't you (-) I've sent you one (-)
8. Phyllis: Rather than us going to London

Phil issues an FAA which functions subversively to challenge Carrie's authority directly (line 5). Carrie attempts to appease Phil somewhat by stating that she'll ask the director to present the information that Phil is requesting, though she does make the point that he already knows this information as she has sent him a précis of this already. This is met with silence. Phyllis then takes the floor to show her support for Carrie, and by using 'us', she implies that the rest of the group also support Carrie's decision.

Shortly after Example 8 has taken place, Carrie issues a bald, on-record directive to Phil which functions as a direct criticism and reprimand. Jane then comes in, using rivalrous humour to criticize Phil which simultaneously shows her support for Carrie's position:

Example 9

Phil is giving feedback on a new post that his department needs to fill

1. Phil: Lyn came back and said that three (-) were interested
2.   in coming back for an interview but she'd get back to
3.   me about whether they were serious in coming back for
4.   an interview or not
5. Carrie: Oh you're gonna have to follow that up
6. Jane: ((smile voice)) That's bizarre
7. Arthur: ((laughs))
8. Carrie: Okay (.) Jackie have you got anything?

From Phil's report (lines 1–4), Carrie assesses that he has not acted appropriately on a task that he is supposed to fulfil and thus issues a directive in a stereotypically masculine style, without any mitigation. Jane invokes rivalrous humour (line 6), using a smile voice to declare that the interview process in which Phil has been involved is 'bizarre'. Arthur signals that he finds Jane's utterance amusing. Carrie then signals Phil's turn has ended, using 'okay' as a discourse marker. She goes on to allocate the floor to Jackie.

The ethnographic information gained from Carrie regarding Phil's actions provides important background knowledge here. Carrie explicitly acknowledged that Phil had been 'hostile' towards her, including her assessment that he was 'being rude' when accusing her of hoarding magazines. She ascribes his confrontational actions to the disciplinary hearing. These specific contextual factors surrounding Phil's position in the business on the day of recording appear to have been an important influence on the manner in which he performed his identity.

Switchboard operators, shopping and sunbathing

There are 24 instances of humour in this meeting. Carrie is responsible for the majority of humorous instances (17), which all function repressively to minimize status differences between herself and her subordinates and enact power covertly (an illustration of which we have already seen in Example 3 above). Only one of these instances is conjoint, and this example co-occurs with small talk. Carrie introduces the topic of one of the switchboard operators going shopping:

Example 10

Phyllis has asked Carrie what to do about telephone calls she has been receiving from the press

1. Carrie: I voted for a block they have actually erm I don't
2.   know whether anybody knows she left here at
3.   [five o'clock   ]
4.   [((laughter from women participants))]
5. Carrie: rather than go shopping and get into work at
6.   twenty past nine (-) so so she won't be back for a while
7.   ((laughter from all women participants))
8. Jane: I don't know that's a convenient excuse isn't it?
9. Carrie: [Yeah
10.   [((laughter from all women participants))
11. Jackie: She wanted a week at ho [me   ]
12. Carrie: [at least] she got back from
13.   the shops I think
14. Jackie: Yeah ((laughs))
15. Carrie: Okay Phyllis anything for you in the next few weeks?

Carrie makes a transition from task-oriented talk to stereotypically feminine small talk in the main body of meeting discourse (line 1), engaging in gossip about one of the switchboard operators. Humour is initiated at line 3, and all women laugh during this episode. Jane and secretary Jackie extend the humour to make the episode conjoint. This example is towards the maximally collaborative end of the conjoint continuum as there are supportive overlaps in the form of laughter at lines 3–4, 9–10 and supportive simultaneous talk at lines 11–12. At line 15, Carrie makes the smooth transition back to business talk, using discourse marker 'okay' to signal that small talk has come to an end. Carrie can thus be seen combining small talk and humour here to function repressively as a way of minimizing status differences, disguising her power by 'gossiping' about an employee from another department in order to enact solidarity and collegiality within her own group. It is notable that it is only the women managers and secretary Jackie who join in. As well as being an example of 'gossip', the topic on which the women are talking is also a stereotypically feminine one: shopping. Therefore, this example acts as a solidarity-building device amongst the women in her team, but arguably not with the men, who do not take part.

There are four other instances of small talk in this CofP. All of these are initiated by Carrie and function repressively to maintain solidarity and collegiality, at least at a superficial level. Four out of the five examples are accompanied by humour, which accords with the findings in the departmental meetings in the retail company. With the exception of Example 1, where small talk takes place at a meeting boundary, all follow the pattern of Example 10: they co-occur with humour, they are initiated by Carrie within the main body of meeting discourse and they include participation from women CofP members only (see Mullany 2006b). As well as this example on the topic of shopping, Carrie's small talk at non-meeting boundaries focuses on the topics of holidays and sunbathing. These issues will be further discussed in Chapter 7. Out of the remaining seven instances of humour, Jane initiates four instances, Phyllis two instances, and secretary Jackie is responsible for one instance. With the exception of Jane's rivalrous humour, also seen above (Example 9), all other instances from Jane, Phyllis and Jackie function to enhance solidarity and collegiality within the group.

From agenda setting to ending

In terms of agenda-setting, after Carrie has completed her initial dissemination of information, she allocates the floor to participants to give their whereabouts in the following manner (see also Example 9, line 8, and Example 10, line 15):

Example 11

1. Carrie: Erm we ought to just see what the whereabouts is gonna be for
2.   everybody (.) Arthur do you want to start?
3. Arthur: Yeah (.) On Tuesday

Carrie uses collective 'we', 'ought' and 'just' and then allocates turns using members first names in interrogative form to mitigate her directive to take the floor. The only exception to this is when Carrie allocates the floor to Phil. Instead of this pattern, with Phil she declares only the product name for which he is responsible, depersonalizing his floor allocation to signal a lack of attention to his face needs. This occurs after

Example 9 has taken place. Once all participants have been allocated the floor, Carrie then asks if everything with her subordinates is 'okay', using a non-authoritarian, informal questioning style to open the floor to all. Jane is the first person to self-select:

Example 12
Members have finished giving details of their whereabouts
1. Carrie: Okay (-) what about up here now? Everything okay up here?
2. Jane: Where did we get to with getting storage?

After all issues have been discussed during the open floor, Carrie closes the meeting as follows:

Example 13
1. Carrie: I think that's it unless you've got any other queries or
2. things to raise? (-) alright (.) thanks

She ensures that she offers the floor one more time to all subordinates, using 'I think' as a hedge, presenting them all with the final chance to bring up any other 'queries' or 'things' that have not already been covered. She officially closes the encounter, expressing thanks to show appreciation of her subordinates.

Summary

To summarize, in the majority of cases Carrie can be witnessed using a range of stereotypically feminine speech styles to enact her managerial identity, minimizing her authority with subordinates by enacting power in a covert manner. She uses small talk to re-establish contact with subordinates, mitigates the majority of her directives, and uses humour and small talk repressively, including small talk at non-meeting boundaries, to attempt to close the status gap between herself and her department by enhancing solidarity and collegiality. She introduces and sets out the meeting structure in a co-operative, non-assertive style, ensuring all participants are allocated a turn. She then gives them the chance to take the floor again before closing the encounter. She expresses approval of subordinates when they have successfully engaged in problem-solving. However, there are occasions where she also uses stereotypically masculine strategies to enact her managerial identity. She issues unmitigated and aggravated directives, one of which co-functions as a bald, on-record challenge when it appears that politeness norms and conventions have been broken by Phyllis. When dealing with Phil, she issues an aggravated directive, responds to an impolite challenge with a direct denial (albeit later mitigated with humour) and allocates his turn to take the floor in a manner that conveys social distance and actively marks him out as different from all other members.

However, she also uses stereotypically feminine strategies with Phil, signalling her attempts to diffuse the difficult situation that develops. She mitigates her criticisms, attempts to accommodate to his needs (Example 8), and also attempts to use humour as a tension releaser. There is clear evidence of Phil using a range of stereotypically masculine strategies throughout. Carrie provides further evidence and evaluation of Phil in her interview which was recorded after Phil had left the business. Her interview data suggest that some of Phil's hostilities could also have been gender-related, as well as being related to the disciplinary hearing. This issue will be thoroughly examined in Chapter 7.

Other members of this CofP can be witnessed using both stereotypically feminine and stereotypically masculine strategies. Jane mitigates her directives and uses humour to invoke solidarity/collegiality with fellow members, though she also uses rivalrous humour to challenge Phil, which simultaneously functions to support Carrie. Phyllis is impolite by disruptively interrupting, though she also mitigates the directive she uses, uses humour to maintain collegiality/solidarity and demonstrates her support and agreement with Carrie when she is having difficulties with Phil. Secretary Jackie uses stereotypically feminine styles, mitigating her directive and using humour to maintain solidarity/collegiality.

Overall, there is evidence of Carrie breaking the stereotypical expectation of feminine speech norms in order to enact her authority, as well as also using a range of stereotypically feminine styles that accord with her gender when managing her subordinates. As one of only two women directors in the manufacturing company, Carrie is frequently evaluated and assessed during my fieldwork, and interviews are conducted with both Carrie and Jane from this CofP. These data are very revealing, and will be thoroughly analysed in Chapter 7 in order to enhance the above analysis, and fully assess the broader gendered discourses within which this CofP operates.

Jane is also a member of the Product Review Team, thus providing the opportunity to examine and compare her interactional style in a different, company-wide CofP.

The Product Review Team

The Product Review Team consists of 6 male and 4 female managers, summarized in Table 6.2. The Product Review Team has been set up with the purpose of improving communication between different departments in order to avoid past problems the company has experienced with sales and stock. These team meetings are thus primarily retrospective, with participants giving feedback on the actions they were allocated to carry out during the last month in order to resolve issues/investigate problems. Problem-solving may take place within the meeting if issues haven't been resolved. The meeting also involves planning ahead, with new tasks being assigned. I was shadowing Sharon on the day of recording, and I accompanied her to this meeting. As summarized in Table 6.2, there are two male directors who belong to this CofP, and Rob occupies the role of Chair. The remaining participants are middle-level managers, with the exception of Julie. Rob is direct superior of John and Julie whilst Craig is the direct superior of Sharon, David and Kim. Keith, Jane and Carl's direct superiors are not part of this team.

This meeting began at 3.30 p.m. on a Monday afternoon in the company's boardroom. It was scheduled for two hours, but over-ran by 30 minutes. Immediately before the meeting Sharon ran through the minutes of the previous meeting with me and informed me of participants'

Table 6.2: Product Review Team members

Gender/number	Name	Professional role and status	Department
MC	Rob	Director (Chair)	Purchasing
M2	David	Middle Manager (M5's subordinate)	Marketing
M3	Keith	Middle Manager	Sales
M4	Carl	Middle Manager	Sales
M5	Craig	Director	Marketing
M6	John	Middle Manager (MC's subordinate)	Purchasing
F1	Sharon	Middle Manager (M5's subordinate)	Marketing
F2	Kim	Middle Manager (M5's subordinate)	Marketing
F3	Julie	Lower Middle Manager (MC's subordinate)	Purchasing
F4	Jane	Middle Manager	Services

roles and the overall 'troubleshooting' purpose of the team. Rob opens the meeting as follows:

Example 14

1. Rob:	Right (.) let's get started good afternoon everybody erm (.)
2.	what I propose we do firstly is just address (.) the action points
3.	from the previous meeting (.) so the first one (.) being to look
4.	at the (.) actual level of stock holding compared to (-) er a week's
5.	cover so that one was down for (.) [Sharon]
6. Sharon:	[me] this is a bit of
7.	continuation

Rob uses a discourse marker and collective 'let's', followed by brief use of small talk through a phatic greeting, inclusively welcoming 'everybody'. He then goes on to agenda-setting, presenting this as a proposal, using collective 'we' and minimizer 'just'. He paraphrases the first action point and indirectly gives the floor to Sharon, who overlaps and then takes the floor. Rob thus opens the meeting in a collective, inclusive manner using a stereotypically feminine style, mapping out the form the meeting will take by making a 'proposal'. He can thus be seen to be minimizing status differences between himself and the members of his team, enacting his power as meeting Chair in a covert manner.

There are 59 directives issued in this encounter. 49 (83.1 per cent) are given by Rob, and all of these are mitigated. He uses a wide variety of stereotypically feminine strategies to achieve this, drawing on the same range of strategies that we have seen other Chairs drawing on in their CofP meetings. A typical illustration of Rob's minimizing strategies can be seen when he is bringing a discussion about stock ordering to a close:

Example 15

The team have been discussing changes to stock ordering

1. Rob:	So we just need to think about how we
2.	[(-) how we can categorize] that [how] we look at it separately
3. David:	[how we categorize on that] [yeah]

Rob's strategies here thus include collective 'we', and 'just' as part of a need statement, as well as modal 'can'. Interestingly, David comes in, using stereotypically feminine supportive simultaneous talk (line 3), stating almost exactly the same thing as Rob at the same time, emphasizing his agreement with Rob's position through the joint production of discourse.

The remaining ten directives are all issued by middle managers. Keith issues five instances, Jane issues two, David and Sharon issue a joint directive to Julie (see Example 23) as well as both issuing one individual directive each. All directives are mitigated apart from two examples issued by Keith, one of which is issued to Jane (Example 19) and the other is issued to his superior, Craig (Example 20). Keith's directives are also notable as they co-occur with either criticisms or challenges, and are accompanied with a range of strengthening and thus stereotypically masculine devices. Four of his directives in total are issued to Jane.

Keith is responsible for a high number of criticisms and challenges in this meeting. He utters 13 out of 18 overall instances of criticism, 10 of which are directed towards Jane, whilst the remaining three are aimed at company outsiders. There are seven challenges issued overall, and Keith is responsible for five of these. Three of Keith's challenges are directed towards the company in general, as well as one to Jane and one to superior Craig. Keith is thus a very assertive, competitive member of this CofP, and his performance, particularly in relation to Jane, is worthy of closer examination.

Keith and Jane

Keith's competitiveness towards Jane starts early on in the meeting, just as the second topic is coming to a close, and continues throughout the remainder of the encounter. Keith takes the floor and raises a topic that is not on the list of action points:

Example 16
Keith has raised a problem with buying too much stock
1. Keith: Why the hell are we still buying {xxx}?
2. Keith: [or {xxx}] ? It doesn't make sense does it
3. David: [mhm   ]
4. Craig: No
5. Keith: If it was my bloody business I wouldn't be doing it
6. Jane: [yeah   ] I think up until now having this team
7. Keith: [it's crazy]
8. Jane: we hadn't had information like that

Keith issues a challenging question to Jane and the Services Department in general (line 1), using the blasphemous term 'hell' to strengthen his point. He then directly states that 'it doesn't make sense', followed by a tag question, to which David and Craig respond. Keith then uses the conditional to introduce his statement that if he was in charge he would not let this happen, strongly implying that he would put a stop to the decisions Jane and the Services Department had been making, using an expletive to strengthen his argument. Jane comes in at line 6, overlapping Keith's comment 'it's crazy' to emphasize further his negative evaluation and annoyance at this product order. Jane then attempts to defend herself and the Services Department in response, making the point that they did not have access to such knowledge until the creation of this team.

The next example of competitive interaction between Keith and Jane begins with Craig making a suggestion to another problem Keith has raised:

Example 17

The group are discussing a problem with too much stock

1. Craig: Can we simplify the range?
2. Keith: Oh well I think the person to have involved on this issue
3.   should be Jason
4. Craig: Mm
5. Jane: Oh yeah but we did [have   ]
6. Keith: [I'm always] the man hard on this I mean
7. Keith: it's not my baby really but I I seem to be getting the grief
8.   over it all
9. Jane: Well [we (.)   ] we have had a meeting with Jason
10. Keith: [from customers]
11. Jane: And erm four years ago I was given the job and we
12.   halved the range four years ago
13.   [(.) cos we had] [loads and loads of stock   ]
14. Keith: [yeah yeah   ] [that's what I (xxx) definitely] (xxx)
15. Rob: Well let's put an action then that we will review this as
16.   a separate item

Keith criticizes Jane at line 2, in conjunction with 'I think' as a strengthening, boosting device, suggesting that she has had the wrong people involved. Keith then directly declares his own idea of who should be involved – this is Jane's direct responsibility. Keith thus strongly implies that Jane has not made the correct decision when carrying out tasks specific to her role. Craig agrees (line 4). Jane attempts to gain the floor to tell Keith that she has already done this (line 5), but Keith uses the stereotypically masculine style of disruptively interrupting. Jane attempts to take the floor again (line 9), but Keith disruptively interrupts once more, albeit briefly. Jane finally gains the floor, informing Keith that she and her team have already met with Jason, and have thus already done what he declared as a different and more effective way forward.

Jane's sole criticism of Keith is mitigated through the use of humour, thus categorized as rivalrous:

Example 18

Jane is informing the group that her department has to order new boxes

1. Jane: I don't know where these things go (.) once sales
2.   have finished [unless they throw] them all round the containers
3. Keith: [there's (xxx xxx)]
4.   ((laughter from many))
5. Keith: We've just plonked a load in the bottom warehouse skips

Humour is created here by Jane's competitive fantasy sequence that Keith's sales staff go to the company's rubbish containers and throw boxes around. Her criticism is thus disguised by humour, resulting in laughter from many of the meeting's participants, though notably not Keith.

The challenge Jane issues to Keith is bald on-record, without mitigation, and occurs in response to a direct, unmitigated directive that he issues to her:

Example 19

Keith is informing Jane of his view on selling surplus stock

1. Keith: We haven't got a problem with this chopping down of ranges
2.   cut them down and we'll do the job of selling the volume
3.   behind it
4. Jane: [it's not about that   ] [it's a different issue]
5. Keith: [it's just we didn't have] [no I know that   ]
6. Keith: No I know it is but a- a- again it's (-) I think that's pretty good
7.   really if we if we do do that going [forward]
8. Jane: [yeah   ]

Keith issues a direct, unmitigated directive to Jane ('cut them down') who responds by challenging him (line 4), directly declaring that he is focusing on the wrong issue. Whilst competing for the floor, Keith agrees with Jane as a floorholding device, repeating his agreement to continue his turn, followed by 'but', 'I think' as a strengthening device, and then a positive evaluation of his own idea that his sales team will fulfil. Jane concedes the point she was trying to make and agrees with him.

Challenging superiors

In addition to his competitive, assertive behaviour towards Jane, Keith is also responsible for issuing a challenge and direct directive to his superior Craig:

Example 20

Keith is discussing problems he had with getting enough stock to his customers due to a product line being discontinued

```
 1. Keith:   That decision was made (.) I accept the decision I haven't got a
 2.          problem with it (.) but what I do have a problem with (.) is when
 3.          we're not informed quickly enough and then I can't re-add then
 4.          [(-)   ]
 5. Craig:   [yeah]
 6. Keith:   so it what I'm suggest- what I'm asking you for is when a decision's
 7.          made at {place name} not to make a certain amount of product lines
 8.          let us know about it early [(.)    ] yeah then I can react
 9. Craig:                             [yeah]
10. Craig:   Yeah okay
```

Craig was ultimately responsible for discontinuing the product line to which Keith is referring. Keith starts off by stating that he is not questioning Craig's decision, but then challenges Craig by overtly stating that he does have a 'problem' with the lack of information that he and his team received, which was also Craig's responsibility. At line 6 he starts by using metadiscoursal 'suggest' and then stops and strengthens the force of this to 'asking' Craig, directly addressing him using the personal pronoun 'you', to give him the information he requires. He issues the direct, unmitigated directive 'let us know about it'. Craig agrees that he will do this (lines 9 and 10). Keith thus uses a range of competitive, stereotypically masculine strategies to challenge and confront Craig in a public setting, gaining agreement from him that it won't happen again.

In addition to Keith's challenge to Craig, there are also five instances of subversive humour in this meeting. Perhaps unsurprisingly, three of these are issued by Keith. However, unlike his earlier instances where the criticisms were directed towards a participant present in the room, these subversive instances are directed towards people who are not members of this CofP. On the following occasion, Keith's challenge is directed towards senior managers who are responsible for authorizing the design of new order forms:

Example 21

Participants are discussing how the company wastes money

1. Keith: A form is a bloody form at the end of the day [for God's] sake
2. Craig: [((laughs))]
3. Keith: why do they [keep bloody changing it for all the time ((xxx))
4. Sharon: [((laughs))
5. Keith: because it pisses me off it really does
6.   ((laughter from all))

Keith uses a succession of expletives (lines 1, 3 and 5) to illustrate his frustration. These terms are the cause of amusement for the meeting's participants, signalling his use of an inappropriate register. Keith thus again displays himself to be an assertive participant, using stereotypically aggressive masculine speech, including expletives, mitigated by humour, to emphasize his point and to criticize the company.

Interestingly, it is Julie, the participant with the lowest status who is responsible for the two remaining examples of subversive humour, again neatly emphasizing the fluidity of power. Furthermore, in contrast with Keith, Julie's subversive humour instances are actually directed at participants in the room, and can thus be seen to be far more risky to her own face. As the participant with the least amount of power and status, Julie's use of the ambiguous tactic of humour to produce challenges to her superiors is very strategic, and she manages to challenge them successfully:

Example 22

The group is discussing surplus stock

1. Carl: I didn't realise we had (-) fifteen pallets worth
2. Julie: hh.
3. David: [It's not true to say but]
4. Julie: [and I can't believe   ] you're saying that I told you
5.   [lot about it] ((laughs))
6. David: [oh right   ]
7.   ((laughter from many))

At line 4 Julie engages in stereotypically masculine jocular abuse with her superiors, assertively and competitively informing them that she cannot 'believe' what they are 'saying' as she 'told' them already, using metadiscourse to strengthen her challenge. She uses laughter to signal humour at the end of her utterance. David responds, followed by laughter from many.

Julie's other instance of subversive humour shows her engaging in jocular abuse, first to challenge David directly, and then to challenge Rob's chairing skills:

Example 23

Julie and Carl have finished discussing stock storage space. This is followed by a lengthy pause

1.		(-)
2.	David:	You got another one Julie?
3.	Julie:	No get lost
4.		((laughter from many))
5.	Sharon:	No you have
6.	David:	monitors and {product name}
7.	Julie:	((smile voice)) what about the one in the middle that Rob's
8.		meant to be [doing exp]lore opportunity of using
9.	Rob:	[me again?]
10.	Julie:	[{company name}] samples there
11.	Rob:	[oh right] okay well I have sent a note

On this occasion Julie insults David by telling him to 'get lost', a register most typically associated with a child's interactional speech strategies. The inappropriate nature of Julie's refusal to take the floor and her insult to David results in laughter from many members. Julie has reported back on the last three action points and has been talking for a lengthy period. David adopts the role of the Chair (line 2), indirectly allocating the floor back to her. However, she rejects David's authority, invoking humour by adopting the role of a disobedient child. Sharon then joins David (line 5) to inform Julie that it is her turn again. Julie consults the action point list, and it transpires that they are wrong. Julie then uses humour to produce an indirect criticism of David, Sharon and Rob, noting that it is actually Chair Rob who should be taking the floor. Julie's challenge, issued under the guise of humour, emphasizes that Rob has been neglecting his chairing duty.

Sharon and David

Sharon's relationship with David is also worthy of examination, particularly in relation to criticism. Sharon is responsible for criticizing David twice. On both occasions she does so by whistling at him. In the first instance, David wants to clarify the date of a future meeting, which has already been announced. Sharon overtly signals her discontent when the topic ends by whistling and uttering 'phew'. On the second occasion, instead of attracting David's attention through speech, Sharon whistles at him again, on this occasion to attract his attention. She continues performing this criticism paralinguistically, waving a sheet of paper in his direction to inform him that the figures he is reading out are incorrect:

Example 24

Sharon and David are jointly reporting on yearly sales figures

1. David: So that's gone up from three something up
2.   on the autumn side it
3. David: [(.) side side   ]
4.   [((Sharon repeatedly whistles))] ((She waves
5.   a piece of paper at David and then throws this
6.   across the room at him))
7. David: I'm SOOO sorry (.) ((picks up a different sheet
8.   but not the one Sharon has thrown))
9. David: on page five of the autumn winter one

Sharon can thus be witnessed using assertive strategies typically associated with a masculine speech style in these examples. By whistling at David, she breaks the norms of this CofP of using speech to attract one another's attention, as well as breaking the norms further by throwing paper at him. The sarcastic tone with which David replies, with his insincere 'apology' signalled through his prosody and excessive and verbose use of intensifier 'so', strongly indicates that he has perceived Sharon's actions to have been impolite. He thus responds in an impolite manner, attacking her face by using sarcasm to indicate his discontent (Culpeper 2005, Mullany 2007b). His response can be classified as an example of rivalrous humour.

Evaluating solutions and agreeing with the boss

Unlike all other meetings examined thus far, Chair Rob is not responsible for any criticisms, nor is he responsible for any expressions of approval. Director Craig also does not issue any criticisms (David is responsible for the two remaining instances of criticism, one to Jane and the other to Carl, both of which are heavily mitigated). However, Craig does express approval on three occasions, at points where he has stepped in to evaluate suggested solutions to problems. Craig shows support by expressing approval of Julie, Jane and Keith following suggestions made by these subordinates. Craig informs Julie that an idea she had is 'excellent', a suggestion that Jane makes is something that 'would be brilliant' and he assesses one of Keith's suggestions as 'a very good idea'. Craig thus demonstrates himself to be supportive and co-operative in these instances, displaying a stereotypically feminine speech style to actively support his subordinates. None of these expressions are acknowledged or commented on by the person being approved, though they all appear to have been taken sincerely and the ideas are listed as suggestions for action points in the meeting's minutes.

There are seven examples of participants expressing approval overall in this meeting. The remainder of these are issued by subordinates to their superiors. Jane issues three instances to superior Craig, and David issues an instance to Rob. In Chapter 4, it was pointed out that if subordinates express approval of superiors, this often functions to signal agreement with them. Indeed, Jane expresses her approval of Craig by praising suggestions that he puts forward on three separate occasions to problems that directly affect her, using the positive evaluative phrase 'good idea', to signal agreement with his suggestion. Similarly, David expresses approval, and thus agreement with Rob, asserting that an idea which will directly impact on David's workload is 'excellent'.

'I polished me Jack boots': Metaphors of war, battle and sport

There are 64 instances of humour given in this meeting, and 24 of these are conjoint. Interestingly, five of these conjoint examples all centrally revolve around Keith as an agent in a metaphorical battle/war with representatives outside of the immediate company. Utilizing figurative language in the form of war/battle and sporting metaphors can be perceived as being indirectly indexed with a masculine style (see Koller 2004). All five examples can be classified towards the minimally collaborative end of Holmes's scale, taking the form of one-liners and quips, again features associated with a stereotypically masculine style of interaction. These conjoint instances involve contributions from men only, though some women managers do signal their amusement through laughter. All of these fulfil the primary function of strengthening solidarity and collegiality. One instance is initiated by superior Craig and functions repressively, superficially maintaining solidarity and collegiality in order to get Keith involved in sorting out a customer problem:

Example 25

David is expressing his concern about a customer who is avoiding communicating with him

1.	David:	He's a bit (.) er we've emailed him the the (.)
2.		[(xxx)]
3.	Craig:	[I think we] should send you in Del sort him out
4.	David:	Well Del was ready [I've asked him
5.	Craig:	[((laughs))
6.	Keith:	I'm coming to the meeting
7.	David:	Del was due to sit in on the meeting tomorrow so er
8.	Keith:	Yeah
9.	David:	Erm
10.	Keith:	I polished me jack boots last night
11.		((laughter from many))
12.	David:	He he is [he's playing for time]
13.	Keith:	[and that's not the first time this year]
14.	Sharon:	((laughs))
15.	David:	I mean back in May and June [he has]
16.	Keith:	[Did you kn]ow
17.		how to set the gun free with me?
18.	Craig:	((laughs)) that's why I said it
19.	David:	He had reason for taking issue with us but those have
20.		all long since gone {xxxx}he's just stringing us along now
21.	Keith:	You can say that again Davey
22.	David:	Yeah

Craig's initiation of repressive conjoint humour (lines 3–4) draws upon masculinist metaphors of war and battle, typifying competition and confrontation, stating that 'Del', should 'sort him out', a phrase with strong connotations of physical violence. Craig and David both use a nickname to refer to Keith, an abbreviation of Keith's surname. The use of this informal referring expression bears a striking similarity to nicknames used in male sporting teams or in combat, functioning to signal a sense of masculine in-group identity and solidarity (Holmes 1995). David had already asked Keith to be involved, pre-empting Craig's idea, providing further evidence that Keith is well known in company for his aggressive style. Keith continues with metaphors of war and battle, making reference to the polishing of his 'jack boots' (line 10) and a 'gun' (line 17). He also reciprocates with use of nicknames, calling David 'Davey' (line 21).

Of the remaining four instances, David initiates one example, whereas the remaining examples are all initiated by Keith himself, including the following where Keith is discussing difficult buyers that he has to deal with:

Example 26
Keith is discussing difficult buyers

1.	Keith:	They're wide boys at the end of the day [(.)] and you have
2.	Craig:	[mm]
3.		to treat them with the contempt they deserve
4.		((laughter from many))
5.	Craig:	I'm sure you're good at that Keith
6.		((laughter from many))
7.	Keith:	They're sharks basically some of them and they'll shaft you
8.		soon as look at you do you know what I mean and you have
9.		to tackle them (.) in a certain way
10.		((laughter from many))

Keith identifies the buyers he liaises with outside the company through the gendered and pejorative referring expression 'wide boys', directly indexing gender here. He goes on to refer to them using the further metaphorical referring expression of 'sharks' who will 'shaft you'. He thus has 'to tackle' them, again a phrase with potentially violent connotations, most commonly associated with sport. Keith invokes humour, initially with the statement that the 'wide boys' have to be treated with 'contempt'. This sentiment goes strictly against the company's ethos and culture of promoting a good working relationship with buyers, and is thus the source of much amusement for team members. Craig then joins in with humour at line 5, issuing a one-liner in the form of stereotypically masculine banter, stating his belief that Keith is good at treating people with 'contempt', further emphasizing the aggressive, competitive and confrontational image that Keith has within the company.

'A great girlie holiday'

There is one instance of the women managers using humour in a gender-exclusive manner, also through the use of conjoint humour. On this occasion, it is only women managers who join in. This example co-occurs with stereotypically feminine small talk:

Example 27
Jane has suggested that the company's design rate should be cut to sell older products

```
1. Keith:    Sell what you've got (-) would help wouldn't it but (.)
2.           [I know that's not] reality is it
3. Jane:     [we'd just say oh ]
4. Jane:     but yeah loads of holidays [(going xxx) ]
5. Sharon:                              [you go every ] year off (xxx xxx)
6.           ((laughter from all women managers))
7. Kim:      And me too (.)
8. Julie:    Kim
9. Sharon:   Kim too ((laughs))
10. Kim:     We could all go on holiday
11. Keith:   It would be (xxx) [like that                        ]
12. Jane:                      [we'd do a great girlie holiday ]
13.          [((laughter from all women managers))]
14. Keith:   [but it's not the reality is it          ]
```

Jane invokes humour and small talk simultaneously here (line 4) after a failed attempt to interrupt Keith (line 3). When Keith completes his turn, Jane shifts talk away from a task-oriented topic towards a social topic, using humour as a tension releaser to joke that she could have numerous holidays if the company followed her suggestion. Sharon supportively overlaps Jane's turn at line 5, highlighting that this instance of conjoint humour can be seen as being towards the maximally collaborative end of the conjoint humour continuum. Jane's comment elicits laughter from all women managers, and Kim then also takes part, including herself in Jane's 'holiday'. Julie and Sharon also join in. Keith gains the floor at line 11, but Jane interrupts and successfully takes the floor from him to continue with the women managers' small talk. At line 12 she directly indexes gender by stating that all the females at the meeting can go on a 'girlie' holiday, which again all women participants find amusing.

This episode can be classified as a 'fantasy' sequence (Holmes 2000b), whereby interlocutors engage in a superficial scenario in order to enhance solidarity and collegiality amongst themselves. Arguably the term 'girlie' works to exclude the men in the CofP. Keith interrupts the women's laughter at line 14, moving the topic straight back to core business talk, with an antagonistic tag question to stress that 'reality' is not like this. Whilst the all-male examples do include laugher from some women participants, the men do not take part at all in this instance where gender in directly invoked (see Mullany 2006b; Chapter 7).

Out of the 64 instances of humour in total in this meeting, Jane actually invokes humour on the most occasions (12 instances). Craig is just behind (10 instances), followed by Rob (nine instances). Julie and David both initiate eight instances, and Keith issues seven instances. Sharon and Carl are next, with five and four instances respectively, followed by Kim, who is responsible for one instance. Of the 64 instances, 38 (59.3 per cent) are initiated by status equals and fulfil the function of maintaining solidarity/collegiality. All of Rob and Craig's 19 instances (29.6 per cent) function repressively, minimizing status differences between themselves and subordinates, (superficially) emphasizing solidarity and collegiality to drive the main purpose of the meeting forward. There are two instances of rivalrous humour (3.1 per cent) in total.

'My daughter's birthday party'

In addition to the 'great girlie holiday' extract, there is only one other example of small talk in this meeting. This is initiated by Rob in response to David. Unlike the previous example, this takes place at a meeting boundary:

Example 28

Sharon and David have been allocated the floor to report on annual sales figures

1. Carl:	We took clearance as what (.) [on this?]	
2. David:		[can can] I just I've got to get
3.	home for my daughter's birthday party would you mind	
4.	[if I actually make] a move?	
5. Rob:	[yeah no no problem]	
6. Sharon:	Mhm	
7. Rob:	Yeah	
8. David:	Just she's only (.) two years old she'll fall asleep if [I'm]	
9. John:		[aahh]
10. David:	not [(-)] there soon sorry about that	
11. Sharon:	[aahh]	
12. Rob:	Okay (.) see you bring in the cake tomorrow David	
13.	[((laughter from some))]	
14. David:	[and jelly and ice cream]	
15. Sharon:	Yeeaaah	
16. David:	[thanks a lot]	
17. Sharon:	[don't forget your wife]	
18. David:	No I'll give her (flowers) (-) thank you all	
19. Rob:	[Don't mention it]	
20. Carl:	[was this one erm] (.) a special Sharon?	

David's request to leave for his daughter's birthday party is especially notable as it is during a turn that has been jointly pre-allocated to him. Rob overlaps his request to give permission, followed by a minimal response from Sharon, who has been jointly allocated the floor. After being granted permission to leave, David provides another justification why he has to leave now, divulging personal details about his family, clearly demonstrating personal emotions. Arguably he starts to move talk towards the social talk end of the small talk continuum, though this utterance is still being used strategically as a justification for his departure and is thus still linked to the work-related part of the small talk continuum. At line 12, Rob initiates small talk proper, combined with humour, to emphasize again that he does not mind David departing. This turns into a brief episode of minimally collaborative conjoint humour, initiated by Rob's request for him to bring in birthday cake, to which David adds (line 14). Sharon continues, telling David not to forget his wife, and David then divulges further personal information about taking her flowers. Rob again assures David that he does not mind his departure (line 19). Whilst he does so Carl overlaps to bring the topic immediately back to business talk, posing a question to Sharon.

This stretch of discourse raises the issue of gender and the work–home balance. David is not abiding by the discourse of scientific modernism here (Brewis 2001), expressing his personal emotions in a formal business context. This example also raises questions surrounding David's commitment to the task at hand, as he leaves half way through a pre-allocated turn. The question of the work–home balance is a particularly prevalent one in studies focusing on gender and organization, and it is a recurrent topic in my interview data. It will be thoroughly analysed in Chapter 7.

Apologies and endings

Rob closes the meeting in the following manner:

Example 29

1. Rob: Okay I apologize that's er (.) gone on a bit but I think erm (.) at the
2.   end of the day we're still very much in the sort of start-up phase in
3.   the sort of processes and procedures that we're talking about as we
4.   crack through some of the things and then going forward it will be a
5.   (.) a bit more streamlined but thanks very much for your time

He chooses a performative speech act to apologize directly for the meeting running over. He then offers his own rationale why he thinks this is the case, using 'sort of' as hedges and 'we' to stress the collective common goal that the team has been working towards. He closes the meeting overall by thanking members for their time. Rob can thus be viewed as using stereotypically feminine styles to close the meeting, including apologizing and stressing the collective aims of the team arguably in an attempt to end the meeting on a note of cohesiveness, despite the inconvenience of running over.

Summary

Overall, Rob can be witnessed using a range of stereotypically feminine styles in this meeting to minimize his status as director and Chair in order to enact power and authority more covertly. He pays attention to the face needs of both subordinates and his status equal, mitigating all directives, and he opens and closes the meeting in a co-operative and inclusive style, functioning to re-affirm collegiality. Director Craig can also be witnessed using stereotypically feminine strategies. He expresses approval of subordinates' ideas, and uses humour repressively to minimize status, attempting to invoke solidarity/collegiality with his subordinates. Additionally, when engaging in humour, on certain occasions Craig draws upon stereotypically masculine metaphors and banter, though these do ultimately fulfil the function of enhancing solidarity, albeit predominately with the male CofP members.

There is one member of this CofP in particular who is very confrontational and assertive throughout. Keith draws upon a wide range of stereotypically masculine styles to invoke his identity. Unlike Phil in the Services meeting, Keith has a pre-existing reputation in the company for acting in this aggressive manner, which can be witnessed through the representations of his identity from other colleagues in the meeting data, as well as being evident in informal talk with a number of managers outside of this immediate CofP. Keith issues unmitigated directives and challenges, he disruptively interrupts and uses a range of tactics to intensify his criticisms, including expletives and blasphemy, the only member of this CofP to do so. He issues subversive humour aimed at the company as a whole, as well as issuing one of his superiors with an unmitigated challenge and directive. The examples of collective, masculinist humour, drawing on banter and war/battle and sport metaphors, all centre around the aggressive and confrontational manner in which Keith performs his identity. Arguably, this is celebrated by other males in this group as an effective manner in which to deal with company outsiders. Keith dominates, criticizes and challenges Jane and her department.

As in the Product meeting, Jane can be witnessed using both stereotypically feminine and stereotypically masculine speech styles. Coming back to stereotypically masculine instances, David and Sharon engage in rivalrous humour, and Julie, the member with the lowest status, displays herself to be an assertive participant, drawing on stereotypically masculine styles of subversive humour to enact power.

To conclude, whilst there is evidence of both stereotypically masculine and feminine strategies being drawn upon in this CofP, arguably, this meeting is more confrontational than any of the other encounters examined so far, and thus more stereotypically masculine. One key reason for this could be the overall specific troubleshooting purpose of the team, from which a degree of conflict and competition may well be expected, a point which Sharon raises in informal talk after the meeting, as well as this CofP having one very competitive member. David, Jane, Kim, Sharon and Julie are all interviewed from this CofP. Evaluations which participants in this CofP make about themselves and each other and the gendered discourses they raise will be fully examined in Chapter 7.

Middle-manager David is the nominated stand-in Chair of the Business Control Team. Sharon and Julie are also members of both CofPs, thus providing the opportunity to observe these managers' interactional strategies in two CofPs.

The Business Control Team

The final meeting to be examined differs from all others as the team leader/Chair is absent. The members who are present thus occupy exactly the same position on the company's institutional hierarchy, with the exception of lower-level manager Julie. The Business Control Team is female-dominated, made up of 6 females and 4 males, summarized in Table 6.3.

Director Simon is the absent Chair, but he is listed as M4; he did not officially attend, but he does enter the room briefly towards the end of the encounter to issue a directive. The Business Control Team has been set up with the purpose of improving inter-departmental communication to avoid the recurrent problems with profit margins. Like the Product Review Team meeting, it is also primarily retrospective, though problem-solving on current issues will also take place if such issues are raised. This meeting takes place on a Tuesday at 1 p.m., and is scheduled to run for an hour and a half. I also accompanied Sharon to this encounter, which took place in the company boardroom. The office of male director Simon who was supposed to be chairing can be viewed from the boardroom, and after approximately half an hour, he returned to his office and could be seen by all members. A recurring topic in the meeting is participants' dissatisfaction with the company's directors, particularly with three new (male) directors who had recently been appointed as part of the company's restructuring: Simon is one of these.

Table 6.3:   Business Control Team members

Gender/number	Name	Professional role and department
MC	David	Middle Manager Marketing
M2	Mark	Middle Manager Purchasing
M3	Martin	Middle Manager Sales
M4	Simon	Director Operations
F1	Sharon	Middle Manager Marketing
F2	Julie	Lower Level Manager Purchasing
F3	Pam	Middle Manager Retail
F4	Carol	Middle Manager Services
F5	Becky	Middle Manager Sales
F6	Kate	Middle Manager Sales

Discussion on this topic was only possible because he was not present at this specific meeting of the CofP; the fact that he was visible to all participants after the meeting was underway appeared to aggravate the situation, and comments surrounding dissatisfaction with the executive intensified. Therefore, whilst arguably this is not a 'typical' encounter of the Business Control Team, it does present the unusual opportunity to observe the team when their direct superior is not present, and this helps to highlight a range of tensions and concerns between middle management and the company's executive.

It is clear from the start of the encounter that David is not happy with Simon's lack of attendance. He opens the meeting as follows:

Example 30

1. David: Right (.) okay err it seems I've been nominated to run
2.   through last week's minutes

After two discourse markers, followed by hesitation, David uses 'seems' which strongly implies negative evaluation of the fact that he has been given the role of Chair, and thus can be seen as a subversive criticism of Simon's decision to pull out at the last minute. Simon approached David in the meeting room before all other members were present to say he was going to another meeting that had not been pre-arranged. Also, David does not officially make any apology for Simon's lack of attendance, despite this being a norm in this CofP's meetings, confirmed by written copies of the minutes from previous encounters, and despite Simon asking him to do so.

There are 31 directives issued in this meeting. All of these directives are mitigated, with the range of strategies that we have seen in all other meetings, with the exception of two aggravated instances, one issued by Martin and the other by David (Examples 32 and 37). David issues 14 (45.2 per cent) directives in total. As he is not the superior of his colleagues, he would not be expected to dominate directive issuance to the extent that all other chairs have done in previous meetings. Some of David's directives relate to items that it is his role to report back on anyway, whereas others relate directly to his role as Chair.

Of the 17 remaining directives, Becky is responsible for five, Carol and Pam both issue three and Sharon, Julie and Martin are responsible for uttering two instances. There are no expressions of approval in this meeting, which arguably could be expected due to all participants (apart from Julie) being status equals. As Simon has the ultimate role of decision-maker and is sole superior in this CofP, it is difficult for the group to come to resolutions without him.

There are 25 criticisms and five challenges issued overall. Interestingly, these criticisms and challenges are on one of only two topics: the company's executive directors and David's chairing skills. Lack of meeting attendance from Simon has thus had a significant impact upon the performance of these speech acts. Nineteen out of 25 criticisms and four out of five challenges are directed either at the company's executive in general, Simon, or another director, and these occur regularly throughout the meeting. Although David is the next most senior person present in terms of experience and length of service, his lack of superior status with the rest of the CofP members can be suggested as a key reason why he is open to criticism. These two topics will now be given closer scrutiny.

The company's executive

All members of the CofP, with the sole exception of Pam, are responsible for issuing at least one criticism of the executive (David is responsible for five instances, Carol and Julie issue three instances, Kate, Mark, Becky all issue two instances, and Martin and Sharon are responsible for one instance each). It is notable that 14 out of these 19 criticisms of the executive co-occur with humour. This fulfils the primary function of subversive humour, but also accomplishes the secondary function of enhancing a sense of solidarity amongst the rest of the members of the CofP. Example 31 illustrates Julie, the CofP member with the lowest status, using sarcasm to criticize Simon:

Example 31

1. Martin: Alright
2. Julie: Has Simon got any other wish lists?
3. Kate: ((smiling)) No that was it ((laughs))
4. Julie: Okay

Although Simon is not present, he asked Kate to bring up an issue on his behalf. When this topic finished, Julie self-selects and uses sarcasm through the term 'wish lists'. Kate acknowledges the humour here and smiles and laughs in response. Julie has already demonstrated herself to be an assertive participant who makes strategic use of humour in the Product Review Team meeting, and this example shows that she also achieves this in Business Control Team.

In the next example, Martin criticizes Becky, though this criticism occurs ultimately due to a problem that has been caused by one of the company's directors:

Example 32

Becky is giving feedback on a problem with one of her customers

1. Becky: I'll do it as a call off [account]   [er]
2. Sharon: [yeah]   [yeah]
3. Martin: The other thing is get estimates from them and
4.   [then we could have that as well   ]
5. Becky: [well that's what I mean that's what I'm working on] (.)
6.   honestly believe me I'm trying to sort it ((smile voice))
7.   I keep getting picked on [and I am trying
8. Martin: [((laughs))
9. Sharon: [((laughs))
10. Becky: [to sort it out   ]
11. Martin: [((smile voice)) we're] not picking on you
12.   ((laughter from all))
13. Becky: the {xxx} can summary come on (xxx)
14. Martin: you'll know when we're picking on you

15. Sharon: ((laughs))
16. Becky: It was actually the uk sales director [who offered
17. Martin: [mhm
18. Becky: it to them ((laughs))
19. Martin: yeah ((laughs))

Becky has presented a solution to her customer problem to which Sharon agrees (lines 1–2). Martin then issues a direct, unmitigated directive, 'get estimates from them'. From Becky's competitive, defensive response, there is evidence of her perceiving Martin to have broken the norms and conventions of the CofP here, and thus his directive has been classified as aggravated, an example of impoliteness. Becky disruptively interrupts Martin, asserting that she is already doing what he commanded (line 5). Arguably, Becky can be seen to be taking issue with the fact that he has issued her with an unmitigated directive, which he does not have the institutional authority to do. Becky draws on rivalrous humour to continue her response, using a smile voice and inappropriate register to invoke humour, accusing Martin of 'picking' on her. As with Julie's example of subversive humour in the Product Review Team meeting (Example 23), Becky uses a register more commonly associated with the performance of a child's identity in interaction, and the inappropriateness of her utterance is the source of laughter for both Martin and Sharon. Martin then adds to Becky's humour, denying that she is being 'picked on', a source of amusement for all. He uses banter (line 14) to function as a denial that he was criticizing her, which helps to rebuild collegiality between them.

Becky deflects responsibility for this problem away from herself (lines 16 and 18), using subversive humour to criticize the company director who is ultimately responsible for creating this problem. Becky refers to this director only by his official job title, acting as a distancing device. Martin then agrees with her, suggesting that ultimately he does not see this as her fault, also signalling an end to this period of tension. As well as defending herself against perceived criticism from Martin, Becky also actively joins in with the subversive critique of the company directors that runs though the meeting, here building solidarity with her colleagues who are present. Martin and Becky both draw on stereotypically masculine strategies during this period of tension. Martin's assertive, aggravated directive leads Becky to compete for the floor. She does mitigate her comments to Martin using humour and by invoking a child-like identity, though she also uses both the competitive categories of rivalrous and subversive humour to do this. Martin uses stereotypically masculine banter to deny Becky's accusation that he is inappropriately 'picking' on her. Ultimately, they both use stereotypically feminine strategies at the end of this episode by supporting and agreeing which one another, signalling resolution and an end to this conflict.

The next example of criticism of the executive is issued by Kate, who uses indirectness to criticize Carrie's abilities, and instead praises absent Chair Simon. Carol reacts negatively to this, and engages in rivalrous humour with Kate:

Example 33

The group are discussing how to avoid the recurrence of a costly stock distribution problem

1.	Kate:	We've just got to hope that now Simon's on board that
2.		somebody's looking at stock and distribution that you can
3.		look at the two together cos before it was always well Carrie did
4.		distribution [didn't she] is that the hold up [side?]
5.	Carol:	[yeah but] [you]
6.		really have come as him ((smile voice)) haven't you
7.	Kate:	Sorry?
8.	Carol:	You really have come as Simon haven't you
9.	Kate:	((brief laughter))
10.	David:	But here we are again at yet another meeting talking about it

In line 5, Carol attempts to interrupt Kate. When she gains the floor she criticizes her, using rivalrous humour, accusing her of attending the meeting disguised as absent superior Simon. Carol's criticism, uttered using a smile voice, makes it very difficult for Kate to formulate a reply. This is the only example throughout the whole of the encounter where any participant issues a comment about Simon that isn't negative. It occurs approximately half-way through the meeting, after Carol has issued direct, unmitigated challenges towards Simon and the executive (see Example 34). Carol thus appears to be reacting negatively to Kate's decision to praise Simon. Kate's comment (lines 3–4) indicates a general feeling within the company that this costly distribution problem had stemmed from Carrie being in charge, thus highlighting negative evaluation of her (see Chapter 7). At line 7, Kate asks for clarification of what Carol said, and Carol re-issues her rivalrous utterance, on this occasion specifically naming Simon for clarification. Kate laughs briefly and ambiguously in response, signalling that she is uncertain of how to react.

Carol thus appears to be questioning Kate's loyalty to her colleagues who have already criticized and challenged Simon on a number of occasions. Kate's positive comment disrupts the us versus them pattern, and

Carol seems to act negatively to this, using humour as a guise to accuse Kate of being the mouthpiece of their absent superior. David then takes the floor to continue with the overall criticism of the executive. The four challenges given to the company executive are all unmitigated. Arguably these challenges can be issued without mitigation as no members of the company executive are present, though openly challenging one's superiors is always risky in an official work context. These challenges are prime examples of stereotypically masculine speech strategies, being competitive, assertive and antagonistic. Two challenges are issued by David, and Carol and Becky both issue one instance. Whilst they serve a subversive function, they also dually function to maintain solidarity between those members of the group who are present at the meeting, strengthening a sense of us versus them. One of Carole's challenges is on the topic of loss of business revenue:

Example 34

The team are discussing lost business due to the executive's policy on product orders

1. Carol: They will never order enough (.) if we wait for them
2.   we'll wait [f-   ] the business'll go down the pan
3. David: [mm]
4. David: I mean Steve Jones tells us that {competing company name}
5.   are (.) smiling all the way to the bank they're on that second
6.   or third drop now in the absence of {product name}
7. Carol: It's absolutely RIDICULOUS

Carol's use of 'they' (line 1) works as a distancing device between the group and the directors. She directly and assertively challenges their actions, using an idiomatic expression (line 2). David supports her, giving information about one of their competitors. Carol then negatively evaluates again, strengthening her challenge using verbosity and 'absolutely' as intensifiers, along with the overall negative evaluation that their actions are 'ridiculous'.

David's chairing skills

The criticisms that David receives whilst enacting his role as Chair will now be examined. Carol initiates two criticisms and Becky, Julie and Mark all initiate one criticism, along with absent Chair Simon, who briefly enters the boardroom and indirectly criticizes David. David's issuance of an aggravated directive occurs on the topic of his chairing style, and he issues this in response to criticism (see Example 36). One instance of criticism does not occur with humour, and this is issued by Sharon:

Example 35

David is discussing the company's stock location system

1. David: You should be able to go into the tracker to see where
2.   you are (.) your own things are [(.) erm]
3. Becky: [mhm]
4. Sharon: It's two twenty-four
5. Becky: Yeah
6. David: When are we supposed to finish?
7. Sharon: two thirty
8. David: Okay

Sharon criticizes David's chairing by assertively declaring the time (line 4), functioning as an indirect criticism. Becky signals her agreement with her. David demonstrates that he has taken the illocutionary force of Sharon's utterance to be a criticism of his timekeeping, questioning her as to what time the meeting is 'supposed' to finish. However, as David has been present at all of these weekly meetings since they began over two months ago, it seems reasonable to assume that he knows what time the meeting should finish, even if he is not the meeting's usual Chair. Pretending not to know this information can be perceived as a tactic to deflect responsibility away from the fact that the meeting is about to run over. Sharon assertively replies, declaring the time again. Sharon's criticism of David can be classified as subversive. Whilst arguably Sharon may only be issuing the criticism because David is her status equal outside the meeting, and could thus be classified as rivalrous (she doesn't criticize superior Rob for time management in the previous encounter); in this particular context, David *is* her superior, and it is his authority as Chair that she is directly challenging. Four out of five of these remaining examples of criticism of David's chairing via humour have been classified as subversive according to the above rationale. The other example issued by absent Chair Simon is classified as repressive humour. Two examples of the subversive humorous instances are conjoint, and involve the women managers only:

Example 36

David is detailing how product codes are calculated

1. David: There are you know thirty, forty different {xxx} codes
2.   depending whether it's colour {red} non-colour {red}

3.   {charcoal} erm you know whatever it might
4.   be [er   ]
5. Carol: [mm]
6.   [((laughter from all women managers))
7. David: [I realize [I'm   ]
8. Becky: [sorry] David we'll all stop [laughing] ((laughs))
9. David: [I realize] I'm boring
10.   you but the scary [there is an important point to all this]
11. Carol: [((laughs)) yes yes come on then   ]
12. David: [there's a scary footnote to all of this erm
13. Kate: [((laughs))
14. David: having looked at the
15.   [export side of things   ]
16. Becky: [((bangs cup on the table repeatedly))]
17. David: Stop hassling me
18. Becky: I wasn't I was giving you a drum roll
19.   ((laughter from all women managers))
20. David: Oh right
21. Julie: Important excit[ing bit   ]
22. Becky: [important]
23.   ((Becky and Sharon bang cups again in the sound of a drum roll))

This extract occurs after Sharon has been critical of David's time-keeping. Carol initiates subversive humour (line 5), with her minimal response 'mm'. The intonation with which she issues this firmly signals that she is disinterested in what David is saying, resulting in amusement from all women managers, shown through their collective laughter. Instead of bringing the meeting to a close, David has opened up another topic and goes into great detail to illustrate his point. He gains the floor again at line 7 but is disruptively interrupted by Becky, who joins in with the subversive humour, superficially apologizing to him whilst continuing to laugh at his expense. David signals that he has interpreted Becky's utterance and the women's laughter as impoliteness towards him, as he retaliates with ('I realize I'm boring you but …') to emphasize his perceived importance of the problem. Carol interrupts this turn, however, continuing the subversive humour by laughing and issuing a direct, on-record directive, redressed only by the fact that she issues this whilst engaging in a period of humour.

Subversive humour continues through Becky's non-linguistic action of banging her cup on the table. It is at this point that David challenges Becky by issuing an aggravated directive, commanding her to stop. This firmly indicates that David perceives Becky's actions to be impolite and challenging. David is not partaking in the episode of humour himself, and the subversive humour directed towards him does not disguise the oppressive intent of his directive (as was the case with Carol's directive six lines earlier). In response, Becky continues with the humour by directly denying that she was 'hassling' him, alternatively claiming that she was giving him a drum roll. The humorous justification for Becky's response makes it difficult for David to challenge this, and he simply acknowledges her explanation with 'oh right'. Julie then joins in, sarcastically mocking David's view that his information is both 'exciting' and 'important', again showing herself to be an assertive participant. Becky engages in supportive simultaneous talk here, repeating part of Julie's turn to signal her support. Sharon then joins Becky in banging their cups, under the guise that they are now both providing David with a 'drum roll'. This example thus demonstrates the women members of the CofP fulfilling the primary function of subversively criticizing David, whilst also simultaneously enhancing a sense of solidarity amongst themselves.

As if to rub salt in the wound, absent Chair Simon then also criticizes David's chairing skills. He briefly puts his head around the door, issuing a declarative which functions both as an indirect directive and a criticism of David's chairing, mitigated by the use of humour:

Example 37

Simon opens the door to the boardroom

1. Simon: I would get out cos you're all gonna die of
2.   asphyxiation
3.   [((laughter from many))]
4. David: [It's a bit warm in here (-)] okay
5.   ((Simon leaves the room))

Sharon informed me whilst we were waiting for participants to arrive that the company's boardroom had bad air circulation. Simon uses this shared background knowledge with hyperbole to invoke humour when he enters, thus attempting to disguise his command that the meeting should be finishing. As with Sharon's critique, David signals agreement. The meeting runs over by ten minutes in total.

The above analysis illustrates the important role played by humour in order to produce criticisms in this meeting. There are 50 instances of humour overall in this encounter. David is responsible for initiating the most (14 instances), followed by Becky and Mark (seven instances), Carol and Sharon (five instances), Pam (four instances), Kate (three instances), Martin and Julie (two instances) and Simon (one instance). Humour fulfils the primary function of maintaining solidarity and collegiality for 64 per cent of the time (32 instances). It functions subversively for 28 per cent of occurrences (14 instances), rivalrous humour accounts for 17 per cent (3 instances) and repressive humour for 2 per cent (1 instance). As already highlighted, Simon's absence accounts for the high instances of subversive humour, with humour being directed either at him, the executive in general, or his chairing replacement. However, it is important to also highlight that whilst subversive humour fulfils the primary function of criticizing/challenging those in power, it also simultaneously fulfils the function of maintaining solidarity/collegiality amongst those who partake in the humour, as any superiors who are being challenged are not present.

'Girls on tour'

There are four examples of stereotypically feminine small talk in this meeting. All of these are initiated by women managers and fulfil the primary function of enhancing solidarity/collegiality. Also, as has been witnessed in the meetings of Amy's Product Department and Carrie's Services Department, all examples co-occur with humour and take place within the main body of meeting discourse. Carol is responsible for initiating two instances which co-occur with conjoint humour towards the maximally collaborative end of the scale, and include participation from all women managers. Pam and Julie initiate the other examples, wherein all participants join in by laughing. Example 38 highlights one of Carol's initiations. This is very similar to Example 27 in the Product Review Team, with gender also being directly indexed here:

Example 38

Becky and Kate have just given the dates they cannot make a special meeting as they are going to be abroad

  1. Carol: ((smile voice)) you're going on the road you're [girls on tour]
  2. Kate: [girls on tour]
  3.   ((laughter from all women managers))
  4. Kate: Thelma and Lou[ise   ]
  5. Carol: [Do you] need any roadies?
  6.   ((laughter from all women managers))
  7. Sharon: Carry your bags miss?
  8. Becky: I'm telling you (.) it's it's hard work you know
  9. Sharon: ((laughs))
10. David: I mean the la- other than Wednesday the seventeenth

Carol invokes small talk and also initiates conjoint humour in line 1. Her turn is supportively overlapped by Kate, demonstrating that this instance of conjoint humour is towards the maximally collaborative end of the scale, with Carol and Kate uttering exactly the same phrase at the same time. After gender is directly indexed through simultaneous use of the term 'girls', Kate continues the humour, drawing parallels between themselves and the protagonists of the feminist road movie, *Thelma and Louise*. By making reference to this film, arguably Kate appears to be acknowledging that her occupation breaks the wider, societal expectations that field sales is a masculine and not a feminine profession. Kate and Becky frequently drive around Europe together selling the company's products, an occupation stereotypically associated with independent male figures. Both Kate and Becky directly acknowledge their awareness that their occupation is stereotypically masculine when interviewed (see Chapter 7).

Carol uses supportive simultaneous talk to expand upon the episode further (line 5), and her question works to maintain both conjoint humour and small talk, as does Sharon's turn (line 7), which again directly invokes gender through use of the directly indexed address term 'Miss'. Becky continues the humour (line 8), signalled by Sharon's laughter. All women managers enhance their solidarity and collegiality with each other by supportively laughing at their overlapping utterances. David then takes the floor (line 10), makes no reference to the previous interaction, and moves straight back to business talk. The women managers thus engage in small talk and conjoint humour as a solidarity-building device amongst themselves (see Chapter 7 for further discussion).

Ending by standing

The Business Control meeting is brought to a close in a rather unconventional manner, by Becky standing up:

Example 39

The team are discussing the lack of meeting agenda

1. David: She said (.) 'but no-one has asked me to pin the agenda together'
2. Sharon: Can you clarify that with Simon then?
3. David: Okay
4. Becky: ((leaves her seat and walks toward David)) David can I just er
5.   talk to you
6.   ((participants begin talking amongst themselves))
7. Sharon: Is that it?
8. Martin: Think so

Sharon requests that David gains clarification on how the group will ensure they have an agenda for the next meeting from Simon. David agrees. Becky then assertively signals the meeting end by leaving her seat and walking towards David to ask if she can talk to him in person. Other participants then begin to talk amongst themselves, causing Sharon to ask if the meeting has finished. Martin replies with 'think so'. The lack of official termination of the meeting from David can perhaps be put down to his ambivalence towards occupying the role of Chair, which he did not want to do in the first place, and for which he has received criticism at various points in the meeting. It is Becky who signals that the meeting is over instead of waiting for official confirmation from the Chair, as we have seen in all previous meetings.

Summary

Overall, this meeting differs from all others examined due to absence of the team's official leader/Chair. However, this has enabled observation of an interesting range of interactional strategies through which participants choose to perform their identities in Simon's absence. David draws on a variety of stereotypically feminine strategies to issue directives, with the exception of one stereotypically masculine, aggravated directive, deliberately attacking the face needs of Becky, signalling that she has broken the norms and conventions of politeness in this CofP. David also draws on a range of stereotypically masculine styles when challenging and criticizing his superiors, albeit co-functioning to establish a sense of solidarity with the managers who are present.

Indeed, all members of the CofP apart from Pam engage in subversive criticism of the executive. As a new appointment to the business, Simon is arguably still seen as an outsider, and the members' resistance to him, as well as to other executive members, is clear. The company had experienced a bad year in terms of profit-making, and morale was low, with those at lower levels of management blaming those at the executive level for the company's problems. There is evidence of all managers apart from Martin initiating criticism of David's chairing style. With the exception of one instance issued by Sharon, these criticisms are mitigated by humour, albeit subversive, in this specific context. Arguably these criticisms of David can be interpreted as part of the broader frustrations the team feels with Simon for double-booking their meeting, appointing David as Chair and then not joining them once he had finished elsewhere.

There is also evidence of stereotypically masculine strategies during the period of tension between Martin and Becky, including evidence of impoliteness from Martin, as well as evidence of conflict between Carol and Kate. Again these episodes are directly related to problems which members attribute to their superiors in the company (the UK Sales director and Carrie, respectively). Despite these periods of tension, Carol, Pam and Julie engage in stereotypically feminine small talk at non-meeting boundaries, functioning to enhance a sense of solidarity and collegiality amongst members. Both of Carol's instances involve women managers only, including the example where gender is directly indexed by Carol and Kate, working to invoke solidarity amongst the women managers. Interviews are conducted with David, Martin, Sharon, Julie, Pam, Carol, Kate and Becky from the Business Control Team.

As in all six CofP meetings examined across both case studies, there is ample evidence of managers breaking stereotypical gendered speech styles in the Business Control Meeting. Any negative evaluation that may result as a consequence of this, along with the broader issues of gender and language and gender more generally within both companies as a whole will now be thoroughly examined in Chapter 7.

7
Gendered Work: Ideologies and Stereotypes in Action

Management and gendered speech styles

In Chapter 2, it was pointed out that stereotypically gendered speech styles are part of the overarching discourse of gender difference. Within this, hegemonic discourses of femininity and masculinity dictate which speech styles are deemed as more appropriate for women and men to use. In reality, there is much evidence of women and men managers using speech styles stereotypically associated with the other gender, and vice versa, as demonstrated in the previous two chapters. With the linguistic variables chosen to analyse stereotypically feminine and masculine speech styles in this study, unlike the older studies highlighted in Chapter 2, there was no evidence of the dominant speech norms in the workplace being masculine norms. The fine-grained, CofP analyses of managerial speech styles has emphasized the complexities involved in the strategies that women and men managers use to enact their workplace identities, depending upon a whole range of contextual factors including the relative power, status and role responsibility that is enacted between participants.

Overall there was a wide range of evidence of women and men managers in all CofPs across both workplaces drawing on similar, stereotypically feminine speech strategies to enact their power and authority more covertly, which perhaps may be indicative of a move towards more stereotypically feminine speech styles as suggested in Chapter 2. However, such an assertion would need to be assessed by a much larger scale, quantitative study. Furthermore, CofP members do utilize stereotypically masculine speech styles, thus according with Marra et al.'s (2006) view of workplace leaders combining both stereotypically feminine and masculine interactional strategies in business meetings depending upon the CofP within which they are interacting, thereby displaying evidence of a wide-verbal repertoire.

However, as was also pointed out in Chapter 2, if interactants produce speech styles that are indirectly indexed with the other gender, then negative evaluation may well occur, often in the form of the double bind, as interactants will have strayed outside of the rigid regulatory frame for appropriate gendered behaviour. It is now important to explore the second layer of gendered discourse analysis further in order to assess how gender ideologies and stereotypes affect how managers are assessed and evaluated in relation to the enactment of their identities in the workplace. This will include an assessment of whether there is any evidence of negative evaluation of managers whom we have seen interacting in the previous two chapters, as a result of them going against the norms and expectations of their gender. As pointed out in Chapter 2, interview data is used as a primary source to assess gendered discourses at this level of analysis, as well as drawing upon other evidence of broader gendered discourses from all other data sources gained via the multi-method approach.

It is the intention that broadening the focus of this project out to examine gendered discourses at this overarching level enables the overall, interdisciplinary nature of this study to be further enhanced. Ultimately, this study builds upon its sociolinguistic focus on workplace talk and takes this a stage further by suggesting a range of broader social and political issues that also need to be addressed, along with language and gender stereotypes and ideologies, if gender inequality in the professional workplace is ever to be resolved. Many of these crucial factors explored in this chapter have been inspired by a range of issues highlighted by workplace members themselves, drawing upon the principles of the importance of involving the researched and their concerns within the project.

The analysis in this chapter will commence with a focus on the two highest ranking women in the meeting data, Amy from the retail company, and Carrie from the manufacturing company. As pointed out in Chapters 5 and 6, a wealth of data has been gathered on Amy, Chair of The Product Department and the Sales Group, as well as on Carrie, Chair of the Services Department in the manufacturing company, and one of only two women to have broken through the glass ceiling in this organization. Analysis of attitudes and evaluations from other CofPs and their members will then be examined. The chapter will go on to analyse other relevant data from managers outside of these immediate CofPs in order to get a broader spectrum of opinion from across both companies.

The discourse of gender difference
and the double bind

In the meeting data analysed in Chapter 5, Amy utilizes a wide variety
of interactional styles, including stereotypically masculine as well as a
range of stereotypically feminine linguistic strategies. Interestingly,
early on in her interview, Amy identifies herself as using language which
is associated with men, and she asserts her belief that this marks her out
as being different. We are talking on the topic of approachability:

Extract 1

Amy: I talk and act more like a man in many of my behavioural
        roles because of what I've worked with in the past [(.)] I'm less
Louise: [mm]
Amy: approachable than some of the men but I think I'm
        probably unique in that respect I think I'm not your
        typical female manager [(.)] and some people find that hard
Louise: [mm]

Amy places herself in opposition with the category of a 'typical female
manager' here, directly aligning herself with talking and acting more like
a man. By invoking these gendered categories, Amy signals her awareness
of different managerial styles that women and men are supposed to have,
and then states her perception that 'some people' in the business find it
'hard' because she acts outside of such expectations for female managers
in the business. In Extract 2, Amy gives more detail on how she deems
these styles to manifest themselves through the language she uses. We
are discussing the company's culture, and I bring up the topic of a business plan which I have observed the upper-middle managers working on.
Amy refers to a video she has been recording as part of the business plan
dissemination, where she appears dressed as a witch on a broomstick:

Extract 2

Louise: This business plan thing's a good idea you know I love the idea
        of that
Amy: Yeah yeah it is quite funny isn't it albeit it when you see us on some
        of the videos I'm not [(.)] quite sure about (-) I'm riding around
Louise: [yeah]
Amy: on a broomstick [at one point ((laughs] I'm not the most erm
Louise: [((laughs))   ]
        I say what I think I'm a manager I say what I think there's no
        cutting corners with people so I suppose if then out of the

management team (-) who is it that's more direct than anyone
it would be me [and it's] sort of like you know some people find
Louise: [right]
my (-) erm directness difficult (.) ((smile voice)) so they're going
Amy: to see me on this broomstick and I can just imagine you know
[they'll be like 'oh oh look Amy's on her broomstick ho ho ho'
Louise: [[((laughs))

Amy initially aligns being direct as part of the expected role of being a
manager, but she then highlights how some people in the company find
this 'difficult' from her. By raising the issue of directness in conjunction
with the gendered image of her dressing up as a witch on a broomstick,
there is a strong implication that being direct aligns her with a negative
image based on gender, an example of why 'some people' find her 'difficult'. Amy's perceptions of her colleagues finding her directness difficult
are certainly borne out in comments from them (see later). The video of
Amy will be shown to all store members. By attempting to invoke
humour through Amy dressing up as a stereotypically evil, domineering
female character, the management team who wrote the video script
(including Amy) appear to be drawing on a well-known, shared perception of Amy being negatively evaluated in the business in order for the
humour to be successful. The dominance of these negative perceptions of
Amy is confirmed by my ethnographic observations also discussed later.

Despite Amy's alignment of herself as a manager who talks 'more like
a man', she also highlights how she changes her managerial style to 'suit
different individuals and circumstances'. In particular, she identifies the
enactment of her managerial identity with her subordinates in the
Product Department in a stereotypically feminine manner, as she identifies her role responsibility as being that of 'nurturer':

Extract 3

I'm supposed to nurture and develop and encourage them (.) I see
that as my role (.) I don't see my having to do that with my peers.

She draws a distinction here between the manner in which she manages
her subordinates and the way she interacts with her peers, presenting
further evidence to explain the differences in interactional styles which
can be seen between the Product Department and the Sales Group meeting encounters. As Amy positions herself within the role of nurturer, it
is interesting to see whether there is any evidence of the supportive and
maternal 'mother role' (outlined in Chapter 2) in her interactions with
her team. Arguably, evidence of this can be seen in Example 19 (Chapter 5)

when discussing new recruit Andrew. She identifies him as a 'really sweet little lad', suggesting that she is framing him from a maternal, nurturing perspective. After this evaluation, she then informs members that he wants to be a policeman, akin to telling them of what the 'lad' wants to do when he grows up. Evidence of the mother role can also be witnessed when Amy checks on the emotional well-being of her new recruits Kirsty and Eddie (Example 21), asking how they are 'feeling'.

However, when members of the two CofPs of which Amy is in charge evaluate her in their interviews and informal talk, she is consistently negatively evaluated, and often this is ascribed to Amy's 'direct' interactional style, thus showing evidence of negative evaluation as a consequence of her using interactional styles indirectly indexed with the other gender. Indeed, negative evaluations of Amy by others within the company were widespread, and they were made evident to me as early as the first hour of the first day when I entered the retail company as a fieldworker. During informal talk with trainee manager Jenny (my main contact) in the staff canteen immediately following my arrival, she informed me that many people found Amy difficult to work with, describing her as 'bossy', 'bombastic' and 'dragon-like'. The following extract is taken from interview with Amy's subordinate Karen, who, as we have seen, is a member of both the Product Department and the Sales Group. We are talking on the topic of chairing styles in meetings:

Extract 4
Amy (.) is a very strong character very straightforward erm says
what she means is very direct (.) and it can be quite an overpowering
experience talking to her.

Karen's comments here accord exactly with Amy's own evaluation of her language use, seen in Extract 2. Karen negatively evaluates Amy's directness as 'quite overpowering'.

Later in her interview, Karen points out that she would prefer to work for a male boss, stating that 'I find it hard to build up a relationship' with Amy. In informal talk which I observed between Karen and Mary whilst they were in the smoking room after the Product team meeting had finished, Mary negatively referred to Amy through the directly indexed gendered term 'Miss bossy boots' in conversation with Karen when they were talking about tasks that they had to fulfil over the next week.

Kelly, Amy's status equal and member of the Sales Group, made the following derogatory comment about female 'tyrants', when talking about approachability, which she later revealed as being directed towards Amy:

Extract 5

Females are more caring generally (.) naturally more nurturing they've definitely got certain qualities that are different to men but some females can be real tyrants.

There is evidence here of a biologically essentialist view, with Kelly stating that women are 'naturally more nurturing', and thus more 'caring' as managers. However, she then negatively categorizes 'some females' who operate outside of this with the pejorative referring expression 'tyrants'. After the interview had officially terminated, Kelly stated that she identifies Amy within this 'tyrant' category. She thus presents Amy as being in opposition with the 'natural' female manager who is more 'nurturing'.

Further negative evaluation of Amy can also be seen in interview data from Lucy, a trainee manager, who used to be directly subordinate to Amy before Amy moved departments. I have asked Lucy if she thinks she is given enough time to express her opinions in business meetings, and she has brought up Amy as an example:

Extract 6

Amy is very domineering (.) when I was younger I'd have said men
would domineer but now Amy's come along (.) Amy is very different
from the rest of the females in the company she's quite honest you know
where you stand with her (.) she's quite abrupt you know as a woman (.)
I can be quite honest with her though sometimes she scares the pants off me.

Lucy directly aligns Amy with the stereotypically masculine trait of 'domineering', and goes on to identify Amy's 'abruptness' as rare from a woman, thus marking Amy's actions out as deviant from the expected gendered norm. Interestingly, Lucy aligns Amy's 'abruptness' with the quality of being 'honest'. Lucy does start to evaluate this positively, stating that this enables her to be honest too, but she then negatively evaluates Amy, stating that 'sometimes she scares the pants off me'. The implicature from Lucy's comments is that women in the retail company are not 'abrupt' are not 'honest'. There is thus evidence here of the traits associated with the dominant discourse of femininity outlined by Fitzsimons (2002, see Chapter 2), that women are manipulative, sly and devious. Lucy appears to be drawing on the stereotypical assumption that women are indirect and thus hide their 'honest' opinions.

A further negative evaluation of Amy is taken from middle-management employee Christine, who also used to be directly subordinate to Amy before she moved departments. Again, we are talking on the topic of approachability:

Extract 7

I find opening up to female managers especially Amy to be more difficult as she is very driven and very ambitious.

Christine negatively evaluates Amy as unapproachable, which she puts down to her being 'very driven and ambitious', traits which are being marked out as deviant here for female managers, but firmly associated with the dominant discourse of masculinity (see Chapter 2). When Amy left Christine's department to move to the Product Department, an upper-middle male manager took over her position. When considering the problems she had with Amy, Christine compares the two managers, and makes the following observation:

Extract 8

Christine: With male managers when I think about my own now
Louise: mm
Christine: I don't feel that I need to know erm (.) a lot about him about his
            personal situation (.)
Louise: mm
Christine: but I found with Amy I did need to I did want to know more about her
            I guess so that I could get a bit more in tune with her maybe

Christine's comments reveal her opinion that subordinates have different expectations of their managers and how they should present their identities to their subordinates based on gender. In order for a woman in a position of authority to set up a good working relationship with her subordinates, Christine believes that she needs them to give her some details of their personal lives so that she can get 'in tune' with them. Indeed, Christine comments with her own subordinates, an all-women team in customer services, that 'I have to give a lot of myself' in order to establish a good working relationship with them. Coming back to Amy, Karen makes a very similar argument to Christine, providing an additional reason why she feels her relationship with Amy is difficult. We are talking on the topic of women in positions of authority:

Extract 9

Karen: With women you always want to get to know them more and you
Karen: need to connect in a different way [and] the relationship takes longer
Louise: [right]

Karen: to work because (.) you could almost be that person and you are
         harder on a woman than you are on a man because you expect them to
         be like more of an outsider (.) but Amy is very closed

The male-as-norm view maintained by the hegemonic discourse of masculinity can be seen in Karen's comments here, and despite being a woman herself, Karen provides evidence of deeply ingrained expectations that she has about who is expected to be in positions of authority, openly admitting that she is harder on women as her superiors as she regards them more as outsiders, and because they are more similar to herself. On the basis of Christine and Karen's comments, it appears that women managers may need to fuse their private and public work lives to some degree in order to be more accepted by their female subordinates. Indeed, Amy is herself conscious that she does not give any personal details about herself away at work, and she directly acknowledges that this can be a problem, particularly with other women in the business. However, Amy equates her decision not to do this as an example of her being a 'professional':

Extract 10

I'm an extremely professional person and nobody knows anything
about me cos I don't ever think to get into that mode when I'm at
work and that sort of switches you off to some degree with people
particularly women who expect it of you as a woman.

Again Amy shows awareness that she is operating outside of the boundaries of expectation for women in the workplace. In commenting that she does not give personal information about herself because she is 'extremely professional', the implicature is that women managers who do give personal information are not as 'professional' as those that do not, and arguably there is evidence of the male-as-norm perspective here. Furthermore, both Amy's comments and the views of her subordinates Karen and Christine demonstrate Lakoff's (2003) point that the boundaries between public and private are far more collapsible for women. Both subordinates argue that, because they lacked details about Amy's personal life, they found it difficult to identify with her, a problem that Christine openly states that she does not have with her new male manager. There is evidence of deeply ingrained stereotypical expectations of women in positions of authority in the workplace here, which place further hurdles in Amy's way, with her women subordinates having greater expectations/needs from women managers (which Amy does not fulfil) in order to establish good working relationships.

To summarize, there is ample evidence here to suggest that, by deviating from the norms and expectations of stereotypically feminine speech styles, Amy experiences negative evaluation at the hands of her peers and subordinates. Despite displaying a wide-verbal repertoire of stereotypically feminine and masculine strategies in interaction, she is negatively evaluated by a number of her colleagues. These negative evaluations can be ascribed to the ideological structural constraints that operate to ensure that the discourse of gender difference, perpetuated by the dichotomous discourses of femininity and masculinity, are firmly entrenched and thus produce and reproduce the deeply ingrained stereotypes of gender-appropriate behaviour.

As if these negative assessments are not enough, there is also evidence of Amy negatively evaluating herself and all other women in the workplace towards the end of her interview on the basis of their use of 'difficult' communicative styles due to biological sex differences. This perspective sits very uneasily with Amy's earlier view that she adapts her communicative styles and talks 'like a man'. Despite acknowledging this, she includes herself in her negative evaluation of women's communicative abilities being innately affected by their hormones. She thus produces evidence of the dominant view, so common in popular culture, of inherent sex differences in language use. We had been talking at length about how Amy misses working with men:

Extract 11

Amy:	I actually get on better with men and I know why
	[(.)] it is because they don't question as much
Louise:	[mm]
Amy:	(.) you know men don't communicate like women
Amy:	do [(.)] women are so much more blooming more difficult
Louise:	[mm]
Amy:	you know hormones (.) we've all got them, I mean Jack I
	think finds me a complete nightmare ... we over-communicate we
	communicate far too much when we don't work you know we
	talk a lot more and [(.)] that's the sort of male female balance isn't it it's
Louise:	[mm]
Amy:	this right left brain thing isn't it you know it's how we're different you
	know the humorous book *Why Men Don't Listen and Women Can't Read*
	Maps [(.)] it's written in a funny vein but actually there's
Louise:	[yeah]
	a lot of sense and a lot of truth in it we are different

The dominant view of inherent differences in language use can be directly witnessed in Amy's comments. She openly states that men communicate differently to women and then negatively evaluates women as being 'more blooming difficult' due to their hormones. Her use of inclusive 'we' here demonstrates that she is including herself in this, despite distancing herself earlier in the interview from women's speech styles. She then goes on to negatively assess herself, stating that she thinks Jack, her direct superior, perceives her as a 'nightmare' because of her hormones (see Extract 26 for further discussion). She then uses collective 'we' again, stating that women 'over-communicate', drawing upon the persistent, pejorative folklinguistic belief that women talk too much (Talbot 2003). She then makes direct reference to Pease and Pease's (1999) management self-help book on workplace communication and the 'scientific' claims it makes about biological sex differences in the brain resulting in men and women being programmed to communicate differently.

Interestingly, this book is one that Talbot (2003) reviews in her discussion on gender stereotyping. She evaluates it as espousing 'an extreme and very crude form of biological essentialism ... rigged up with an illusion of "scientificity"' (2003: 481). Despite the fact that Amy has acknowledged earlier in her interview that she talks 'more like a man', and thus breaks with any such biological predetermination, she appears to accept the findings of Pease and Pease. Amy's reactions to this book neatly highlight the damaging impact that these popular culture publications can have when they espouse such biological determinism. Overall, Amy's comments provide evidence of the powerful overarching discourse of gender difference, often justified by the view of inherent biological differences in language use. The persistence of this discourse results in the dominance of views such as Amy's, that women are more 'difficult' to communicate with, and thus women are seen as less-suited for the workplace. Amy's comments in Extract 11 also illustrate Holmes and Meyerhoff's (2003: 9) point, outlined in Chapter 1, that 'in everyday life it really is often the case that gender is essential'.

We'll now move on to examine evidence of the discourse of gender difference in Carrie's CofP in the manufacturing company. When Carrie is interviewed, she makes the following positive evaluations about women managers' communicative skills when we are discussing the topic of men and women chairing meetings:

Extract 12

Carrie: I think women can be much more sophisticated
          communicators to be honest the women I've known that
          have been successful anyway [(.)   ] very good very
Louise: [mhm]

Carrie: sort of chameleon like maybe maybe verging on
           manipulative but erm much better at changing themselves
           to get someone to understand them erm I think men can be
           more men are very much 'this is me and this is why I'm
           doing it and it's up to you to understand me' kind of thing
           they're not as receptive to different styles.

Carrie thus reports her belief that there are differences in the manner in which women and men communicate, starting off by positively evaluating women managers as more 'sophisticated communicators', a perspective which accords with the aforementioned wide-verbal-repertoire that women managers have been observed using (Holmes and Stubbe 2003a). Indeed, Carrie herself was witnessed using a whole range of different styles in Chapter 6 (including stereotypically feminine and stereotypically masculine styles), adapting herself depending upon her interlocutor and the specific circumstances of the interaction within her CofP. Interestingly though, whilst this begins as a form of positive evaluation, there is evidence of the dominant discourse of femininity here when Carrie suggests that women managers verge on being 'manipulative'. Therefore, by responding to different circumstances and changing communicative styles, instead of simply being praised for being adaptable, Carrie also gives negative evaluation that, when women do this, it verges on manipulation. Also, despite her general praise for women managers' communicative styles, later in her interview she makes the following negative comment which accords with one of the most persistent and damaging folklinguistic beliefs about women's language use, which we have just seen Amy drawing on in Extract 11: the belief that women talk too much (Talbot 2003):

Extract 13

Carrie: Women are much more likely to say things and I suppose that
           can be a downfall of women (.) as they become more senior is
           that urge to fill the silences and actually the silence is quite a lot of
           power [(.)] and people ask questions and women try and answer
Louise: [mm]
Carrie: them it's a sort of eagerness (.) it's a bit like a erm an eager spaniel
           and as it gets to be bigger and a more important person it's got to
           shut up and er just sit quiet a bit longer and let some other little
           spaniel speak (.) often for men silence is the most comfortable thing

Carrie therefore accuses women as they rise through the ranks of businesses of failing to recognize the power of silence, and instead continuing with the wish to please by answering questions and talking too much. Furthermore, Carrie also goes on to state her belief that men's opinions are still taken more seriously:

Extract 14

I still think male opinions do seem to count a lot more (.) that's the male authoritative figure that's my gut feel about it.

These comments are made in reference to Carrie's experiences interacting at the executive level of the company. Therefore, even though she has broken through the glass ceiling, Carrie still feels that male opinions count more, with men automatically being seen as having more authority. Carrie's belief suggests evidence of the persistence of the dominant view of the male manager/director as the norm.

A recurrent theme with Carrie's evaluations of herself in interview, along with her perceptions of how she feels others view her in the business, is strongly influenced by the fact that she had just returned from maternity leave after giving birth to her second child. When talking about how her colleagues relate to her in terms of her approachability as a manager, Carrie makes the following comments:

Extract 15

Carrie: I've kind of noticed that coming back off maternity leave I'm a lot
          bigger (.) than before [(.)   ] and err you know I think there's quite a
Louise: [mm]
Carrie: change in attitude towards me because of that (-)
Louise: Really?
Carrie: Yeah so I'm on a diet now (-)
Louise: More of a maternal figure do you think?
Carrie: Yeah yeah in in for people underneath [(.) yes] much more switched
Louise: [mm   ]
Carrie: on to me [(.)   ] erm for erm people above or whatever are much more
Louise: [yeah]
Carrie: (.) don't take you so seriously when you're fatter definitely definitely
          I'm sure about that [(.)   ] so we'll see when I've been on a diet
Louise: [mhm]
Carrie: [((laughs))] and I'm not getting younger either
Louise: [((laughs))]

Carrie's comments raise a number of fundamental issues regarding image in the workplace and the social pressures that women managers can face as a result of their bodily image. Carrie expresses her belief that, becoming fatter during pregnancy, combined with the fact that she is getting older, has affected how seriously her opinions are taken by senior colleagues. The dominant discourse of femininity in terms of image and sexual attractiveness can be clearly seen here in Carrie's discourse. Her perspective implies that, in order for women's opinions to be taken seriously in the workplace, they need to be sexually attractive, fulfilling the idealized criteria of being slim and young. Carrie is not the only female interviewee to raise the importance of female image in the manufacturing company (discussed later). When there was a long pause I was keen to pursue this topic further, particularly in terms of whether Carrie thought there were changes directly as a result of her now being a mother. I thus asked if she thought she had become more of a maternal figure. Her response illustrates her perception that she has had a positive reaction from her subordinates, with them being more 'switched on' to her. There is evidence of this from Jane in her interview when she positively states that 'Carrie can be like our mum (.) she looks out for us.'

However, despite this positive evaluation, there is a range of evidence that Carrie is subject to negative evaluation in the business on gender grounds. As we have already witnessed in Chapter 6, Business Control Team member Kate negatively evaluates Carrie's professional performance (Example 33), when she suggests that Carrie was responsible for failing to maximize the potential of a product which cost the company a large amount of money in lost revenue. Carrie decided to take longer off work with her maternity leave than originally expected. This happened at what is regarded as the busiest time in the company's four-year production cycle. Carrie's commitment to her professional role has been seen to be lacking as a consequence, leading to a general perception of her being viewed as ineffective at her job. In interview with David, Chair of the Business Control Team and member of the Product Review Team, the problem of this particular product came up, and he comments that 'Carrie being off for ages did not help matters at all.' In her own interview, Carrie describes that, despite her initial projection of how long she would be off work, she had a change of priorities and chose to stay on maternity leave for longer than originally intended:

Extract 16

I took more time on maternity leave because you kind of get things a bit more in balance you just think what's the point in just rushing back.

There are observable consequences of Carrie's decision to prioritize her family, and she has been negatively evaluated in the company as a result. Carrie also comments in her interview that she is currently finding the work–home balance very difficult to manage, and had just brought in a time-management consultant to help her attempt to organize her time more effectively. The issue of the work–home balance is of crucial importance when considering gender inequality in the workplace, and it will be expanded upon later.

Carrie's 'hostile' encounter with Phil was a key focus of the Services Department encounter. As highlighted in Chapter 6, Carrie attributed Phil's negative behaviour to the disciplinary hearing that was to take place later in the day. However, when Carrie was interviewed, she had more information available to her as Phil had since handed in his resignation. When he did so he cited one of the reasons for his departure was due to Carrie making the department 'too feminine'. Carrie produces the following vignette, using direct reported speech, to present me with the conversation she had with Phil:

Extract 17

He said to me 'there are too many women in your department you ought
to take on more men' and I said 'have you any idea how sexist that is?'
'That's not sexist that's just equalling the balance a bit' he said 'there just
aren't enough men' and I could understand that kind of whole atmosphere
might become too female ... he finds it threatening and I found it shockingly
stupid to be honest but it made me stop and think ... is it too female has
everything gone pink and fluffy and it hadn't.

As a traditionally male-dominated arena, there is evidence of resistance to a change in the workplace demographic here from Phil. Carrie interprets his reaction as a consequence of him finding it 'threatening'. As males have dominated in the workplace for so long, a male-dominated team has been regarded as the norm. However, this is no longer the case in the 'Supply' section of the Services Department where Phil belonged, with four women and two men and now an equal number of women and men managers overall (see Table 6.1). Unsurprisingly, there are no examples of any interviewees suggesting that a team is too male and that more women should be employed. When Carrie reports this incident, she directly accuses Phil of being 'sexist' followed by her personal assessment of his opinion as 'shockingly stupid'. However, Phil's comments still led her to question her actions, and assess whether she thought her department had become too feminine, which she negatively defines using the stereotypically feminine adjectives 'pink' and 'fluffy'. Carrie's characterization of a feminine department here and the pejorative terms that she uses to describe this can be seen as evidence of an underlying assumption that femininity is not traditionally associated with the workplace, thus also invoking the view of masculinity as the workplace norm. The reverse equivalent, a junior woman accusing her male superior of making his department too masculine would obviously not be expected due to the historical predominance of men in the public sphere, combined with the view of male as norm. Furthermore, Robert negatively evaluates Carrie's chairing in informal talk with me after the Services meeting for 'going on about trivia'. In the meeting analysis, there are four examples of small talk, all initiated by Carrie on stereotypically feminine topics, where only women managers choose to join in. It seems likely that these are examples of what Robert refers to as 'trivia', with small talk often negatively evaluated for being non-task related and thus 'trivial', despite the important role it plays in workplace talk (see Chapter 4).

David provides further negative evaluation of Carrie in his interview when talking about the women at a higher level of management in the manufacturing company:

Extract 18

There's two senior females here we have one exec member Carrie
who is very strong willed and I have no doubt that she uses her gender
with her strong will to very good effect and I would find it hard working
for that person (.) but certainly I have no problem working with a female
boss at all.

David accuses Carrie of sexual manipulation here by stating that she 'uses her gender', in conjunction with her 'strong will' to 'good effect', something that he would find difficult to work with. He contradicts himself by stating that he would have 'no problem' working for a female boss 'at all'. In light of his preceding utterance it appears that he would have a problem if this was Carrie. Interestingly, Carrie is not the only woman manager that David accuses of sexual manipulation in the company (see later).

In summary, there is a range of evidence that Carrie is subject to negative evaluation in the workplace as a result of the positioning of her gender identity. Carrie, like Amy, can be witnessed utilizing a range of both stereotypically feminine and stereotypically masculine speech styles in her meeting. Carrie positively evaluates her own use of a range of different communicative styles, which directly accords with the manner in which she performs her managerial identity. However, unlike Amy, Carrie does not experience negative evaluation for behaving in a stereotypically masculine manner. Instead, it is Carrie's femininity that comes under attack. First, there is her own suggestion that her opinions are not taken so seriously since she has given birth due to the fact that she has put on weight. Interrelated with this is a perception of her being ineffective due to the fact that she took time out of the business to go on maternity leave. There is also the accusation that she has made her department too 'feminine', and therefore inappropriate for organizational life. Finally, she is negatively evaluated by David when he accuses her of using her gender in a sexually manipulative and cunning manner.

Coming back to the retail company, in the Technical Department meeting, there is much evidence of male Chair Steve using a range of stereotypically feminine strategies in order to enact his managerial identity. Indeed, in the linguistic features studied, Steve can be witnessed using humour in a stereotypically masculine manner, but all other strategies on this occasion of recording are stereotypically feminine. Steve engages in informal talk with me briefly during a break in the Technical Department meeting when Sue leaves the room to get her display board to show him a task she completed whilst he was on holiday. When Sue leaves, Steve engages in informal talk with me (the only other person present), where he spontaneously gives his own assessment of his managerial style:

Extract 19

Sue:	Two seconds [and I'll just] ((Sue leaves the meeting room))
Steve:	[two seconds]
Steve:	((addressing me)) That's the reaction I was hoping for (.)
Louise:	yeah
Steve:	gives them the chance to assert themselves like that instead of me telling them what to do (.) you know [I don't] like the team to feel like
Louise:	[mm]
Steve:	a pecking order with me at top (.) ((Sue re-enters with her display board))

Steve's evaluation of his own managerial style directly equates with a stereotypically feminine approach. He explicitly mentions that he does not like to be authoritarian, and that he tries to minimize any sense of hierarchy. There is evidence here of Steve actively adopting an interactional style that goes against the stereotypical norms and expectations for his gender. However, there is no evidence to suggest that Steve receives any negative evaluation as a result of this. In interview with Sue, she makes the following evaluation of Steve:

Extract 20

Sue:	Steve's great to work for (.) I feel he listens that I am able to speak freely to him (.) you are allowed to make mistakes and there's a lot of trust put in you (.) but there's no hierarchical system [(.)] when you ask for help you get
Louise:	[mm]

Sue: it you never get shouted out (.) I haven't had one negative response from
             him in the eighteen months I've been here

Sue's evaluation of Steve accords with the speech styles that we have
seen him use in the Technical Department meeting. Sue positively evaluates him for being non-hierarchical, a good listener, being helpful and
for trusting her with responsibility, as well as stating that Steve has never
responded negatively to her. The traits that Sue draws upon to assess
Steve so positively provide further evidence of him as a manager who
favours a stereotypically feminine style to enact his power and authority. However, unlike Amy, who is negatively evaluated for going against
the gendered norms and expectations, Steve does not experience any
negative evaluation as a consequence of this. In fact, he is praised for
being a co-operative and effective leader by Sue. These findings accord
with Cameron's (2003) observations that men will often experience positive evaluation for using co-operative, feminine speech styles instead of
being negatively evaluated for going against the norms and expectations
of their gender.

    In the Technical Department meeting, there is also ample evidence of
Sue using stereotypically feminine speech styles. Sue's role responsibility
within the Technical Department is head of security, a stereotypically
masculine job. In her interview, she comments that she takes a 'softer'
approach to this role:

Extract 21

In security I take a much softer approach (.) you can all talk to the security
team and they will stop and help shop floor workers and customers (.) but
sometimes people say it is too soft (.) too womany.

Sue directly accords the 'softer' approach she takes as one where security
members engage in interaction with other store workers and customers,
but she then comments that this has been subject to negative evaluation
by some for being 'too soft' and 'too womany'. Therefore, when Sue
enacts her stereotypically feminine style within security, including
training her (male) staff to use these 'feminine' styles, they have been
subject to negative evaluation by some outside of their department.
Three months after I interviewed Sue, she left her post in security and
transferred to manage the cash office.

    In terms of evaluations of the male chairs in the manufacturing com-
pany, Jane and Sharon are the only members of the Product Review
Team to provide brief assessments of Chair Rob. Both of these are positive. In her interview, Jane states that 'Rob's good at being supportive (.)

he doesn't interfere when you're making a point'. In informal talk after the meeting had taken place, Sharon stated her opinion that Rob 'lets you have your say and then brings stuff together so you know what you're doing'. Both these comments support Rob's style, positively identifying him as an effective meeting chair. Like Steve in the retail company, Rob can be seen as utilizing stereotypically feminine strategies to enact power and authority without any form of negative evaluation.

Also in the Product Review Team, the use of masculinist metaphors of war/battle and sport can be viewed within the overarching discourse of gender difference. Following Koller's (2004) work, war metaphors can be identified as masculinizing business discourse, promoting and reinforcing the dominant hegemonic discourse of 'macho' masculinity, serving to reinforce traditional gender bias. There are two occasions in the manufacturing company where women managers directly index gender, thus showing their own ability to invoke in-groups and out-groups and thus resistance to dominant masculinist discourses. These occasions will be discussed in the section on 'resistant discourses' later.

In the Business Control Team Meeting, there is clear evidence that David's power and authority as Chair are criticized and challenged. As has already been pointed out in Chapter 6, one of the main consequences for this was due to a broader frustration that members felt, including David, with lack of attendance from director Simon. Indeed, David's lack of enthusiasm for his enforced role as chair is notable. However, it is interesting to explore this issue further, as David's chairing style is also evaluated in interviews with Business Control Team members Sharon and Becky. Sharon comments on the amount of talking time David takes up, stating that 'David if we let him he'd sit there all day', and similarly Becky comments that 'there's certain people that do want to discuss the whole thing (.) David will go on all day'. However, it is notable that both Sharon and Kate clearly attribute David's inefficient chairing style to his 'personality', and not his gender. Sharon claims that 'it's person rather than the gender though' and similarly Kate states that with David 'it's not a male thing it's his personality'.

It is perhaps possible that these findings may be indicative of a broader pattern which could be another consequence of the male-as-norm view in the professional workplace: in both of these companies, when women's managerial styles are negatively evaluated, such negativity is attributed to their gender. In contrast, when David is negatively evaluated, it is simply attributed to his personality traits. This suggests that gender is more salient an issue for women in the workplace due to men still being viewed as the norm, though this assertion would need to be put to the test in a larger-scale study.

Business Control Team members Kate and Becky provide further evidence of the dominant discourse of masculinity with the view of male-as-norm embedded within this in the following observation about their job roles in interview when talking about how seriously they think their opinions are taken in business meetings:

Extract 22

Kate: If we were men in this role if I'm totally honest if we were men
          in this role we'd have far more of a mark on the business than we do
Becky: And a bit more respect
Kate: Yeah definitely

Kate expresses her 'honest' belief that if she and Becky were men they would have had far more of an impact on the business. Becky supports this viewpoint, adding that they would also receive 'a bit more respect', strongly indicating that they do not get the respect they deserve because they are women managers.

The above examination of evidence of the discourse of gender difference in all six CofPs, particularly focusing on Chairs and leaders, has produced a wealth of evidence of the dominance of this overarching discourse. Another key discourse which can be seen as part of the overarching gender differences approach is the specific discourse of female emotionality/irrationality (Mullany and Litosseliti 2006), whereby women are seen as inappropriately placed in the workplace due to their biological tendency to be emotional and irrational. This sits at odds with the discourse of scientific modernism, the need to be unemotional and irrational in order to occupy the role of manager (see Chapter 2). There is also evidence of this damaging discourse in my data. Such instances, along with consideration of negative consequences of these discourses, will now be explored. There is a remarkable amount of uniformity between the evidence of these discourses found in both companies, suggesting that these findings may be indicative of shared opinions, attitudes and evaluations in wider society.

The discourse of female emotionality/irrationality

Martin from the Business Control Team presents rather condemning opinions through which the discourse of female emotionality/ irrationality can be observed. In interview with him, I asked whether he had a preference to work for a woman or a man. He draws upon the following life history narrative to illustrate his perspective on this topic:

Extract 23

Martin: When I did have a woman boss they (-) do they do tend
          to be a bit more emotional than men you know I think men can be
          pretty hard but probably straighter [(-)   ]
Louise: [mhm]
Martin: whereas women tend to be (-) I don't know some some women
          can play (.) the fact that they are a woman (.) and other
          women erm just tend to be more emotional I've found th-
          than men which isn't someone I particularly want to wor-
          I I don't particularly want to be working for a person who's (.)
          got emotional highs and lows you know I want to be working
          for someone that I know where I am (.) when I'm with them

The biologically essentialist position can be clearly seen here in Martin's
narrative. He reduces women managers into two distinct categories,
ones that can 'play the fact that they are a woman', and others who are
'more emotional', albeit minimized somewhat by Martin's use of
diminutive 'bit'. His first identity category strongly implies that such
women use their sexuality in a manipulative and cunning manner (see
later). The second category, the 'emotional' woman boss, is negatively
evaluated by Martin, who states his preference for a male boss as the
'straighter' option. His reasoning illustrates how he views women in
positions of authority as inappropriate due to their 'emotional highs
and lows', which is seen in direct opposition to the rational and efficient
characteristics which he indirectly attributes to men.

   Martin elaborates further on his views on emotionality, making a
more general comment which he applies to all women in the workplace,
adding further weight to the argument that he sees women and the
stereotypical behaviour he associates with them as inappropriate for the
public sphere:

Extract 24

I just find men in general I mean in the workplace and in general I just
find them to be more stable and straight really than women ... if you look
at sort of even just on the biological clock you know you've got one week
a month when women are you know not as they are the other three weeks
of the month you know and and that is bound to have an effect I mean that
is whatever people say about men and women are the same they're not
because we- you know men don't go through that women do and it's very
rare a woman who says she isn't affected for that week of the month so if
you're working for someone and you get them in that week you know it's

they will be emotionally they will be more susceptible to emotional swings and not making decisions erm with the kind of same sort of accuracy that they normally would.

Martin here overtly espouses the sexist, stereotypical view that for a 'week' of every month, women are incapable of making rational decisions due to their hormones, thus placing all women managers in direct opposition with the rationality, effectiveness and efficiency associated with the discourse of scientific modernism. The fact that Martin openly expressed his viewpoint to me, a female interviewer in what I would characterize as a very co-operative interview encounter, arguably suggests that he felt he was stating a universal 'truth' due to the inherent biological essentialism that runs through his perspective. A most intriguing part of his response is where he corrects himself from stating 'we', claiming solidarity and common ground with myself as the interviewer. As I am inappropriately classified with the collective, inclusive pronoun, Martin corrects this and replaces it first with a verbal filler, and then follows this with 'men' as a more distant term of reference.

In the retail company, male interviewee Peter expresses a similar opinion to Martin's in response to the same question. Peter directly mentions John Gray's publications as a preamble, followed by the view that we are 'wired up differently', showing evidence of the biologically essentialist view that men and women are inherently programmed to talk and act differently (also similar to Amy's view in Extract 11):

Extract 25
There's the book you know the Venus Mars book and there's all that
thing going on about men and women being wired up differently (.)
and erm you know I firmly believe that there is a difference in the way
that we think (.) the managerial working relationships that really work for
me (.) erm are the ones where (.) it's very open you know it's almost like
there are no holds barred you know you can say what you like and
it's not going to upset the other person and vice versa and erm (-) and
I've had erm (-) erm yeah I think the the best (.) managerial working
relationships are the ones where (.) there's no hidden agenda there's no
politics (.) it's all very open and above board and erm I seem to get
that with male managers more.

Whilst Peter does not deny the possibility of having an 'open' and 'above board' relationship with women managers, he firmly equates such traits as being primarily associated with males, where you can be sure that you will not encounter emotionality and where you can be honest. There is evidence again here of the dominant discourse of femininity, with women being viewed as devious, sly and manipulative, interacting with hidden agendas, and hiding their 'honest' opinions. Again, the rational, objective principles of the dominant discourse of scientific modernism are being clearly equated with men as opposed to women managers, based on inherent biological difference.

However, as mentioned earlier, it is not just men who expound such damaging opinions about women's emotions. We have already seen evidence of Amy openly stating her opinion that hormones make women 'more blooming difficult' to work with. There is a long pause after she states she thinks Jack finds her a 'complete nightmare'. I encourage her to continue and she goes on to state the following:

Extract 26

Amy: I mean Jack I think finds me a complete nightmare (-)
Louise: Really?
Amy: Oh yeah I yeah I mean like I have been so hormonal since I've
         been here it's untrue I'm the most unemotional person in the
         world and then suddenly I will burst into tears

The inconsistency in Amy's perspective in terms of her biological sex dictating her behaviour can be seen again here. Whilst Amy describes herself as the most 'unemotional person in the world', she then contradicts this by stating that since she joined the retail company she has been at the mercy of her hormones, and 'suddenly' starts crying. Amy thus positions herself in direct opposition to the unemotional and rational behaviour that is set as the norm for those who are successful in the managerial workplace.

Two middle-level women managers also present evidence in their interviews of how they perceive certain male colleagues to negatively evaluate them for expressing 'emotional', 'irrational' opinions in business meetings. When talking about whether they think their gender affects how seriously their opinions are taken in meetings, both Christine in the retail company and Jane in the manufacturing company report their concerns. Christine feels that her comments would be taken more seriously if they were uttered by a man:

Extract 27

Christine: I think people think I'm talking about the (.) I'm talking about
             people things the squishy things [the] nice things and its sometimes
Louise: [mm]

Christine:	people see me sort of 'oh look at that girl girlie comment [you] can't
Louise:	[mm]
Christine:	put the boxes there and take an extra two grand this weekend (.)
	[cos] Christine thinks you can't see the signs for the toilets duh'
Louise:	[yeah]
Christine:	whereas I think if I was a man talking about those things I think (.)
	I feel it would be perceived by some people as more important

Christine directly invokes gender here, reporting her feeling that others in the business perceive her to be concerned about emotional 'girlie' things which are in direct opposition with the rational judgement required to fulfil the corporate aim of making money. Christine clearly perceives there to be a distinct difference in how her views are treated because of her gender. In the manufacturing company, whilst Product Review Team member Jane feels her prior experience in the company does count towards her colleagues at least listening to her opinions, she still expresses a concern that certain males will negatively evaluate her for being an 'emotional female', and attributes this to being 'a general thing in their head':

Extract 28

I think in all the meetings I go in if my opinion (-) I think they look
at my experience and what I've proven to do over the years here and
I think (-) they'll go with it (-) erm or listen to it at least ... but I think
a couple of (.) in a couple of meetings men will sit there thinking (.)
oh here she goes again emotional oh God (.) female and you know
I think they probably do think that as a general thing in their head.

Furthermore, Kim, also from the Product Review Team, reports that she has actually overheard men coming out of meetings in the manufacturing company making such comments, thus providing evidence for Jane's perspective:

Extract 29

I've heard comments at {company name} when a woman has got
angry at a meeting you know I've heard male colleagues come out of
the meeting and say 'oh she's just emotional' you know they find it difficult
or they put it down as a silly emotion.

Later in her interview Kim draws a distinct difference between men and women on the topic of emotionality by stating that men are not emotional:

Extract 30

Women are more personable women can tolerate emotion more and
men are just not emotional and I think with a male boss if a woman

reportee does show emotion it's not the thing to do whereas with a woman a woman is more forgiving of that.

Kim argues here that women should not show emotion with men in the workplace, but it is okay to do this with women as they can be 'forgiving'. Kim thus presents women's emotionality as something that needs to be forgiven, and strongly suggests it is something that is inappropriate in a workplace context.

Further aspersions cast regarding the irrationality of women in the workplace can be viewed through the negative portrayals of women's judgement due to a tendency to be 'bitchy'. Both men and women managers in the retail company comment on how women can be 'bitchy'. Middle-manager Jake commented that 'groups of females tend to be like an old-biddies club and can be quite bitchy'. Christine reports that in her experience of running an all-woman team 'you get bitchiness which causes an atmosphere and you don't get this with males'. Interviewee Lucy provides an essentialist justification for the connection between women and bitchiness, presenting it as something that is beyond their control, as 'we just do it':

Extract 31

We've got a lot of women in our department and (.) there is quite a lot
of erm bickering and bitchiness behind people's backs which annoys me
(.) and I think we're all guilty of it as women we just do it.

Trainee manager Jenny states her dislike of working with women due to the 'bitchy' environment:

Extract 32

I generally get on better with men (.) I don't like working in a team
where there's a lot of women (.) it can be really bitchy catty and backstabbing.

In the manufacturing company, Business Control Team member Becky reports her belief that 'all men together can be as bitchy as all women together'. Whilst her perspective acknowledges than men can also be responsible for 'bitchy' and thus stereotypically feminine behaviour, her comment simultaneously reinforces the view that women are bitches in the first place. By focusing on women's alleged propensity to be 'bitchy', there is evidence of both women and men managers implicitly questioning whether women have the capacity for rational judgement due to their 'bitchy' predisposition. Following Brewis's (2001: 299) argument, the fact that women also engage in this negative 'bitchy' evaluation of both themselves and their female colleagues demonstrates that they are caught in the double bind. They too are responsible for negative evaluation, placing women in direct opposition with rational, non-judgemental values typically associated with the dominant workplace discourse of scientific modernism.

Discourses of motherhood and the family

Career progression and motherhood

The work–home balance was a common point of discussion in many interviews, as well as in informal talk with managers, through which participants' discursive positioning according to the discourses of motherhood and the family can be observed. There was an observable correlation between the opinions women managers had across both companies towards the work–home balance, depending on whether or not they had children. A concern of all women interviewees aged 24–33 without children in both companies was that the decision to have children would negatively affect their career progression. Some interviewees also reported that they had encountered stereotypical presumptions that they would automatically want children, regardless of their own personal desires, simply by virtue of the fact that they are female. Product Review Team member Kim comments on how she believes the assumption that all women will want children could prejudice an interviewing panel's decision against her either if she went for promotion or if she wanted to move to another company:

Extract 33
The cynical part of me thinks that well people are gonna be thinking
if I come up against a man then they'll be thinking oh well she'll probably
be off wanting to start a family.

Kim's discursive positioning can be seen through her opinion that there will be assumptions automatically made about her because she is female that would not be made about a male interview candidate. The dominant discourse of motherhood, with its expectation that women will take greater domestic responsibility, can be seen as part of the overarching discourse of gender difference, which then places women in direct opposition with the discourse of scientific modernism, making them less likely candidates for promotion.

In the retail company, middle-manager Christine (aged 30) is currently contemplating having children, though she comments on her awareness that she may well experience negative evaluation for this from some male colleagues, based on her observations of when other women managers in the business were pregnant:

Extract 34

Some men around the business see pregnancy and maternity leave as an inconvenience (.) as a wasted resource but it's fine for their wives to go off work having children.

Christine highlights her perception of a double standard that exists between the attitude certain men have towards their female colleagues, and the attitude they have towards their own private lives.

Childless female interviewees in both companies (aged between 36–44) who had progressed up the career ladder *all* reported their belief that not having children was a fundamental reason why they had managed to progress so far with their careers. As the highest ranking woman on the organizational hierarchy in the retail company, Amy openly acknowledged that her prospects of progression were greatly improved by the fact that she did not have either children or a partner and was thus 'highly mobile'. She believed that this would put her in a highly advantageous position over other females in making the final step up the ladder to become a store manager. Indeed, eight months after the interview took place, Amy had re-located to gain promotion to store manager over 200 miles away from her previous job.

In the manufacturing company, whilst director Carrie does have children as we have seen, in informal talk she commented that she made the conscious decision to climb up the career ladder before having them. Judy, the only other female director in the manufacturing company is considering moving to a different company, and she sees not having children as a positive advantage in such a recruitment process:

Extract 35

I've probably got an advantage cos I don't have children so I don't
fall into the 'oh well she'll probably leave and have children' category
or 'oh she'll have problems at home and therefore won't be around'
you know 'she'll dash off at the last minute' so that's an advantage.

The first category that Judy reports directly accords with Kim's concerns raised earlier when discussing perceptions in job interviews. Business Control Team middle-management member Pam also made a similar point during her interview, commenting that she felt she had an 'advantage over other females' in terms of gaining promotion in the manufacturing company as she is not 'tied down to doing child-related tasks'.

All of these comments demonstrate that Amy, Judy and Pam are clearly aware of the negative attitudes and evaluations that exist towards women managers who have children. Indeed, ample evidence of this has already been witnessed when examining how Carrie is evaluated. There was also evidence in the interview data of Judy passing on such opinions to her more junior colleagues. During interview with Kate and Becky, Kate reports a conversation she had with Judy on this topic:

Extract 36

Kate: I remember going out for a meal it was the first meal for the {xxx} Committee [and] the {job title} director was there and there
Louise: [mm]
Kate: was a few people there and I remember her saying 'you you don't want kids you'll be a career woman' and I said 'no actually I do want kids' and it was quite ((puts on a mocking voice)) 'no no you can't' ((laughs)) no I *can't* have them
Louise: ((laughs))
Becky: ((laughs)) yeah I remember that it is though something that you probably don't mention [like we] might talk to each other about
Louise: [no   ]
Becky: it but it wouldn't be a thing which we'd tell our boss about like what we plan to do

Kate's narrative report of Judy's comments highlights how Judy perceives there to be two distinct and incompatible female identities, either as a 'career woman' or as a mother. Kate uses direct speech here for additional emphasis when telling her narrative, and invokes humour to report what Judy had said to her. Kate's reporting of Judy's viewpoint suggests that Judy perceives there to be a distinct difference between women with children and women with careers, demonstrating that it is not just males who have stereotypical opinions about women with children in organizational life. Becky states that it is not something that she would mention. Kate goes on to report that she is contemplating having children, but confirms Becky's point that she would never mention this:

Extract 37

Kate: you never mention kids or anything you leave it totally out 'oh no no I'm very much a career woman' and like most of us deep down are all thinking well oh well I'm 31[and we never mention it do we]
Becky: [it's funny that actually   ]
Becky: no we never

Kate: once you get a job you are quite conscient- conscious that you know that it
        could stop your career [progression]
Becky: [yeah   ]
Kate: I don't like having to keep quiet about it an- and acting as if you know I am
        totally career orientated cos really you know I would like kids

Kate and Becky engage in supportive simultaneous talk, agreeing that
you do not mention children in the workplace, with Kate using hypo-
thetical reported speech to illustrate how she responds if people ask her.
She draws upon the dichotomous categories Judy mentioned here,
reporting that she is a 'career woman' instead. Kate directly states that
she is aware that having children could stop career progression, and also
expresses discontent with not being able to express her true plans. This
evidence accords with Halford and Leonard's (2001) observation
that women need to hide their personal lives at work in order to protect
their professional reputations. In contrast, they report that men have far
more freedom on this issue, and are able to acknowledge openly their
home lives and children, as well as have a fully integrated work and
home life. This is illustrated by David in the Product Review Team meeting, where he overtly states that he needs to go home for his daughter's
birthday party. There are no such examples of women mentioning their
home lives in meeting data or during any of my ethnographic observations of workplace interaction in either company. The comments made
by Kate and Becky firmly suggest that women would not have this
option open to them without being negatively evaluated.

Work–home balance

On the broader topic of work–home life more generally, in both companies, women and men managers commented that women work harder.
Becky comments that she puts in far longer hours than her male status
equals as she feels she has to actively demonstrate that she is worthy of
her career, and that she does not have to go and be a 'housewife' instead.

Extract 38

At the moment I know the reason why we tend to put in more
hours because we try to think you know erm (-) look I haven't
got to go and be a housewife and try to prove to them I haven't
got to go and be a housewife you know I've got my career now
whereas a man doesn't have to justify that.

There is clear evidence of 'male manager as norm' view here, with
Becky stating that men do not have to justify their presence – they are

automatically expected to be in the workplace anyway, not in the home. After Becky's comments, Kate agrees and makes a similar point, stating that women 'have to work harder women have to justify their ambition', again as a consequence of the fact that women are not traditionally perceived to be part of the professional workplace. Carrie also comments on the women within her department, including Jane, working longer hours than their male counterparts:

Extract 39

Women are very prone to over-work ... the guys definitely are much
more of a nine-to-five slot than the women – five o'clock they're off
I know it's a lack of self-esteem with women.

Carrie equates long hours with a lack of self-esteem, which arguably can also be seen to stem from the persistent male-as-norm view. David's decision to leave the Product Review meeting when it was scheduled to finish provides evidence to support Carrie's observation that men tend to leave as soon as it is 'officially' time to go.

There are also comments in interview data from the retail company that women work harder than their male counterparts. Trainee manager Jenny reports the following:

Extract 40

Women have to work that extra bit harder (-) to be able to be seen as
being as important and saying the right thing (-) you know (.) knowing
what they are talking about.

Her viewpoint accords with those from the manufacturing company, that the image of a male manager is still the stereotypical norm in workplaces, and women thus feel that they have to work harder in order to gain kudos and authority for themselves in the public sphere. Peter comments that women work harder in his experience, though he expresses uncertainty as to why this is the case, presenting two potential reasons:

Extract 41

I don't know if it's because in reality females have to work harder
to be able to do the same job or whether they think they need to work
harder to do the same job that manifests itself in that way.

The first part of Peter's utterance reveals an underlying sexist attitude that women may need to work harder in order to be able to achieve what men automatically achieve. Again, the discourse of scientific modernism, imbuing the perception of males as the workplace norm can be seen here through Peter's comments, though he also gives the option that it may be the internalization of this attitude which causes women to work longer hours. Peter therefore categorizes women managers into either one of two negative stereotypical categories, as less competent or as insecure.

A further issue regarding the work–home balance is raised in interview by Becky, when she refers to an unequal division of labour in the home:

Extract 42

For men they go home ... they don't then have to then start go and making the tea and doing the housework and doing whatever cos despite you know however liberal your husband is I still think to a degree you're expected to do more in the house ... we finish yeah but then we've got to go home and start again.

Indeed, Becky's colleague David openly acknowledges that he takes less responsibility for household labour than his wife in his interview:

Extract 43

Like er an awful lot of blokes I don't share certain functions as much as my wife would like namely cooking and washing ... I struggle after a hard day to think what the hell are we going to have for tea.

These comments accord with Franks's (1999) observations regarding the sexual division of labour in the home. Drawing on numerous surveys from the 1970s onwards, Franks (1999: 109) concludes that even if both partners are in full-time employment, statistics show that women still do more work in the home, with male contributions being regarded as something 'extra, in the sense that men do not own these tasks' (Franks 1999: 109). Expectations of male roles thus have not changed despite women entering the workforce in vast numbers. Recent statistics demonstrate that this is still very much the case (EOC 2006). Again, the dominant discourse of family, which includes assumptions about the sexual division of labour within a family unit, can be seen to be positioning women at an overall disadvantage in both work and home life.

Dominant discourses of femininity: Image and sexuality

The topic of feminine image recurs as an important issue during the interview data. The importance of image, in particular, the idealized image of the slim, attractive female, has already been highlighted above through Carrie's comments that she is no longer taken seriously by her superiors since she has put on weight. Coates (1997: 295) points out that one of the dominant discourses of femininity is that women should care about their image and appearance; in particular, they should attempt to stay slim. Carrie's comments demonstrate that failing to abide by these expectations leads to negative consequences for her in the workplace. Carrie's subordinate Jane also comments on her image, stating that her 'sex' and 'the way you look' affects how seriously she perceives her opinions to be taken in certain meetings. Jane reports her perception of how her gendered image leads to more senior male colleagues perceiving her as incapable of doing her job:

Extract 44
They see me as this girl with a ponytail and fresh skin and you know
they just look at me and they think (-) I can't do the job

Jane perceives male colleagues to view her negatively as a young 'girl' as opposed to a professional adult, and thus see her as unable to fulfil her professional role. She elaborates on this, reporting that since she gained promotion to middle-management she has come across sexist attitudes in certain company-wide meetings (including the Product Review Team) from two male colleagues in particular:

Extract 45
I've come across comments (-) ermm which are completely related to
your sex and the way you look I've had comments made like erm oh that
must have been interesting for you ((laughs)) ... (-) erm I've often got my
hair in a ponytail or up like I have today I don't wear make-up ... I I I
distinctly get the impression from a lot of men in meetings that they look
at me as if I'm a kind of twenty-one-year-old being given an opportunity
to sit in and listen ... the meetings where those two gentlemen are in (-)
I do tend to end up putting on a bit of eye liner and wearing something
slightly smarter ... you'll get kind of (-) the male chauvinist he'll sit on
the desk and kind of lean over and go 'oh well-done' when you when
you do something and you think it's my job and you know there have
been a lot of men in decision (.) roles you do start to think well will
they look at you just as this young little female and will that affect me.

By putting her hair in a ponytail and not wearing make up, Jane implies that she has broken an expectation surrounding the expected feminine image for a professional woman in the workplace. There is also evidence of a combination of gender and age ideologies in Jane's comments. Whilst Jane is the youngest member of Product Review Team in terms of her chronological age (30), she has considerable experience in her role, having been with the company for over eight years and a manager for five years. However, she believes it is not her actual chronological age/experience but the age she is perceived to be, combined with gender, that results in men viewing her as 'this young little female', superseding the wealth of experience she has in her role, resulting in negative evaluation.

The view perpetuated by the dominant discourse of femininity regarding feminine image appears to be that, in order to succeed and be taken seriously in the workplace, women need to fulfil the heterosexual imperative: style their hair, wear make up and 'smart' clothes, thus fulfilling the expectation that they have attempted to make themselves attractive to men. Jane reports on how she has actively begun to change her appearance by putting on make up and wearing 'smarter' attire in an attempt to gain some respect from the two male colleagues who have patronized her in the past. Jane later identifies one of these males as Keith from the Product Review Team (only a year older than Jane). Jane's reporting of Keith's actions sheds further light on their working relationship, with Jane perceiving these factors to be part of the reason for his confrontational interactional strategies and negative evaluation of her in business meetings.

Another tactic that Jane employs, in addition to changing her appearance, is to stress that she has been with the company a long time when giving her opinion, in order 'to continually remind them' that she is not just a 'young little female' but 'an experienced professional who has been with the business for a good long time'. There is empirical evidence of Jane doing this on eight occasions in the company-wide, Product Review Meeting. For example, when commenting on a problem the company has been experiencing with overproduction of a certain item of stock Jane begins her suggested solution with the preface 'from being here a reasonable length of time and knowing the personalities ...' Jane can be seen using this tactic when Keith criticizes and challenges her (see Chapter 6, Example 17). There is no evidence of any males in the interactional data sample who had been with the company for a similar length of time doing this, arguably suggesting that males may automatically get the authority and kudos associated with their status, role and length of service. In the retail company, Kelly perceives her gendered image, combined with her age, to be a problem when she needs to enact authority with older males in the business:

Extract 46

I've had to talk to people that are older than me (.) males that
were older than me and I've thought 'ohhhhh' you know (.) I don't
want them to think this is like 'who's this silly little woman telling me'
you know so it has to be done in a different way (.) very professional.

Kelly expresses her concern that when attempting to enact authority
with older males she may be evaluated negatively through their perceived image of her as a 'silly little woman'. In order to combat this, she
argues that she has to be 'very professional', firmly implying a male-as-
norm view here.

Further evidence of the dominant discourse of femininity surrounding female image in particular relation to sexual attractiveness is highlighted in the manufacturing company in David's interview when he is
talking about a recent appointment he made:

Extract 47

I had a number of female applicants as well er I suppose I'd be
lying if I didn't say it's nice to have attractive women around the
office if I had to be honest but you know that's only a- (-) that that
doesn't form any serious part of any judgement erm erm I'm just
being perfectly honest.

David hesitates and appears to stop himself during this utterance, pausing and then changing his comment from 'that's only a-' to a denial that
the attractiveness of a female candidate 'doesn't form any serious part of
any judgement'. His comment thus implies that a woman's sexual
attractiveness may be playing at least some part in his judgement. The
dominant discourse of femininity in terms of the sexualization of female
appearance is clearly in evidence here, with David openly acknowledging that he likes to have sexually attractive women in the workplace,
highlighting a tendency to treat women in the office as sexual objects.
David appears to be displaying an attitude which Cockburn (1991: 157)
observes, that sexually attractive women may find that they are initially
welcomed into their place of work 'because their presence adds sexual
spice to the working day'.

However, as we have already seen above, David objects to Carrie as he
feels she uses her 'gender' to unduly influence men in the business.
Therefore, it appears that whilst David likes looking at 'attractive
women', there is a fine balance here, and he encounters difficulties if he

fears that women may be 'using' their sexuality, drawing on the devious and manipulative stereotypically feminine traits ingrained in the dominant discourse of femininity.

As well as Carrie, David accuses Sharon of such behaviour, and also levels the same accusation at Becky and Kate, all three being colleagues from the Business Control Team. When talking on the topic of career progression, David embarks upon the following life history narrative to illustrate his perspective. Approximately two months after the Product Review Team and Business Control Meetings had been recorded, Sharon moved to another company. David's interview took place after she had left:

Extract 48

David: In recent history erm erm I felt until three years ago I'd got on (.)
         very well in this business [(.)   ] through my own abilities
Louise: [mm]
David: erm (-) and err more recently (.) erm (.) a new person came in who
         you will know but who's no longer with us Sharon Jones (.)
David: who was brought in by one of the exec (.) directors (.) erm (.)
         and who was a previous colleague of that person [(.)   ] so they
Louise: [mhm]
David: brought 'em in er and I (-) I have no (.) doubt in my mind that
         she used her sexual (-) erm wiles if that's the right
Louise: [mm]
David: word [(((laughs)))] er you know (-) to get what she wanted in the
Louise: [(((laughs)))]
David: business and that probably to some degree (.) er had a negative
         [effect] on me (.)] so I I found myself (.) less able to exert (.) my
Louise: [mm]
David: influence based on skill [(.)   ] er in the light of others er ability to
Louise: [right]
David: (.) apply their sexual influences if you like

Whilst David does question his use of the term 'wiles', this does not detract from the fact that he draws a clear distinction between his own ability to manage using his 'skill', whereas Sharon's managerial ability is solely based upon her 'sexual wiles'. Later in the encounter, David again draws on his perception of females being sexual manipulators, accusing both Becky and Kate of using their gender to get their own way, and he strongly implies that they have done this in the direction of their superiors in order to enhance their career progression:

Extract 49

Two female account managers here are not slow to use the combination of will and gender to good effect when they can see an opportunity to do

so and that's usually in the direction of a male person get what they want
I've no doubt about it ... that's causing erm resentment from other males
you know there are other account managers who were who were certainly
were at the same level as them who feel they're dropping behind because
of the ability of the two females to exert their will gender mix to good effect.

David's sexist opinions are evident here once again as he reports a more
general feeling of resentment from other male managers towards female
managers who are overtaking them on the career ladder, not through
their own merit as good managers, but through their ability to use their
'gender' and 'will' to 'good effect'. David presents Becky and Kate as cunning and manipulative women who are unfairly thwarting the career
progression of men in the manufacturing company. David later states
that Martin is one of the males who believes they have hampered his
own career progression. Like David, Martin's comments in the above
section illustrate his belief that some women managers 'play' their gender in order to manage. There is ample evidence here of David and
Martin accusing their female colleagues of invoking the gendered identity role of seductress, particularly aimed at those in positions of power, in
order to manipulate to get their own way. It is worth comparing their
opinions with Kate and Becky's assessment of their own positioning in
the business (Extract 22), where they state their belief that they would
have had a much bigger impact on the business as well earning more
respect if they were men. David and Martin's comments certainly provide
evidence that they do not appear to respect Kate and Becky for their
'achievements'. There is a clear difference here in terms of how the impact
of gender identity is evaluated by male and female colleagues. Within
David and Martin's comments there is evidence of the view of masculinity being 'in crisis', a currently popular notion, perpetuated by the mass
media, that due to the feminist movement and women's advancement
men have been plunged into crisis (Johnson 1997; Swann 2003). Johnson
(1997) argues that one tactic that can be witnessed within popular culture
in response to this is a move towards stressing innate, biological differences between men and women in order to reassert men's superiority.
Indeed, Martin does just this in his comments (Extracts 23 and 24) when
he declares that women's biological differences mean that they are incapable of making decisions for one week of each month.

Resistant discourses

In terms of resistance to specific dominant discourses that have been
illustrated in this chapter, there is evidence of Carrie resisting the

dominant discourse of femininity in relation to image, albeit at the expense of other women who work for different departments in the company. Carrie frequently jokes about other women who *do* always wear feminine clothes and have perfectly made up faces with other female members of her team, including Jane. After her interview had officially terminated, Carrie told me that they have nicknamed Pam from the Business Control Team 'Colour Me Beautiful', a humorous reference to the consistently 'perfect' state of Pam's make-up, providing evidence of them drawing on alternative, resistant discourses, albeit at Pam's expense. Whilst engaging in such discourse does not challenge the status quo in terms of the manner in which women are evaluated by their image, it is the source of solidarity-building amongst Carrie and members of her team, and illustrates that women are not just unreflexive and passively trapped by these dominant discourses.

There are two occasions in the manufacturing company meeting data where women managers directly invoke gender as an identity category, and these instances can be interpreted as examples of resistant feminist discourses. On both occasions women managers directly index gender, using the terms 'girlie' and 'girls' serving to deliberately mark themselves out as different from their male colleagues. On both occasions these instances can be seen as women managers drawing attention to gender differences in a positive, celebratory way in order to invoke humour and enhance solidarity and collegiality amongst themselves in mixed-gender settings. Whilst 'girl' has been identified as a pejorative term to refer to an adult woman (Cameron 1992), the women managers use it positively as an in-group identity marker, raising the idea of a 'girlie holiday' and the concept of 'girls on tour'. The women managers thus draw on feminist discourses of liberation and freedom, invoking solidarity and in-group identity by suggesting that they all go away together without any men. Kate's analogy in Example 39 of themselves and the fictional feminist icons in the film *Thelma and Louise* adds further credence to the argument that dominant discourses governing expectations for feminine behaviour and traditional feminine occupations are being subverted. In both of these examples the women managers take advantage of the stereotypically feminine interactional strategies of conjoint, collaborative humour and small talk to enhance solidarity and collegiality and simultaneously accrue power for themselves by building a sense of female in-group identity and solidarity.

A further example of resistant discourse comes from when Lucy in the retail company informs me of how both she and her fellow women managers 'laugh and joke' about the physical nature of the work they do, demonstrating their awareness that they have broken the stereotypical expectations associated with traditional gender roles in the workplace:

Extract 50

I think you have to be a boy cos you're doing a lot of physical work
a lot of drilling we always laugh and joke and say if our mothers could
see what we do now they think we do all these nice little displays they
don't know that we're getting our hands in doing electrics and we're
doing painting and things like that.

The humour that Lucy and her colleagues invoke here emanates from the subversion of the dominant discourses of femininity and the family. They draw on assumptions of the type of employment mothers stereotypically expect their daughters to engage in. Lucy reports their mother's perception of them creating 'nice little displays' in the design department (note the Lakoffian gendered speech terms here), when in reality they are engaged in manual labour, partaking in activities stereotypically associated with male manual labourers. Lucy highlights how the subversion of their role expectation as women is the source of the humour for this group of women managers.

Furthermore, despite all of the deeply engrained problems that are raised by the foregoing analysis, there was some evidence in the retail company of them actively seeking to promote more women to senior management, which had become a part of the company's equal opportunities discourse. Amy informed me of the following conversation she had with one of the senior members of the company:

Extract 51

It's very encouraging as a female wanting to be in that next phase
you know having a conversation with the {xxx} manager saying well
actually it's a positive advantage you know we'll not discriminate
against men who are you know who are as good as you or better
than you but you know if we've got two people one's a man and
one's a woman and there's nothing to pick between them the fact
that you're a women is actually going to give you just that bit of extra
help so I'm not complaining about that holding me back for once.

Amy states how this part of the company's equal opportunities discourse has had a positive impact on 'encouraging' her to strive for promotion and break through the glass ceiling. Amy makes the point that this is different from situations that she has encountered in the past, when stating that 'for once' being female will be an advantage. Indeed, it is important to point out that Amy did break through the glass ceiling after this interview had been conducted in spite of the all of the negative evaluation she faced. However, it is notable that Amy did need to re-locate over 200 miles away, which, by her own admission was easily achievable because she did not have children or a family. Amy's subor-dinate Karen also comments in her interview on the positive elements of the company's equal opportunities discourse in terms of being a female who wants to break through into senior management in future:

Extract 52

The company have said that they need more females in
higher managerial positions in order to balance things (.)
not just based on gender it's also based on ability as well
but it looks like being female will be an advantage.

Like Amy, Karen stresses the positives of being female, stating that she thinks it will be an 'advantage' in terms of gaining promotion in future. She is also careful to stress that the company is aiming to promote women, not just to redress the balance, but will instead base promotion decisions on merit *and* sex. However, it is important to point out that, whilst such policies have had a positive impact, there are a range of complex social and political reasons why the glass ceiling remains. Just actively seeking to promote more women will not result in an equal bal-ance of women and men at a senior level, though the retail company's attempts should be seen as a step in the right direction. Riley (2002) points to a more fundamental problem with the dominant view of equality in Western societies of it being based on 'merit', the discursive positioning which both Amy and Karen express. Riley argues that this conceptualization of equality is androcentric, and fails to address the dominant ideologies that are so deeply ingrained in social structures which underpin gender inequalities.

Summary

A range of evidence has been presented in this chapter which demon-strates how women can be placed at distinct disadvantage in the profes-sional workplace due to the persistence of gender ideologies and stereotypes and the role they play in maintaining gender inequalities. By examining the broader gendered discourses within the retail and manufacturing companies, the analysis has demonstrated that women managers are judged and evaluated very differently from their male counterparts, particularly as a consequence of the overarching dominance of the discourse of gender difference. This includes the dominant stereotypical view that there are distinct gender differences in the language that women and men use.

McConnell-Ginet (2000) reports very similar findings, and the discriminatory pattern that she describes is clearly evident in both of my case studies:

> The disturbing documented sex differences in workplace achievement still found are differences in how people are judged and evaluated ... both women and men expect different things of women and of men, and these expectations lead them to respond to and evaluate women and men quite differently, often in professional contexts undervaluing women's talents and work and over-valuing men's. This happens in various ways even from people who are sincerely committed to promoting equality. (McConnell-Ginet 2000: 269)

What can be done as a result of this evidence in order to attempt to bring about gender equality in the professional workplace? This issue will be explored in the final chapter.

8
Towards the Future: Breaking the Stereotypes of Gendered Work

The dominance of difference

By conducting this empirical study of gendered discourses in the professional workplace, a range of reasons as to why gender inequalities are still in place have been discovered. The analysis of gendered speech styles in managerial interaction has produced a wealth of evidence of both women and men managers breaking stereotypically gendered expectations with the speech styles they use to perform their identities. It highlights how a range of complex factors affect the manner in which managers perform their identities through the interactional strategies they use. However, a broader examination of gendered discourses through the analysis of attitudes and evaluations of women and men managers has shown how powerful gendered discourses, based on gender stereotypes and maintained by gender ideologies, work to emphasize distinct differences between them. This includes managers' perceptions that women and men communicate in very different ways.

Therefore, despite my empirical interactional findings to the contrary, there is evidence of managers in this study aligning themselves with the dominant, stereotypical view, perpetuated by the overarching discourse of gender difference, that there are distinct gender differences in language use. Indeed, the negative impact of the overarching discourse of gender difference is clear in both companies studied here. Hegemonic discourses of femininity and masculinity play a key part in this, working to position women at a disadvantage at a managerial level by emphasizing gender differences between them and men, with the male figure still being perceived as the managerial workplace norm. Many of these perceived differences between men and women's behaviour are explicitly attributed to innate biological differences, thus according with the highly questionable but nevertheless dominant view within popular culture of the existence of innate, essentialist differences between women and men which make them speak and act differently (Holmes and Meyerhoff 2003). There is evidence of women managers being subject to the double bind in both companies, being negatively evaluated if they use stereotypically masculine speech styles, and vice versa. There is also evidence that women are perceived as less suited for leadership roles as a result of the view of biological essentialism. Women are presented by both women and men managers as being at the mercy of their hormones, displaying emotional and irrational behaviour which is considered less suitable for the public sphere.

The dominant discourses of family and motherhood which maintain that women should take the primary domestic role can also be seen in my data, with women managers expressing concerns that the decision to have children, or the taken-for-granted perception from others that they will want to have children in the future, will hamper their career progression. These discourses do not have any negative impact on men's working lives. If a woman takes a key role in the family, especially by becoming a mother, then she leaves herself open to negative charges that she is not fully committed to her professional role. She may end up on what has been referred to as the *mommy track* instead of on the company's 'official' ladder of career progression (Davidson and Burke 2000).

Hegemonic discourses of femininity which work to disadvantage women include how women are negatively assessed on the grounds of their gendered image, how ideologies of age interact with gender ideologies, working to question women's abilities and effectiveness, and how women are sexualized in the workplace, seen either as passive objects of male pleasure or as devious and manipulative beings who use their sexuality to make gains, at the expense of the genuine skills and abilities of their male counterparts. Such observations directly accord with Lakoff's (2003) viewpoint about the persistence of the double bind in the public sphere in twenty-first-century Western society. She argues that women who have managed to accrue power for themselves are treated in the following manner:

> Powerful women are variously sexualized, objectified, or ridiculed ... objectification, via elaborate discussion of appearance, usually negative, is disempowering ... Being the passive object of the gaze is presupposed for women, never for heterosexual men. (Lakoff 2003: 173)

Despite such pessimism, in both case studies there is also some evidence of resistance in the form of feminist discourses displayed by certain women managers. Equal opportunities discourses are also evident in both companies, including a commitment by the retail company to attempt to recruit more women at senior levels.

However, the findings of the two ethnographic studies indicate that there is still a long way to go before workplace equality will be achieved. Whilst it is important to acknowledge that these findings are from two case studies only, there is a remarkable amount of uniformity between the observable gendered discourses in these two different businesses. Furthermore, these findings also directly accord with the findings from a wide range of recent research that has been conducted within organizational studies and management studies in the United Kingdom, Canada and the United States on the topic of gender inequalities in the professional workplace. Indeed, evidence of the discourse of gender difference and women managers being subject to a double bind can be seen in the work of Olsson and Walker (2003) and Oshagbeni and Gill (2003). The perpetuation of the view of male-as-norm and the 'think manager, think male' stereotype has been found consistently in the work of Olsson (2000), Appelbaum et al. (2002), Powell and Butterfield (2003), Vinnicombe and Singh (2003) and Powell and Graves (2003). Women managers being sexualized in the professional workplace and negatively evaluated or sexually discriminated against has been discovered in the work of Appelbaum et al. (2002) and Olsson and Walker (2003). The dominant discourses of family and motherhood can also be seen through a range of studies, which have highlighted the lack of family-friendly policies and ingrained sexism in terms of the work–home balance as major reasons why gender inequalities in the workplace still exist, particularly when women managers have children (Mavin 2000; Elmuti et al. 2003; Vinnicombe and Singh 2003; Drew and Murtagh 2005).

By going beyond an investigation of interactional strategies and examining these findings as part of broader gendered discourses, the importance of addressing broader social questions surrounding the role of women and men in wider society has been raised. It is clear that it is not just language attitudes but also a range of broader social/political issues that need to be addressed if gender equality is ever to be achieved, further highlighting the importance of taking an interdisciplinary approach. This includes questions of the work–home balance and the sexual division of labour in the home, and changes in social policy on issues including childcare (cf. Franks 1999). These points bring us back to McElhinny's (1997) view, highlighted in Chapter 1, that the dichotomization of the public and the private needs to be resisted. Instead, these spheres should be viewed in conjunction with one another from the perspective of governmental policy in order to bring about social change. If they continue to be viewed as separate worlds, then the manner in which they are inextricably interlinked will continue to be overlooked.

Cameron (2006) argues that, in twenty-first-century Britain, it is a popular conception that the public sphere is equally open to both sexes and that we now live in an age of equal opportunity. However, whilst there are now more women in managerial positions than ever before (EOC 2006), it is crucial to realize that entry into the professions by no means guarantees equal treatment. As Cameron (2006: 4) points out, women have found it difficult to participate in the discourse of public institutions on equal terms once they have made it inside, with both 'prejudice' and 'internalized anxiety' still very much in evidence. A useful terminological notion to consider in reference to women managers here is the 'interloper' (Eckert 1998). Despite the large numbers of women now participating in managerial workplaces, they are still being negatively evaluated for interacting in a social space and enacting social roles that do not traditionally belong to them. The various gendered discourses that have been highlighted in this book can be seen to go some way towards providing explanations as to why the notion of the interloper persists.

It was pointed out in Chapter 1 that once a language and gender study has explored the existence and nature of its chosen political problem it then needs to go beyond this and ask 'what is to be done?' (Cameron 2006: 18), particularly in terms of considering how such findings can be put to practical use in order to attempt to bring about social change. I will now consider how the findings of my study can be put to practical, applied use in order to attempt to contribute towards redressing the problem of gender equality in the professional workplace. This includes a consideration of how these findings were reported back to those communities who took part in the research.

Moving forward: Challenging gendered discourses

In light of the evidence that has been produced in this study, it is clear that the dominance of a whole range of hegemonic gendered discourses needs to be broken if the workplace is ever to become a more egalitarian environment in which women will achieve equality, including equal numbers of women advancing through the glass ceiling into the higher ranks of management. On the basis of these findings, a key principle that can be of applied practical relevance is the aim of raising awareness of the gender stereotypes that managers hold, and present evidence which challenges these gender stereotypes. This was one of the key aims when reporting back to the companies that took part in the research, as part of the agreed research aim to investigate the persistence of the glass ceiling. However, as also pointed out in Chapter 1, this study and its recommendations go beyond the interests of just the two companies, in order to fulfil broader academic and political aims and objectives. These recommendations as to what can be done as a result of my findings therefore have a much wider applicability in addition to their immediate relevance to the companies and managers who took part.

Even when using the same behaviour, men and women evaluate each other very differently. In particular regard to the stereotypes that uphold the views of distinct differences in language use, including the persistence of the essentialist view of males and females being biologically predetermined to use particular communicative styles, the empirical meeting data can be used as practical evidence to highlight that in reality these preconceptions of gender and language use are not accurate. Managers instead draw upon on a whole range of specific factors related to their role, their fellow interlocutors and the features that are specific to the particular context and team within which they are interacting. Interactants do not automatically produce speech patterns because they are men or women. Instead, a whole range of complex issues affects the manner in which interlocutors engage in the sophisticated process of interacting with one another. Another important aim to achieve when giving feedback was to dispel the myth of the popular culture, self-help books that reify differences and result in reinforcing existing power relations, including those directly referred to by interviewees in the retail company, Pease and Pease's (1999) management communication book, and John Gray's *Mars and Venus* series.

It is the intention that this awareness-raising will go some way towards fulfilling Holmes and Stubbe's (2003a: 595) aim for sociolinguistic language and gender research in the workplace, that it is the researcher's job to challenge 'generalizations which constitute the inevitable stereotypes that develop in a community'. Researchers should then give 'detailed evidence to unravel and complexify the stereotypes themselves, moving a stereotype in the direction of a more accurate "social type"', and overall, fulfil our ultimate responsibility as sociolinguists: to show what people are achieving through discourse, using analytical approaches, such as the CofP framework, which enable us to 'capture more satisfactorily the complexities of meaning negotiated through discourse in workplace interaction' (2003a: 595). To clarify the distinction between a *stereotype* and a *social type*, Holmes and Stubbe make reference to Talbot's (2003) work. Talbot (2003) draws on Hall (1997) and defines *social typing* as a process we all engage in order to sense-make. This includes the need to impose classification systems, including systems that we draw upon in order to classify individuals. In specific relation to individuals, Talbot (2003: 470–471) points out that 'we *type* people according to the complexes of classificatory schemes in our culture, in terms of the social positions they inhabit, their group membership, personality traits and so on'. *Stereotyping* contrasts with social typing as stereotyping 'reduces, essentializes, naturalizes and fixes "difference" ... facilitates the "binding" or bonding together of all of Us who are "normal" into one "imagined community"; and it sends into symbolic exile all of Them' (Hall 1997: 258, cited in Talbot 2003: 471).

Therefore, in order to move from stereotyping to social typing, academic research should aim to highlight the negatives of stereotyping, demonstrating how it essentializes, reduces and simplifies, with the intention of encouraging people to think in social types without the negative reduction. This is a rather tall order, and in order to bring this about successfully, a good deal of social and political change in terms of the wider hegemonic power structures is required. However, if gender ideologies can be changed to ones where 'more positive experiences for women' are offered and encouraged, then this is a step in the right direction (Philips 2003: 272). Indeed, there is cause for optimism.

When Lakoff (2003: 177) concludes her consideration of the positioning of women in power in public spheres, she expresses the rather positive belief that 'change is coming'. She observes that, if we look back 30 years, the social and political changes that have taken place since would then have been thought unimaginable, and thus is cause for much optimism. Similarly, changes in gender practice that have occurred as a consequence of feminism lead Eckert and McConnell Ginet (2003: 51) to posit that 'life and daily living are about to change' by pushing upon the space that exists 'by the incomplete hold of ideologies and institutions'. Therefore, it is important to remember that as dominant gendered discourses are maintained by hegemony, by agitating for political change these commonsensical assumptions can be challenged and changed so that the experiences of women in the workplace and in general are improved.

One way of raising awareness that the expectations and norms of gendered behaviour are just stereotypes which *prescribe* appropriate gendered behaviour and are not biologically determined programmes for how men and women behave, is to demonstrate that current stereotypes are just one version of what is currently deemed to be 'appropriate' behaviour, the version which has come to be naturalized as part of society's dominant hegemonic masculinist discourses. Indeed, Talbot (2003: 478) argues that producing evidence which challenges stereotypes works to undermine the 'naturalization of gender categories and destabilize the link between them and particular attributes of behaviour'. Therefore, whilst gender stereotypes for appropriate and acceptable behaviour appear to be natural to managers, and are justified on the basis of this naturalness, it is important to point out to them that in reality they have come to be seen as naturalized due to the dominance of a particular political perspective, and have thus come to be accepted as commonsensical norms.

Coming back to the self-help material, it is vitally important to begin to change perceptions towards this material as soon as possible. The publications and programmes that have been designed so far are based upon the outdated dominance and difference frameworks, which work only to reinforce and reify stereotypes of gendered behaviour. When providing feedback to both companies, the flaws with the self-help literature that abound in wider society were pointed out by drawing on evidence of communication in their own workplaces which disproves the assumptions found in these books, video materials and courses. To illustrate this further, it is useful to reproduce a typical extract from a handout from one of these gender awareness classes for improving workplace communication, cited in Mullany and Litosseliti (2006: 144):

WOMEN say 'we' more, play down achievements, downplay certainty, ask more questions, use ritual apologies and ritual compliments, soften feedback, nod to indicate listening. MEN say 'I' more, talk up achievements, minimize doubts, want answers, avoid apologies, give to-the-point feedback, use bantering, nod to indicate agreement.

These listings of men's and women's styles can be seriously questioned by drawing upon the empirical evidence of meeting data produced in Chapters 5 and 6, where there are numerous examples of women and men producing speech styles that are said to be associated with the other gender, and vice versa.

Furthermore, the assertiveness training (AT) movement, another form of self-help for women in the workplace, can also be rejected for drawing on the view that stereotypically masculine speech styles of dominance and assertiveness are the norm for communication in the workplace (Cameron 1995). Despite suggestions put forward in Chapter 2 which indicated that stereotypes of effective communication in the workplace appeared to be changing towards more stereotypically feminine models of communication, the assertiveness training movement for women in businesses is still burgeoning (for example, see http://www.amanet. org/seminars, http://www.cmctraining.org/ and http://www.ivillage. co.uk/workcareer/survive/). As with the other self-help materials, the assertiveness training movement is based upon the outdated deficit, power/dominance or culture/difference approaches to language and gender, in conjunction with naïve conceptualizations of language, based on little/no linguistic knowledge of the complexities involved when participants engage in interaction. Instead, much assertiveness training material simply comes up with terribly simplistic prescriptions such as 'be direct' (see Cameron 1995). If the evidence presented in my two case studies is anything to go by, stereotypically masculine speech styles are not dominant, and both women and men communicate in much more sophisticated ways, in reaction to the specific settings they are in, drawing upon a range of both stereotypically masculine and stereotypically feminine interactional styles. Therefore, instead of helping women, the AT movement works to do nothing more than reify the difference between men's and women's speech. It promotes the stereotypical assumption that the speech norms stereotypically associated with femininity are inappropriate for public discourse, thus maintaining the inaccurate view that workplace norms are masculine norms. Ten years ago, Coates (1997) made the following comment on the subject of assertiveness training which is still applicable today. It also applies to the field of self-help tools more generally, predominantly aimed at and purchased by women:

The rhetoric that women need some kind of training perpetuates the idea that it is women who don't fit in the public sphere and therefore women who have to change. (Coates 1997: 289)

In addition to changing people's attitudes towards self-help material, and providing evidence that dominant stereotypes about language use are inaccurate, I also presented both businesses with details of the dominant gendered discourses I found within their organizations. In order to avoid using obfuscating language, I dropped any reference to 'discourses' or 'hegemony' and instead presented these as 'themes' which had co-occurred during my investigations. The feedback I gave to both businesses demonstrated how managers had highlighted the following themes which indicated potential problems and tensions in terms of gender in the workplace: women as emotional and irrational, family and motherhood, feminine image and sexuality and the theme of 'think manager, think male'.

By naming these 'themes' and bringing them to the direct attention of managers, it was the intention that they could be brought to the fore and become topics of discussion within the companies themselves, with the ultimate aim of encouraging the managers to be aware of and consider ways of attempting to redress such problems. This is similar to the approach that Baxter (2003) took when naming the discourses she identified with the managers in her study. Again, she did not use academic terminology but instead changed her dominant discourses into what she terms 'colloquial sound bites' (2003: 193). In drawing managers' attention to these discourses through the rhetoric of 'themes' my intention was to highlight the omnirelevance of gender, and show how even with equal opportunities policies in place, there are a whole range of problems and issues relating to gender which may be leading to disadvantage. Obviously some of these issues are broader, societal problems, which go way beyond the scope of the individual businesses themselves. However, it is still important to raise awareness of these issues in order to highlight that these broader social and political problems exist.

Giving feedback which contained the above points to the manufacturing company in the form of a written report, their chosen method of results dissemination, went smoothly. However, this was more problematic with the retail company. The personnel director who had initially granted me access to the retail company told me in the first private conversation I had with him during my first week of fieldwork that I should not produce a report that would 'rock the boat', as the company was quite happy with its equal opportunities policies and the manner in which gender was viewed within the organization. This is one of the problems associated with the complex relationship of negotiation between the researcher and researched (see Mullany 2008 for further discussion).

Another problem with both companies was with the length of time it takes to produce a linguistic transcription. As Myers (2005: 540) points out 'academic timescales are radically different from those of non-academics'. Often managers would want 'hot' feedback (Sarangi and Candlin 2003: 277), immediately after a meeting had taken place, or immediately after shadowing had finished. The delay in giving feedback appeared to affect the level of interest in the project in the fast-moving world of business. Nevertheless, the findings in both companies were received with much interest. Within the retail company, I felt obliged to produce a report that didn't 'rock the boat'. However, I did include details of the aforementioned language stereotypes versus realities of usage, the 'themes' on the topic of gender and the critique of the self-help literature. However, in order not to 'rock the boat', I used very careful rhetoric throughout the report. I presented the findings very much as problems within wider society that needed to change, and agreed at various points with the personnel director's opinion that the company had very positive equal opportunities policies in place.

It is difficult to know what impact my findings had overall on these two businesses, and whether any changes came about as a result of my reports. As Mullany and Litosseliti (2006) point out, 'it is not easy to see (and much less to control) which components of academic research are taken on board in organizations, and which research findings are used to shape their policies and practices'. One potential way around this would be to engage with companies in an official 'consultancy' or 'consultative role'. Sarangi (2006: 201) emphasizes the difference between these two approaches, arguing that the former is where the researcher is viewed as 'an expert trouble shooter', whereas the latter is a 'collaborative exploration of professional practice' with practitioners. However, such approaches come with their own range of ethical and practical problems (see Roberts and Sarangi 2003; Sarangi 2006).

Towards an integrated interdisciplinary approach

Overall, this study has emphasized that traditional sociolinguistic approaches which focus on the analysis of interactional speech styles in particular social contexts do not take us far enough. As McConnell-Ginet (2000) points out, producing linguistic analyses and raising awareness of language use in the workplace by language and gender scholars will not result in a change of the positioning of women. The linguistic strategies that managers use when interacting in workplaces are just one component of what is a very complex picture of the enactment of gender relations in formal, institutionalized settings.

The broader analysis of gendered discourses that has taken place in this study, within which a sociolinguistic analysis of stereotypically gendered speech styles is embedded, has raised a range of complex social and political issues (of which language use and language ideologies are just one part) suggesting reasons why the glass ceiling persists, and why gender inequalities in general remain in existence.

By conducting this centralist interdisciplinary study, it is the overall intention that the benefits of broadening research horizons by looking outside of the sub-discipline of sociolinguistics and the discipline of linguistics more generally has been emphasized as a starting point. The problem of gender inequality in the professional workplace, and indeed in workplaces as a whole, is a complex and multifaceted one. The analysis of gendered discourses in this study has pointed to a whole range of social and political changes that need to be brought about before larger numbers of women are able to break through the glass ceiling and thus equalize the balance of women and men in the higher echelons of power.

However, this study firmly indicates that there is a real need for more collective political action if significant social change is to be brought about. I firmly agree with McConnell-Ginet (2000: 259) that 'collective action' is required in order to trigger 'the systemic social changes that are needed' for workplace gender equality to be achieved. This call for collective action firmly enhances the case for moving towards integrated interdisciplinary research in order for the problems of gender inequalities in the workplace to be properly explored, evaluated and resolved.

For instance, in future studies, research teams consisting of analysts from a range of different academic backgrounds, including workplace practitioners, could be created with the common aim of investigating gender inequalities in professional workplaces. This will enable expertise to be combined in order to tackle the problem of inequalities from a range of different perspectives. Then perhaps one day, gender equality in the professional workplace may be finally achieved with the help of academic research.

Appendix

Data summaries

Summary of CofP members: The retail company meetings

No.	Name	Sex	Age	CofP
1	Steve	M	37	Technical Department
2	Sue	F	36	"
3	Mike	M	36	"
4	Matt	M	35	"
5	Amy	F	37	Product Department and Sales Group
6	Karen	F	29	Product Department and Sales Group
7	Mary	F	32	Product Department
8	Kirsty	F	29	"
9	Tony	M	29	"
10	Eddie	M	30	"
11	Kelly	F	30	Sales Group
12	Janet	F	32	"
13	Sara	F	34	"
14	Sybil	F	31	"
15	Gary	M	36	"
16	Jack	M	35	"
17	Billy	M	35	"
18	James	M	35	"
19	Paul	M	32	"

Summary of CofP members: The manufacturing company meetings

No.	Name	Sex	Age	CofP
1	Carrie	F	42	Services Department
2	Jill	F	40	"
3	Jane	F	30	Services Department and Product Review Team
4	Jackie	F	36	Services Department
5	Phyllis	F	30	"
6	Joan	F	38	"
7	Jim	M	41	"
8	Phil	M	36	"
9	Robert	M	34	"
10	Doug	M	37	"
11	Arthur	M	42	"
12	Rob	M	42	Product Review Team
13	David	M	42	Product Review Team and Business Control Team
14	Keith	M	31	"
15	Carl	M	36	"
16	Craig	M	41	"
17	John	M	36	"
18	Sharon	F	32	Product Review Team and Business Control Team
19	Kim	F	33	Product Review Team
20	Julie	F	34	Product Review Team and Business Control Team
21	Mark	M	35	Business Control Team
22	Martin	M	42	"
23	Pam	F	41	"
24	Carol	F	40	"
25	Becky	F	32	"
26	Kate	F	31	"
27	Simon	M	42	"

Interview data summary: The retail company

No.	Name	Sex	Age	Managerial level	Department	Meeting attendance
1	Amy	F	37	Upper-middle	Product	Product, Sales
2	Kelly	F	30	Upper-middle	Building	–
3	Peter	M	38	Upper-middle	Systems	–
4	Simon	M	36	Upper-middle	Business	–
5	Sue	F	37	Middle	Technical	Technical
6	Christine	F	30	Middle	Logistics	–
7	Janice	F	34	Middle	Systems	–
8	Karen	F	29	Middle	Product	Product, Sales
9	Jenny	F	24	Lower-middle	Systems	–
10	Lucy	F	25	Lower-middle	Building	–

Interview data summary: The manufacturing company

No.	Name	Sex	Age	Managerial level	Department	Meeting attendance
1	Carrie	F	42	Director	Services	Services
2	Judy	F	44	Director	Logistics	–
3	Becky	F	32	Middle	Sales	Business
4	Carol	F	40	Middle	Services	Business
5	Jane	F	30	Middle	Services	Services, Product
6	Kate	F	31	Middle	Sales	Business
7	Kim	F	33	Middle	Marketing	Product
8	Pam	F	41	Middle	Retail	Business
9	Sharon	F	32	Middle	Marketing	Product, Business
10	David	M	42	Middle	Marketing	Product, Business
11	Martin	M	42	Middle	Sales	Business
12	Julie	F	34	Lower-Middle	Purchasing	Product, Business
13	Susan	F	42	Lower-Middle	Logistics	–

References

Adler, N. (2003) Preface. In G. Powell and L. Graves. *Women and Men in Management*. Third Edition. Oxford: Blackwell, pp. i–x.

Alvesson, M. and Y. Billing. (1997) *Gender, Work and Organization*. London: Sage.

Alvesson, M. and S. Deetz. (2000) *Doing Critical Management Research*. London: Sage.

Appelbaum, S., L. Audet and J. Miller. (2002) Gender and leadership? Leadership and gender? A journey through the landscape of theories. *Leadership and Organization Development* 24(1): 43–51.

Ashcraft, K. and D. Mumby. (2004) Organizing a critical communicology of gender and work. *International Journal of the Sociology of Language* 166: 19–43.

Austin, P. (1990) Politeness revisited: the dark side. In A. Bell and J. Holmes (eds), *New Zealand Ways of Speaking English*. Clevedon Avon: Multilingual Matters, pp. 277–293.

Bargiela-Chiappini, F. and S. Harris. (1997) *Managing Language: The Discourse of Corporate Meetings*. Amsterdam: Benjamins.

Baron, B. and H. Kotthoff. (2001) *Gender in Interaction: Perspectives on Femininity and Masculinity in Ethnography and Discourse*. Amsterdam: Benjamins.

Baxter, J. (2003) *Positioning Gender in Discourse: A Feminist Methodology*. Basingstoke: Palgrave.

——. (2006a) (ed.) *Speaking Out: The Female Voice in Public Contexts*. Basingstoke: Palgrave.

——. (2006b) Introduction. In J. Baxter (ed.), *Speaking Out: The Female Voice in Public Contexts*, Basingstoke: Palgrave, pp. xiii–xviii.

——. (forthcoming) *The Language of Leadership*. Basingstoke: Palgrave.

Bem, S. (1993) *The Lenses of Gender*. New Haven, CT: Yale University Press.

Bergvall, V. (1999) Towards a comprehensive theory of language and gender. *Language in Society* 28(2): 273–93.

Bergvall, V., J. Bing and A. Freed. (1996) (eds), *Rethinking Language and Gender Research: Theory and Practice*. New York: Longman.

Billig, M. (2000) Towards a critique of the critical. *Discourse and Society* 11(3): 291–292.

Bing, J. and V. Bergvall. (1996) The question of questions: Beyond binary thinking. In V. Bergvall, J. Bing and A. Freed (1996) (eds), *Rethinking Language and Gender Research: Theory and Practice*. New York: Longman, pp. 1–30.

Boden, D. (1994) *The Business of Talk: Organizations in Action*. Cambridge: Polity Press.

Boxer, D. (2002) *Applying Sociolinguistics: Domains and Face-to-Face Interaction*. Amsterdam: Benjamins.

Brewis, J. (2001) Telling it like it is? Gender, language and organizational theory. In R. Westwood and S. Linstead (eds), *The Language of Organization*. London: Sage, pp. 283–309.

Brown, P. (1980) How and why are women are more polite: Some evidence from a Mayan community. In S. McConnell-Ginet, R. Borker and N. Furman (eds), *Women and Language and Literature in Society*. New York: Praeger, pp. 111–136.

Brown, P. and S. Levinson. (1978) Universals in language usage: Politeness phenomena. In E. Goody (ed.), *Questions and Politeness: Strategies in Social Interaction*. Cambridge: Cambridge University Press, pp. 56–311.

——. (1987) *Politeness: Some Universals in Language Use*. Cambridge: Cambridge University Press.

Bucholtz, M. (1999a) "Why be normal?": Language and identity practices in a community of nerd girls. *Language in Society* 28(2): 203–223.

——. (1999b) Bad examples: Transgression and progress in language and gender studies. In M. Bucholtz, A. Liang and L. Sutton (eds) (1999) *Reinventing Identities: The Gendered Self in Discourse*. Oxford: Oxford University Press, pp. 3–24.

——. (2001) Reflexivity and critique in discourse analysis. *Critique of Anthropology* 21(2): 165–183.

Bucholtz, M. and K. Hall. (1995) Introduction: Twenty years after *Language and Woman's Place*. In K. Hall and M. Bucholtz (eds), *Gender Articulated: Language and the Socially Constructed Self*. London: Routledge, pp. 1–23.

Bucholtz, M., A. Liang and L. Sutton. (eds) (1999) *Reinventing Identities: The Gendered Self in Discourse*. Oxford: Oxford University Press.

Burke, R. and S. Vinnicombe. (2005) Supporting women's career advancement. *Women in Management Review* 21(1): 1–3.

Butler, J. (1990) *Gender Trouble: Feminism and the Subversion of Identity*. New York: Routledge.

——. (1993) *Bodies that Matter: On the Discursive Limits of Sex*. New York: Routledge.

——. (1999) *Gender Trouble: Feminism and the Subversion of Identity*. Second Edition. New York: Routledge.

Cameron, D. (1992) *Feminism and Linguistic Theory*. Second Edition. Basingstoke: Macmillan.

——. (1995) *Verbal Hygiene*. London: Routledge.

——. (1996) The language-gender interface: Challenging co-optation. In V. Bergvall, J. Bing and A. Freed (eds), *Rethinking Language and Gender Research: Theory and Practice*. New York: Longman, pp. 31–53.

——. (1997a) Theoretical debates in feminist linguistics: questions of sex and gender. In R. Wodak (ed.) *Gender and Discourse*. London: Sage, pp. 21–36.

——. (1997b) Performing gender identity: Young men's talk and the construction of heterosexual masculinity. In S. Johnson and U. H. Meinhof (eds), *Language and Masculinity*. Oxford: Blackwell, pp. 47–64.

——. (2000) *Good to Talk: Living and Working in a Communication Culture*. London: Sage.

——. (2003) Gender and language ideologies. In J. Holmes and M. Meyerhoff (eds), *The Handbook of Language and Gender*. Oxford: Blackwell, pp. 447–467.

——. (2006) Theorising the female voice in public contexts. In J. Baxter (ed.) *Speaking Out: The Female Voice in Public Contexts*. Basingstoke: Palgrave, pp. 3–20.

Cameron, D., E. Frazer, P. Harvey, B. Rampton and K. Richardson. (1992) *Researching Language: Issues of Power and Method*. London: Routledge.

Candlin, C. N. (2000) General editor's preface. In J. Coupland (ed.) *Small Talk*. Harlow: Pearson, pp. xiii–xx.

Case, S. S. (1988) Cultural differences not deficiencies: an analysis of managerial 'women's language'. In L. Larwood and S. Rose (eds), *Women's Careers: Pathways and Pitfalls*. New York: Praeger, pp. 41–63.

Case, S. S. (1995) Gender, language and the professions: Recognition of wide-verbal-repertoire speech. *Studies in the Linguistic Sciences* 25(2): 149–192.

Cheshire, J. (1982) *Variation in an English Dialect: A Sociolinguistic Study.* Cambridge: Cambridge University Press.

——. (2002) Sex and gender in variationist research. In J. K. Chambers, P. Trudgill and N. Schilling-Estes (eds), *The Handbook of Language Variation and Change.* Oxford: Blackwell, pp. 423–443.

Christie, C. (2000) *Gender and Language: Towards a Feminist Pragmatics.* Edinburgh: Edinburgh University Press.

Coates, J. (1988) Gossip revisited: Language in all-female groups. In J. Coates and D. Cameron (eds), *Women in their Speech Communities.* London: Longman, pp. 92–121.

——. (1995) Language, gender and career. In S. Mills (ed.), *Language and Gender: Interdisciplinary Perspectives.* London: Longman, pp. 13–30.

——. (1996) *Women Talk.* Oxford: Blackwell.

——. (1997) Competing discourses of femininity. In H. Kotthoff and R. Wodak (eds), *Communicating Gender in Context.* Amsterdam: Benjamins, pp. 285–313.

——. (1999) Changing femininities: The talk of teenage girls. In M. Bucholtz, A. Liang and L. A. Sutton (eds), *Reinventing Identities: The Gendered Self in Discourse.* Oxford: Oxford University Press, pp. 123–144.

——. (2003) *Men Talk.* Oxford: Blackwell.

——. (2004) *Women, Men and Language.* Third Edition. Harlow: Pearson.

——. (2007) Gender. In C. Llamas, L. Mullany and P. Stockwell (eds), *The Routledge Companion to Sociolinguistics.* Abingdon: Routledge, pp. 62–68.

Coates, J. and D. Cameron. (eds) (1988) *Women in their Speech Communities.* London: Longman.

Coates, J. and M. E. Jordan. (1997) Que(e)rying friendship: Discourses of resistance and the construction of gendered subjectivity. In A. Livia and K. Hall (eds), *Queerly Phrased: Language, Gender and Sexuality.* Oxford: Oxford University Press, pp. 214–232.

Cockburn, C. (1991) *In The Way of Women.* London: Macmillan.

Coupland, J. (2000) Introduction: Sociolinguistic perspectives on small talk. In J. Coupland (ed.), *Small Talk.* Harlow: Pearson, pp. 1–25.

Coupland, J., N. Coupland and J. Robinson (1992) 'How are you?' Negotiating in phatic communion. *Language in Society* 21 (2): 207–230.

Coupland, N., S. Sarangi and C. N. Candlin. (2001) Editor's preface. In N. Coupland, S. Sarangi and C. N. Candlin (eds), *Sociolinguistics and Social Theory.* Harlow: Pearson pp. xiii–xv.

Crawford, M. (1995) *Talking Difference: On Gender and Language.* London: Sage.

——. (1997) Review of Holmes's 'Women, Men and Politeness'. *Language in Society* 26 (3): 426–429.

Culpeper, J. (1996) Towards an anatomy of impoliteness. *Journal of Pragmatics* 25: 349–367.

——. (2005) Impoliteness and entertainment in the television quiz show: The Weakest Link. *Journal of Politeness Research: Language, Behaviour, Culture* 1 (1): 35–72.

Davidson, M. and R. Burke. (eds) (2000) *Women in Management: Current Research Issues Volume II.* London: Paul Chapman.

Deetz, S. (1992) *Democracy in the Age of Corporate Colonization: Developments in Communication and the Politics of Everyday Life.* Albany NY: State University of New York Press.

Drew, E. and E. Murtagh. (2005) Work/life balance: senior management champions or laggards? *Women in Management Review* 20(4): 262–278.

Duranti, A. (1997) *Linguistic Anthropology*. Cambridge: Cambridge University Press.

Eakins, B. and R. Eakins. (1979) Verbal turn-taking and exchanges in faculty dialogue. In B-L. Dubois and I. Crouch (eds), *The Sociology of the Language of American Women*. San Antonio, TX: Trinity University, pp. 53–62.

Eckert, P. (1989) *Jocks and Burnouts: Social Categories and Identity in the High School*. New York: Teachers College Press.

——. (1997) Age as a sociolinguistic variable. In F. Coulmas (ed.), *The Handbook of Sociolinguistics*. Oxford: Blackwell, pp. 151–167.

——. (1998) Gender and sociolinguistic variation. In J. Coates (ed.) *Language and Gender: A Reader*. Oxford: Blackwell, pp. 64–75.

——. (2000) *Linguistic Variation as Social Practice*. Oxford: Blackwell.

——. (2003) Language and gender in adolescence. In J. Holmes and M. Meyerhoff (eds), *The Handbook of Language and Gender*. Oxford: Blackwell, pp. 381–400.

Eckert, P. and S. McConnell-Ginet. (1992a) Communities of practice: Where language, gender and power all live. In K. Hall, M. Bucholtz and B. Moonwomon (eds), *Locating Power: Proceedings of the Second Berkeley Women and Language Conference*. Berkeley CA: Berkeley Women and Language Group, pp. 89–99.

——. (1992b) Think practically and look locally: Language and gender as community-based practice. *Annual Review of Anthropology* 21: 461–490.

——. (1999) New generalizations and explanations in language and gender research. *Language in Society* 28(2): 185–201.

——. (2003) *Language and Gender*. Cambridge: Cambridge University Press.

Edelsky, C. (1981) Who's got the floor? *Language in Society* 10: 383–421.

Eelen, G. (2001) *A Critique of Politeness Theories*. Manchester: St. Jerome.

Ehrlich, S. (2003) Coercing gender: Language in sexual assault adjudication processes. In J. Holmes and M. Meyerhoff (eds), *The Handbook of Language and Gender*. Oxford: Blackwell, pp. 645–670.

Elmuti, D., J. Lehman, B. Harmon, X. Lu, A. Pape, R. Zhang and T. Zimmerie (2003) Inequality between genders in the executive suite in corporate America: Moral and ethical issues. *Equal Opportunities International* 22(8): 1–19.

Equal Opportunities Commission (2006) *Sex and Power Index*. London: Equal Opportunities Commission UK.

Fairclough, N. (1989) *Language and Power*. New York: Longman.

——. (1992) *Discourse and Social Change*. Cambridge: Polity Press.

——. (1995) *Critical Discourse Analysis: The Critical Study of Language*. New York: Longman.

——. (2001) *Language and Power*. Second Edition, New York: Longman.

——. (2003) *Analysing Discourse*. London: Routledge.

Fishman, P. (1978) Interaction: The work women do. *Social Problems* 25(4): 397–406.

Fitzsimons, A. (2002) *Gender as a Verb: Gender Segregation at Work*. Aldershot: Ashgate.

Fletcher, J. (1999) *Disappearing Acts: Gender, Power and Relational Practice at Work*. Cambridge MA: MIT Press.

Foucault, M. (1972) *The Archaeology of Knowledge*. London: Routledge.

——. (1978) *The History of Sexuality: An Introduction: Volume I*. New York: Random House.

——. (1979) *Discipline and Punish*. Harmondsworth: Penguin.

224   *References*

Foucault, M. (1981) The order of discourse. In R. Young (ed.), *Untying the Text: A Post Structuralist Reader*. Boston: Routledge and Kegan Paul, pp. 48–78.

Franks, S. (1999) *Having None of It: Women, Men and the Future of Work*. London: Granta.

Freed, A. (1996) Language and gender in an experimental setting. In V. Bergvall, J. Bing and A. Freed (eds), *Rethinking Language and Gender Research: Theory and Practice*. New York: Longman, pp. 54–76.

——. (2003) Epilogue: Reflections on language and gender research. In J. Holmes and M. Meyerhoff (eds), *The Handbook of Language and Gender*. Oxford: Blackwell, pp. 699–721.

Gal, S. (1979) *Language Shifts*. New York: Academic Press.

——. (1991) Between speech and silence: The problematics of research on language and gender. In M. di Leonardo (ed.), *Gender at the Crossroads of Knowledge: Feminist Anthropology in the Postmodern Era*. Berkeley, CA: University of California Press, pp. 175–203.

——. (1995) Language and gender: An anthropological review. In K. Hall and M. Bucholtz (eds), *Gender Articulated: Language and the Socially Constructed Self*. London: Routledge, pp. 169–182.

Gee, J., G. Hull and C. Lankshear. (1996) *The New Work Order*. London: Allen and Urwin.

Geertz, C. (1973) *The Interpretation of Cultures*. New York: Basic Books.

Gherardi, S. (1996) Gendered organizational cultures: Narratives of women travellers in a male world. *Gender, Work and Organization* 3(4): 187–201.

Goffman, E. (1967) *Interaction Ritual*. New York: Anchor Books.

Goodwin, M. H. (1980) Directive-response speech sequences in girls' and boys' activities. In S. McConnell-Ginet, R. Borker and N. Furman (eds), *Women and Language and Literature in Society*. New York: Praeger, pp. 157–173.

Graddol, D. and J. Swann. (1989) *Gender Voices*. Oxford: Blackwell.

Gramsci, A. (1971) *Selections from the Prison Notebooks* (trans. Q. Hoare and G. Nowell-Smith), New York: Lawrence and Wishart.

Grant, D., T. Keenoy and C. Oswick. (1998) Introduction. Organizational discourse: Of diversity, dichotomy and multi-disciplinarity. In D. Grant, T. Keenoy and C. Oswick (eds), *Discourse and Organization*. London: Sage, pp. 1–17.

Gray, J. (2002) *Mars and Venus in the Workplace*. New York: HarperCollins.

Green, J. and D. Bloome. (1995) Ethnography and ethnographers of and in education: A situated perspective? In F. Flood, S. Heath, D. Alvermann and D. Lapp (eds), *A Handbook for Literary Educators*. New York: Macmillan.

Grice, P. (1975) Logic and conversation. In P. Cole and J. L. Morgan (eds), *Syntax and Semantics 3: Speech Acts*. New York: Academic Press, pp. 41–58.

Gumperz, J. (1974) Linguistic anthropology in society. *American Anthropologist* 76: 785–798.

——. (1982) *Discourse Strategies*. Cambridge: Cambridge University Press.

Gunnarsson, B-L., P. Linell and B. Nordberg. (1997) Introduction. In B-L. Gunnarsson, P. Linell and B. Nordberg (eds), *The Construction of Professional Discourse*. London: Longman, pp. 1–12.

Halford, S. and P. Leonard. (2001) *Gender, Power and Organisations: An Introduction*. Basingstoke: Palgrave.

Hall, S. (1997) The spectacle of 'other'. In S. Hall (ed.), *Representation: Cultural Representations and Signifying Practice*. London: Sage, pp. 223–290.

Hammersley, M. and P. Atkinson. (1995) *Ethnography: Principles in Practice*. Second Edition. London: Routledge.

Harris, S. (2001) Being politically impolite: Extending politeness theory to adversarial political discourse. *Discourse and Society* 12: 451–472.

Hearn, J. and W. Parkin. (1988) Women, men, and leadership: A critical review of assumptions, practices, and change in the industrialized nations. In N. Adler and D. Izraeli (eds), *Women in Management Worldwide*. London: M.E. Sharpe, pp. 17–40.

Heller, M. (2001) Critique and sociolinguistic analysis of discourse. *Critique of Anthropology* 21(2): 117–141.

Hennessy, R. (1993) *Materialist Feminism and the Politics of Discourse*. New York: Routledge.

Hester, S. and D. Francis. (1994) Doing data: the local organization of a sociological interview. *British Journal of Sociology* 45(4): 675–696.

Holmes, J. (1995) *Women, Men and Politeness*. New York: Longman.

———. (2000a) Women at work: Analysing women's talk in New Zealand. *Australian Review of Applied Linguistics* 22(2): 1–17.

———. (2000b) Politeness, power and provocation: How humour functions in the workplace. *Discourse Studies* 2(2): 159–185.

———. (2000c) Victoria University of Wellington's Language in the Workplace Project: An overview. *Language in the Workplace Occasional Papers* 1: 1–18.

———. (2000d) Doing collegiality and keeping control at work: Small talk in government departments. In Justine Coupland (ed.), *Small Talk*. Harlow: Pearson, pp. 32–61.

———. (2003a) Women's talk at the top. *Boardroom: The Journal of the Institute of Directors* May 2003: 1–2.

———. (2003b) How top women talk. *Paanui*. Ministry of Women's Affairs. June 2003: 6–7.

———. (2005) Power and discourse at work: Is gender relevant? In M. Lazar (ed.), *Feminist Critical Discourse Analysis*. Palgrave, pp. 31–60.

———. (2006a) *Gendered Talk at Work*. Oxford: Blackwell.

———. (2006b). Sharing a laugh: Pragmatic aspects of humour and gender in the workplace. *Journal of Pragmatics* 38(1): 26–50.

Holmes, J. and M. Marra. (2002) Over the edge: Subversive humour between colleagues and friends. *Humor* 15(1): 1–23.

———. (2004) Relational practice in the workplace: Women's talk or gendered discourse? *Language in Society* 33: 377–398.

Holmes, J., M. Marra and L. Burns. (2001) Women's humour in the workplace: A quantitative analysis. *Australian Journal of Communication* 28(1): 83–108.

Holmes, J. and M. Meyerhoff. (1999) The community of practice: Theories and methodologies in language and gender research. *Language in Society* 28(2): 173–183.

———. (2003) Different voices, different views: An introduction to current research in language and gender. In J. Holmes and M. Meyerhoff (eds) *The Handbook of Language and Gender*. Oxford: Blackwell, pp. 1–17.

Holmes, J. and S. Schnurr (2005) Politeness, humor and gender in the workplace: Negotiating norms and identifying contestation. *Journal of Politeness Research: Language, Behaviour, Culture* 1(1): 121–149.

Holmes, J. and M. Stubbe. (2003a) 'Feminine' workplaces: Stereotype and reality. In J. Holmes and M. Meyerhoff (eds), *The Handbook of Language and Gender*. Oxford: Blackwell, pp. 573–599.

——. (2003b) *Power and Politeness in the Workplace: A Sociolinguistic Analysis of Talk at Work*. Harlow: Pearson.

Holmes, J., M. Stubbe and B. Vine. (1999) Constructing professional identity: 'Doing power' in policy units. In S. Sarangi and C. Roberts (eds), *Talk, Work and Institutional Power: Discourse in Medical, Mediation and Management Settings*. Berlin: Mouton de Gruyter, pp. 351–385.

Holstein, J. and J. Gubrium. (1995) *The Active Interview*. London: Sage.

Hymes, D. (1974) *Foundations of Sociolinguistics: An Ethnographic Approach*. Philadelphia: University of Pennsylvania Press.

Johnson, S. (1997) Theorizing language and masculinity: A feminist perspective. In S. Johnson and U. H. Meinhof (eds), *Language and Masculinity*. Oxford: Blackwell, pp. 47–64.

Johnson, S. and U. H. Meinhof (eds) (1997) *Language and Masculinity*. Oxford: Blackwell.

Jones, D. (2000) Gender trouble in the workplace: 'Language and gender' meets 'feminist organisational communication'. In J. Holmes (ed.), *Gendered Speech in Social Context: Perspectives from Gown to Town*. Wellington: Victoria University Press, pp. 192–210.

Journal of Politeness Research. (2006) Special Issue: *Politeness at work*.

Kanter, R. (1977) *Women and Men of the Corporation*. New York: Basic Books.

Kendall, S. (2003) Creating gender demeanors of authority at work and at home. In J. Holmes and M. Meyerhoff (eds), *The Handbook of Language and Gender*. Oxford: Blackwell. pp. 600–623.

——. (2004) Framing authority: Gender, face and mitigation at a radio network. *Discourse & Society* 15(1): 55–79.

——. (2006) Positioning the female voice within work and family. In J. Baxter (ed.), *Speaking Out: The Female Voice in Public Contexts*. Basingstoke: Palgrave, pp. 179–197.

Kendall, S. and D. Tannen. (1997) Gender and language in the workplace. In R. Wodak (ed.), *Gender and Discourse*. New York: Longman, pp. 81–105.

——. (2002) Discourse and gender. In D. Schiffrin, D. Tannen and H. Hamilton (eds), *The Handbook of Discourse Analysis*. Oxford: Blackwell, pp. 548–567.

Koester, A. (2006) *Investigating Workplace Discourse*. Abingdon: Routledge.

Koller, V. (2004) *Metaphor and Gender in Business Media Discourse: A Critical Cognitive Study*. Basingstoke: Palgrave.

Kotthoff, H. (2000) Gender and joking: on the complexities of women's image politics in humorous narratives. *Journal of Pragmatics* 32: 55–80.

Kotthoff, H. and R. Wodak. (1997) Preface: Gender in context. In R. Wodak and H. Kotthoff (eds), *Communicating Gender in Context*. Amsterdam: Benjamins, pp. vii–xxv.

Labov, W. (1972) *Language in the Inner City: Studies in the Black English Vernacular*. Philadelphia: University of Pennsylvania Press.

——. (1982) Objectivity and commitment in linguistic science. *Language in Society* 11: 165–201.

Labov, W. and D. Fanshel. (1977) *Therapeutic Discourse: Psychotherapy as Conversation*. New York: Academic Press.

Lakoff, R. (1975) *Language and Woman's Place*. New York: Harper Row.
——. (1990) *Talking Power: The Politics of Language*. San Francisco: Basic Books.
——. (2003) Language, gender and politics: Putting 'women' and 'power' in the same sentence. In J. Holmes and M. Meyerhoff (eds), *The Handbook of Language and Gender*. Oxford: Blackwell, pp. 161–178.
Lave, J. and E. Wenger. (1991) *Situated Learning: Legitimate Peripheral Participation*. Cambridge: Cambridge University Press.
Linstead, S. (1988) 'Joker's Wild': Humour in organisational culture. In C. Powell and G. Paton (eds), *Humour in Society: Resistance and Control*. Basingstoke: Macmillan, pp. 123–148.
Litosseliti, L. (2006) Constructing gender in public arguments: The female voice as emotional voice. In Judith Baxter (ed.), *Speaking Out: The Female Voice in Public Contexts*. Basingstoke: Palgrave, pp. 40–58.
Litosseliti, L. and J. Sunderland (eds) (2002) *Gender Identity and Discourse Analysis*. Amsterdam: Benjamins.
Livia, A. and K. Hall (eds) (1997) *Queerly Phrased: Language, Gender and Sexuality*. Oxford: Oxford University Press.
Marra, M., S. Schnurr and J. Holmes. (2006) Effective leadership in New Zealand workplaces. In J. Baxter (ed.), *Speaking Out: The Female Voice in Public Contexts*. Basingstoke: Palgrave, pp. 240–260.
Martin-Rojo, L. and C. Gómez Esteban. (2002) Discourse at work: When women take on the role of manager. In G. Weiss and R. Wodak (eds), *Critical Discourse Analysis: Theory and Interdisciplinarity*. Basingstoke: Palgrave, pp. 41–71.
——. (2005) The gender of power: The female style in labour organizations. In M. Lazar (ed.), *Feminist Critical Discourse Analysis*. Basingstoke: Palgrave, pp. 66–89.
Mavin, S. (2000) Approaches to careers in management: Why UK organisations should consider gender. *Career Development International* 5(1): 13–20.
McCarthy, M. (2000) Mutually captive audiences: Small talk and the genre of close-contact service encounters. In J. Coupland (ed.), *Small Talk*. Harlow: Pearson, pp. 84–109.
McConnell-Ginet, S. (2000) Breaking through the glass ceiling: Can linguistic awareness help? In J. Holmes (ed.), *Gendered Speech in Social Context: Perspectives from Gown to Town*. Wellington: Victoria University Press, pp. 259–282.
McElhinny, B. (1997) Ideologies of private and public language in sociolinguistics. In Ruth Wodak (ed.), *Gender and Discourse*. London: Sage, pp. 106–139.
——. (1998) 'I don't smile much anymore.' In J. Coates (ed.), *Language and Gender: A Reader*. Oxford: Blackwell, pp. 309–327.
——. (2003) Theorizing gender in sociolinguistics and linguistic anthropology. In J. Holmes and M. Meyerhoff (eds), *The Handbook of Language and Gender*. Oxford: Blackwell, pp. 21–42.
McRae, S. (2004) *Language, Gender and Status in the Workplace: The Discourse of Disagreement in Meetings*. Unpublished PhD Thesis. Milton Keynes: Open University.
Meyerhoff, M. (1996) Dealing with gender identity as a sociolinguistic variable. In V. Bergvall, J. Bing and A. Freed (eds), *Rethinking Language and Gender Research: Theory and Practice*. New York: Longman, pp. 202–227.
Mills, S. (1995) *Feminist Stylistics*. London: Routledge.
——. (1997) *Discourse*. London: Routledge.

Mills, S. (2002) Rethinking politeness, impoliteness and gender identity. In L. Litosseliti and J. Sunderland (eds), *Gender Identity and Discourse Analysis*. Amsterdam: Benjamins, pp. 69–89.

——. (2003) *Gender and Politeness*. Cambridge: Cambridge University Press.

Milroy, L. (1987) *Observing and Analysing Natural Language*. Oxford: Blackwell.

Milroy, L. and M. Gordon. (2003) *Sociolinguistics: Method and Interpretation*. Oxford: Blackwell.

Milroy, J. and L. Milroy. (1997) *Authority in Language: Investigating Standard English*. Third Edition. London: Routledge.

Morrison, A., R. White and E. van Velsor (1987) *Breaking the Glass Ceiling: Can Women Reach the Top of America's Largest Corporations?* Reading MA: Addison-Wesley.

Mulac, A., D. Seibold and J. L. Farris. (2000) Female and male managers' and professionals' criticism giving: differences in language use and effects. *Journal of Language and Social Psychology* 19(4): 389–415.

Mulkay, M. (1988) *On Humor*. New York: Basil Blackwell.

Mullany, L. (2002) 'I don't think you want me to get a word in edgeways do you John?' Re-assessing (im)politeness, language and gender in political broadcast interviews. *English Studies: Working Papers on the Web* 3: http://www.shu.ac.uk/wpw/

——. (2004) Gender, politeness and institutional power roles: Humour as a tactic to gain compliance in workplace business meetings. *Multilingua* 23 (1/2): 13–37.

——. (2006a) Narrative constructions of gendered and professional identities. In G. White and T. Omoniyi (eds), *The Sociolinguistics of Identity*. London: Continuum, pp. 157–172.

——. (2006b) 'Girls on tour': Politeness, small talk and gender identity in managerial business meetings. *Journal of Politeness Research: Language, Behaviour, Culture* 2(1): 55–77.

——. (2007a) Speech Communities. In C. Llamas, L. Mullany and P. Stockwell (eds), *The Routledge Companion to Sociolinguistics*. London: Routledge: 84–91.

——. (2007b) 'Stop hassling me!' Impoliteness in the workplace. In D. Bousfield and M. Locher (eds), *Impoliteness in Language*. Berlin: Mouton de Gruyter.

——. (2008) Negotiating methodologies: Making language and gender relevant in the professional workplace. In K. Harrison, L. Litosseliti, H. Sauntson and J. Sunderland (eds), *Gender and Language: Theoretical and Methodological Approaches*. Basingstoke: Palgrave.

Mullany, L. and L. Litosseliti. (2006) Language and gender in the workplace. In L. Litosseliti (ed.), *Gender and Language: Theory and Practice*. London: Arnold, pp. 123–148.

Mumby, D. (1988) *Communication and Power in Organizations*. Norwood NJ: Ablex.

Musson, G. (1998) Life histories. In G. Symon and C. Cassell (eds), *Qualitative Methods and Analysis in Organisational Research: A Practical Guide*. London: Sage, pp. 10–27.

Myers, G. (2005) Applied linguists and institutions of opinion. *Applied Linguistics* 26(4): 527–544.

Ochs, E. (1992) Indexing gender. In A. Duranti and C. Goodwin (eds), *Rethinking Context: Language as an Interactive Phenomenon*, Cambridge: Cambridge University Press, pp. 335–358.

Olsson, S. (2000) Acknowledging the female archetype: Women managers' narratives of gender. *Women in Management Review* 5(6): 296–302.

Olsson, S. and R. Walker (2003) Through a gendered lens? Male and female executives' representations of one another. *Leadership and Organization Development* 24(7): 387–396.

Oshagbemi, T. and R. Gill. (2003) Gender differences and similarities in the leadership styles and behaviour of UK managers. *Women in Management Review* 18(6): 288–298.

Pateman, T. (1980) *Language, Truth and Politics: Towards a Radical Theory for Communication.* London: Jean Stroud.

Pease, A. and B. Pease. (1999) *Why Men Don't Listen and Women Can't Read Maps.* New South Wales: Pease Training International.

Philips, S. (2003) The power of gender ideologies in discourse. In J. Holmes and M. Meyerhoff (eds), *The Handbook of Language and Gender.* Oxford: Blackwell. 252–276.

Pizzini, F. (1991) Communication hierarchies in humour: Gender differences in the obstetrical/gynaecological setting. *Discourse & Society* 2: 477–488.

Powell, G. and D. Butterfield. (2003) Gender, gender identity, and aspirations to top management. *Women in Management Review* 1(2): 88–96.

Powell, G. and L. Graves. (2003) *Women and Men in Management.* Third Edition. Oxford: Blackwell.

Rampton, B., K. Tusting, J. Maybin, R. Barwell, A. Creese and V. Lytra. (2004) UK Linguistic Ethnography: A Discussion Paper. *UK Linguistic Etnography Forum.* http://www.lancs.ac.uk/fss/organisations/lingethn/

Roberts, C. (2001) 'Critical' social theory: Good to think with or something more? In N. Coupland, S. Sarangi and C. N. Candlin (eds), *Sociolinguistics and Social Theory.* Harlow: Pearson, pp. 323–333.

Roberts, C. and S. Sarangi. (2003) Uptake of discourse research in professional settings: Reporting from medical consultancy. *Applied Linguistics* 24(3): 338–359.

——. (2005) Theme-orientated discourse analysis of medical encounters. *Medical Education* 39: 632–640.

Romaine, S. (2003) Variation in language and gender. In J. Holmes and M. Meyerhoff (eds), *The Handbook of Language and Gender.* Oxford: Blackwell, pp. 98–118.

Sacks, H., E. Schegloff and G. Jefferson. (1974) A simplest systematics for the organisation of turn-taking in conversation. *Language* 50: 696–735.

Sarangi, S. (2006) The conditions and consequences of professional discourse studies. In R. Kiely, P. Rea-Dickens, H. Woodfield and G. Clibbon (eds), *Language, Culture and Identity in Applied Linguistics.* London: Equinox.

Sarangi, S. and C. Candlin. (2003) Trading between reflexivity and relevance: New challenges for applied linguistics. *Applied Linguistics* 24 (3): 271–285.

Sarangi, S. and C. Roberts. (1999) The dynamics of interactional and institutional orders in work-related settings. In S. Sarangi and C. Roberts (eds), *Talk, Work and Institutional Order: Discourse in Medical, Mediation and Management Settings.* New York and Berlin: Mouton de Gruyter. pp. 1–57.

Sarangi, S. and T. van Leeuwen. (2003) Applied linguistics and communities of practice: Gaining communality or losing disciplinary autonomy? In S. Sarangi and T. van Leeuwen (eds), *Applied Linguistics and Communities of Practice.* London: Continuum, pp. 1–7.

Schwartzman, H. (1989) *The Meeting: Gatherings in Organizations and Communities*. New York: Plenum Press.

Shaw, S. (2006) Governed by the rules? The female voice in parliamentary debates. In J. Baxter (ed.), *Speaking Out: The Female Voice in Public Contexts*. Basingstoke: Palgrave, pp. 81–102.

Silverman, D. (1999) Warriors or collaborators: Reworking methodological controversies in the study of institutional interaction. In S. Sarangi and C. Roberts (eds), *Talk, Work and Institutional Order: Discourse in Medical, Mediation and Management Settings*. Berlin: Mouton de Gruyter, pp. 401–425.

Silverman, D. (2000) *Doing Qualitative Research: A Practical Guide*. London: Sage.

———. (2001) *Interpreting Qualitative Data: Methods for Analysing Talk, Text and Interaction*. Second Edition. London: Sage.

Singh, R. (1996) *Towards a Critical Sociolinguistics*. Amsterdam: Benjamins.

Speer, S. (2005) *Gender Talk: Feminism, Discourse and Conversation Analysis*. London: Routledge.

Spencer-Oatey, H. (2000) *Culturally Speaking*. London: Continuum.

Spiers, J. (1998) The use of face work and politeness theory. *Qualitative Health Research* 8(1): 25–47.

Stewart, A. (1998) *The Ethnographer's Method*. London: Sage.

Stubbe, M., J. Holmes, B. Vine and M. Marra. (2000) Forget Mars and Venus: Let's get back to earth! Challenging gender stereotypes in the workplace. In J. Holmes (ed.), *Gendered Speech in Social Context: Perspectives from Gown to Town*. Wellington: Victoria University Press, pp. 231–258.

Sunderland, J. (2004) *Gendered Discourses*. Basingstoke: Palgrave.

Sunderland, J.and L. Litosseliti. (2002) Gender identity and discourse analysis: Theoretical and empirical considerations. In L. Litosseliti and J. Sunderland (eds), *Gender Identity and Discourse Analysis*. Amsterdam: Benjamins, pp. 1–39.

Swann, J. (2002) Yes, but is it gender? In L. Litosseliti and J. Sunderland (eds), *Gender Identity and Discourse Analysis*. Amsterdam: Benjamins, pp. 43–67.

Swann, J. and J. Maybin. (2008) Sociolinguistic and ethnographic approaches to language and gender. In K. Harrison, L. Litosseliti, H. Sauntson and J. Sunderland (eds), *Gender and Language: Theoretical and Methodological Approaches*. Basingstoke: Palgrave.

Talbot, M. (1998) *Language and Gender: An Introduction*. Cambridge: Polity Press.

———. (2003) Gender stereotypes: Reproduction and challenge. In J. Holmes and M. Meyerhoff (eds), *The Handbook of Language and Gender*. Oxford: Blackwell, pp. 468–486.

Tannen, D. (1989) *Talking Voices: Repetition, Dialogue and Imagery in Conversational Discourse*. Cambridge: Cambridge University Press.

———. (1994) *Talking from 9 to 5. Women and Men in the Workplace: Language, Sex and Power*. New York: Avon.

———. (1999) The display of (gendered) identities at work. In M. Bucholtz, A. Liang and L. Sutton (eds), *Reinventing Identities: The Gendered Self in Discourse*. Oxford: Oxford University Press, pp. 221–240.

Thimm, C., S. Koch and S. Schey. (2003) Communicating gendered professional identity: Competence, cooperation, and conflict in the workplace. In J. Holmes and M. Meyerhoff (eds), *The Handbook of Language and Gender*. Oxford: Blackwell, pp. 528–549.

Trudgill, P. (1974) *The Social Differentiation of English in Norwich*. Cambridge: Cambridge University Press.

——. (1984) *Applied Sociolinguistics*. London: Academic Press.
van Leeuwen, T. (2005) Three models of interdisciplinarity. In R. Wodak (ed.), *New Agendas in Critical Discourse Analysis*. Amsterdam: Benjamins, pp. 3–18.
Vine, B. (2004) *Getting Things Done at Work*. Amsterdam: Benjamins.
Vinnicombe, S. and V. Singh. (2003) Locks and keys to the boardroom. *Women in Management Review* 18(6): 325–333.
Wajcman, J. (1998) *Managing Like a Man*. London: Sage.
Walsh, C. (2001) *Gender and Discourse: Language and Power in Politics, the Church and Organisations*. London: Longman.
——. (2006) Gender and the genre of the political broadcast interview. In J. Baxter (ed.), *Speaking Out: The Female Voice in Public Contexts*. Basingstoke: Palgrave, pp. 121–138.
Watts, R. (2003) *Politeness*. Cambridge: Cambridge University Press.
Wenger, E. (1998) *Communities of Practice*. Cambridge: Cambridge University Press.
Wenger, E., R. McDermott and W. Synder. (2002) *Cultivating Communities of Practice*. Cambridge MA: Harvard Business School.
West, C. (1990) Not just 'doctor's orders': directive–response sequences in patients' visits to women and men physicians. *Discourse & Society* 1(1): 85–112.
——. (1995) Women's competence in conversation. *Discourse & Society* 6(1): 107–131.
West, C. and D. Zimmerman. (1987) Doing gender. *Gender and Society* 1: 125–151.
Wodak, R. (1997a) Introduction: Some important issues in the research of gender and discourse. In R. Wodak (ed.), *Gender and Discourse*. London: Sage, pp. 1–20.
——. (ed.) (1997b) *Gender and Discourse*. London: Sage.
——. (1997c) 'I know we won't revolutionize the world with it, but … ': Styles of female leadership in institutions. In H. Kotthoff and R. Wodak (eds), *Communicating Gender in Context*. Amsterdam: Benjamins, pp. 335–370.
——. (2003) Multiple identities: The roles of female parliamentarians in the EU Parliament. In J. Holmes and M. Meyerhoff (eds), *The Handbook of Language and Gender*. Oxford: Blackwell, pp. 671–698.
Wodak, R. and G. Benke. (1997) Gender as a sociolinguistic variable: New perspectives on variation studies. In F. Coulmas (ed.), *Handbook of Sociolinguistics*. Oxford: Blackwell, pp. 127–150.
Women and Work Commission (2006) *Shaping a Fairer Future*. London: Women and Work Commission.
Yieke, F. (2005) Gender and discourse: Topic organisation on workplace management committee meetings in Kenya. Paper presented at *Theoretical and Methodological Approaches to Gender* BAAL/CUP Seminar, University of Birmingham, 18 November.

Index

emotionality, 43, 44, 47, 116, 171,
185, 207, 227
see also gendered discourses
equal opportunities policies, 5, 14, 55,
58, 67, 214, 215
Equal Opportunities Commission (EOC),
13, 223
essentialism, 18, 23, 25, 26, 46, 172,
176, 186–7, 190, 207, 210
ethnicity, 25, 27, 40
ethnography, 22, 26, 28, 49, 50–4, 55,
57–8, 60, 63–9, 79, 82, 91, 123,
130, 132, 170, 194, 208, 220, 224,
225, 226, 229, 230
expletives, 140, 143, 152

face, 77–86, 89–90, 98, 101, 104–5,
108, 124, 128, 129, 134, 143, 145,
152, 165, 220, 226, 230
face-attack acts (FAAs), 78, 86, 120,
131
face-threatening acts (FTAs), 77, 79,
83, 86
see also impoliteness; politeness
family, 14–15, 151, 179, 204, 208, 226
see also gendered discourses
Feminism, 10, 12, 18–20, 21, 30,
36–9, 42, 44, 66, 77, 164, 202,
220, 221, 224, 225, 226, 227, 228,
230
third-wave, 19, 42
see also gendered discourses
*Feminist Post-Structuralist Discourse
Analysis* (FPDA), 36
feminist sociolinguistics, 12, 20
field notes, 51, 59, 64, 66–7, 69, 87
floorholding, 79–80, 141
see also turn-taking; interruptions
folklinguistics, 34, 41, 177

gendered discourses
emotionality/irrationality, 185–91
equal opportunities, 41, 203–4, 208
of the family, 191–4, 196, 203, 207,
214
of femininity, 38, 40, 43, 167, 172,
175, 177, 179, 188, 196–201,
202, 203, 206–7, 222
feminist, 202, 208

of gender difference, 35–6, 37–8, 40,
41, 43, 47, 163, 167, 169, 175,
176, 184, 185, 191, 205, 206,
208
image and sexuality, 170, 178–9,
195, 196–201
of masculinity, 37–8, 40, 43–4, 173,
174, 184–5, 212
motherhood, 191–6, 207–8, 214
mother as main parent, 40–1
gendered domains, 43
gendered speech styles, 30–6, 41,
45–8, 52, 74–6, 79–94, 99, 108,
120, 122, 128, 130, 135–6, 143,
145, 146, 152, 159, 166, 167–8,
175–6, 181, 183, 203, 206–7,
212–13, 215, 226, 227, 230
gendered work, 167–205
glass ceiling, 1, 6, 13–16, 44, 56–8, 65,
70, 168, 178, 203–4, 209–10,
215–16, 227, 228, 229
gossip, 76, 93, 112, 133, 222
see also small talk

hedges, 98, 99, 151
hegemony, 29, 37–40, 43–4, 46, 167,
174, 184, 206–7, 209, 211, 212, 213
humour, 44, 61, 75–6, 80, 86–90, 93,
96, 100, 101–3, 105, 106–14, 116,
120–4, 127, 131–6, 141–51, 152,
156–64, 165, 170, 182, 193, 202,
203, 225, 227, 228, 229
banter, 100, 103, 105, 120, 123,
148, 152, 157–8
conjoint, 88, 100, 102, 105, 112–14,
121–2, 133, 146–7, 148–9, 151,
160, 163–4, 202
contestive, 88
one-liners, 102–3, 105, 148
repressive, 89, 90, 93, 99, 103, 110,
112, 116, 121, 123, 129, 147,
160, 163
rivalrous, 89, 90, 120–1, 123, 132,
134, 136, 141, 145, 150, 152,
157–8, 160, 163
sarcasm, 105, 145, 156
solidarity/collegiality forming, 100,
112, 121, 124, 136, 150, 152,
163

metaphors, 107, 146–7, 148, 226
masculinist, 147, 152, 184
minimal responses, 99, 150, 161
motherhood, *see* gendered discourses
mother role, *see* sex-role stereotyping
multi-methods, 48, 50, 59, 168

narrative, 186, 193, 200, 228
new work order, 46, 62, 224
see also power

observer's paradox, 54, 67–9
one-at-a-time floor (OAT), 79–80, 88, 100
see also floorholding
organizational communication, 6
organizational studies, 6, 7, 16, 18, 36, 41, 43, 46, 50, 87, 208
overlaps, 80, 92, 97, 99, 101, 112, 113, 122, 129, 133, 138, 140, 149, 150, 151, 164

participant observation, 53–4, 59, 60–2
patriarchy, 37–8
pay gap, 13, 20, 25
performative, *see* speech acts
performativity, 18, 19, 22–6, 32, 33, 42, 89, 104, 105, 109, 118, 139, 145, 157, 179
phatic communion, *see* small talk
politeness, 40, 73, 74–86, 88–90, 93, 94, 105, 120, 128, 131, 135, 165, 225, 228
see also face; impoliteness
power, 1, 3, 13, 15–16, 18, 21, 23, 25, 27, 28, 33, 35–42, 44, 46, 48, 62, 73–6, 80, 81–6, 88–90, 93, 97, 99, 104, 105, 108, 115, 117, 129, 133, 135, 138, 143, 152, 163, 167, 177, 183, 184, 201, 202, 207, 210, 211, 216, 223, 225, 226, 227, 228
coercive, 21, 46, 74
consent, 21, 46
oppressive, 37, 39, 46, 74–5, 83, 162
repressive, 36, 46, 74–5, 83, 88, 89, 90, 93, 99, 103, 110, 112, 116, 121, 123, 129, 147, 160, 163

power/dominance approach, 11, 19, 24, 33, 76, 213
practical relevance, 9–12, 28, 36, 42, 55–7, 210
pregnancy, 13, 178, 192
private spheres, 3–5, 46
public spheres, 1, 3–5, 43–4, 46, 47, 181, 186, 195, 207, 209, 213

rationality, 43–4, 47, 185–91
see also discourses, scientific
modernism
reflexivity, 3, 19, 53, 79, 229
research ethics, 9, 68, 215

sex, 4, 11, 13, 21, 22, 24–6, 31, 42, 45, 69, 175, 176, 188, 197, 204, 205, 221
sexism, 180, 187, 195, 197, 201, 208
sex-role stereotyping, 24, 45
dragon lady, 44, 171
iron maiden, 44
mother role, 44, 45, 170–1
the pet, 44
the seductress, 44, 201
sexual division of labour, 5, 76, 196, 200
sexuality, 25, 44, 179, 181, 186, 207, 214, 222, 223, 227
see also gendered discourses
shadowing, 51, 59, 61–2, 64, 66, 70, 96, 106, 117, 126, 137, 214
silence, 132, 177, 224
small talk, 62, 75, 76, 80, 90–4, 96–8, 105, 106, 111–13, 116, 121, 122, 123, 126, 133–4, 135, 138, 148–51, 163–4, 166, 181, 202, 222, 228
social class, 20–1, 25, 27, 28, 38, 40, 71, 223
social psychology, 6
social structure, 28–9
see also power
social talk, 62, 111, 151
see also small talk
social theory, 5–6, 7–8, 16, 18, 22, 229
social types, 210–11
sociology, 5, 6, 8, 16, 18, 36, 43

236   *Index*